Islamic Social Finance

Sherin Kunhibava · Aishath Muneeza ·
Maryam Binti Khalid · Zakariya Mustapha ·
Thong Ming Sen

Islamic Social Finance

Law and Practice in Malaysia

Springer

Sherin Kunhibava
Faculty of Law
University of Malaya
Kuala Lumpur, Malaysia

Maryam Binti Khalid
Faculty of Law
University of Malaya
Kuala Lumpur, Malaysia

Thong Ming Sen
Faculty of Law
University of Malaya
Kuala Lumpur, Malaysia

Aishath Muneeza
INCEIF
Kuala Lumpur, Malaysia

Zakariya Mustapha
Faculty of Law
University of Malaya
Kuala Lumpur, Malaysia

ISBN 978-981-97-1409-4 ISBN 978-981-97-1410-0 (eBook)
https://doi.org/10.1007/978-981-97-1410-0

This Springer imprint is published by the registered company Springer Nature Singapore Pte Ltd.
The registered company address is: 152 Beach Road, #21-01/04 Gateway East, Singapore 189721, Singapore

Paper in this product is recyclable.

Foreword by Prof. Dr. Jason Chuah

Writing a Foreword, especially for a book that promises to be a significant contribution to learning, is an absolutely pleasure and privilege. As the writer of this Foreword, one does have a sense of guilt stealing some of the spotlight and glory for a work that has been brought about by others! Thank you to the contributors for the kind invitation to write this Foreword. As Dean of the country's leading Law Faculty in spearheading innovative and impactful research, I feel terribly humbled by the scholarship and dedication of the panel of contributors to this writing project. Important works are increasingly the culmination of much hard work and dedication from many people. This work is no different. The authors, Dr. Sherin Kunhibava, Professor Aishath Muneeza, Dr. Maryam Binti Khalid, Mr. Zakariya Mustapha, and Mr. Thong Ming Sen, have clearly seen this not merely a project of the mind but of the heart.

I have also been impressed at the very diverse team of contributors—from thoroughly well-established specialists to doctoral researchers—all played a critical role in ensuring that different perspectives are accommodated. Knowledge is a joint enterprise.

Financing is increasingly seen as a philanthropic wrap-around. From moral and ethical perspective, this combination has often led to some tension in the legal and regulatory response—how should the law discourage irresponsible borrowing and encourage responsible lending? Given these moral considerations, Islamic social finance principles bring to the fore some clarity as to these imperatives. Islamic social finance seeks to empower the financially powerless in society. The subject under study intersects with so many different socio-economic needs and interests in Malaysia that a careful delineation of the regulatory framework is essential to enable Islamic social finance to achieve the full complement of its objectives in Malaysia. This book serves that up in a manner which is both readable and exploratory. There is, *inter alia*, in-depth discussion about global Islamic financial markets as drivers, the role of "Islamic" fintech and Islamic legal concepts directly applicable to social finance.

The Faculty of Law is very proud to have been involved in the funding of the research under the so-called Breaking the Silo Research Grant. Administrative support from our Research Office should of course not be forgotten. As I alluded to earlier, a magisterial accomplishment such as this could not have been made without the work and generosity of many.

Many congratulations to the entire team for a job well done!

Prof. Dr. Jason Chuah
Dean
Faculty of Law
Universiti Malaya
Kuala Lumpur, Malaysia

Foreword by Jeffrey Salim Waheed

Our faith encompasses the notion that social justice is the beating heart of our society, and intrinsic to all aspects of our lives. Unfortunately, this aspect of 'shari'ah compliance' and Islamic finance has only barely been elaborated in the financial structures and institutions of many Muslim nations. While Islamic Commercial Finance is now evermore established, the notion of Islamic social finance has yet to be widely adopted. In this book, its authors take a much needed step toward providing a comprehensive and in-depth analysis of financial products and instruments within the realm of Islamic social finance, providing both a theoretical and practical perspective to their application.

Islamic commercial financing institutions and methods have gained momentum across Muslim societies around the world, and are increasingly welcomed by the nations that host these communities. Though practiced by Muslims since inception of Islam, the institutionalization of Islamic social finance is slow compared to Islamic Commercial Finance, and is too often practiced in the informal sector of the economy due to a lack of awareness regarding available support structures. As such, it is clear that this book will have a place in bridging the existing gap, not only in academic research, but also in the overall awareness on Islamic social financial institutions and tools, as this book has adopted a balanced approach in discussing both Islamic commercial and social modes of financing as alternative financing modalities for the conventional financial system.

Over recent financial crises, and especially in the wake of the COVID-19 pandemic, the resilience of Islamic financial systems has become clear. Providing a different set of products from conventional financial systems, and focusing on utilizing shari'ah compliant contracts, Islamic finance is based on financial products that strive to achieve the higher objectives of Shari'ah (*Maqasid al Shariah*) by ensuring that the people, planet, and collective prosperity remain at the core of its endeavors, in an effort to ensure that no one is left behind.

I welcome this book as a source of knowledge and inspiration to those who are searching for an alternative financial system. The practical application of this knowledge goes beyond academic discourse, being practically applicable for practitioners and policymakers who aspire to transform the lives of their constituents, through implementing ethical and social financial systems that are consistent with their faith. My warm thanks to the authors of this book, for its immense contribution to the field of Islamic economics and Islamic finance, and for paving the for future research, contributions and practical developments in this field.

Malé, Republic of Maldives

Jeffrey Salim Waheed
Former Deputy Minister,
Ministry of Foreign Affairs,
Republic of Maldives

Preface

Islamic social finance, rooted in the teachings of the Quran and Sunnah, has evolved into a dynamic and impactful field encompassing various instruments and institutions. This textbook delves into the legal foundations and practical aspects of Islamic social finance in Malaysia, offering insights through digital case studies. The chapters explore key components such as Zakat, Sadaqah, Waqf, Qard Hassan, Islamic Microfinance, Social Sukuk, and Social Takaful, providing a comprehensive understanding of their legal frameworks and digital applications.

Chapter 1 lays the groundwork by examining the historical development of Islamic social finance, its instruments, and the profound impact it has on society. It also explains Islamic social finance as a tool to accomplish Maqasid al-Shariah. The exploration extends to its relationship with blended finance, alternative finance, and the circular economy, highlighting the interconnectedness of Islamic social finance with contemporary financial paradigms.

Chapter 2 focuses on Sadaqah, Zakat, and Qard Hassan, elucidating their definitions, differences, and legal frameworks. Digital case studies showcase innovative applications of technology in these realms, shedding light on advancements in philanthropy-based and cooperation-based social finance.

In Chapter 3, the discussion shifts to Waqf, exploring its essence, distinctions from other forms of social finance, and the legal framework in Malaysia. Digital case studies, including Finterra's Waqfchain and Bank BJB Syariah's Wakaf Ikhlas, exemplify how technology has been integrated to enhance the impact of Waqf.

Chapter 4 takes a comparative approach, drawing lessons from Zakah and Waqaf frameworks in Indonesia and Singapore to provide valuable insights for Malaysia. The examination of legal, regulatory frameworks, and practices contributes to a richer understanding of the diverse landscape of Islamic social finance.

Islamic Microfinance takes center stage in Chap. 5, dissecting its definition, differences from conventional microfinance, and the legal framework in Malaysia. Case studies on AIM and TEKUN Nasional showcase the transformative potential of Islamic Microfinance in empowering communities.

Chapter 6 delves into Social Sukuk, unraveling its concept, distinctions, and legal framework. Innovative case studies such as Sukuk Prihatin (Malaysia) and Sukuk

Wakaf Indonesia illustrate the application of Social Sukuk and the integration of technology in their issuance.

Social Takaful, explored in Chap. 7, unfolds its meaning, differences from other social finance tools, and the legal framework in Malaysia. Case studies on mySalam (Malaysia), Takaful and Karama (Egypt), and Uplift Mutuals Biradaree (India) showcase the transformative role of Social Takaful.

The concluding Chap. 8 addresses contemporary issues and challenges in Islamic social finance, emphasizing the need for integration, standardized reporting, updated regulations, and the utilization of digital databases. The way forward envisions a digital era for Islamic social finance, ushering in a new paradigm of efficiency and inclusivity.

This textbook serves as an invaluable resource for academics, practitioners, and policymakers seeking a comprehensive understanding of Islamic social finance in Malaysia, coupled with practical insights from case studies. Designed as a textbook, it is a crucial companion for students of Islamic social finance, providing a foundational framework for those aspiring to study and research in this emerging discipline within Islamic finance.

This book is dedicated to all patrons of Islamic finance who seek a profound understanding of the legal paradigm of Islamic social finance. In the current landscape, finding a comprehensive resource on this subject can be challenging. However, this textbook is meticulously crafted to bridge that gap, providing a thorough exploration of the legal foundations and practical applications of Islamic social finance in Malaysia.

Kuala Lumpur, Malaysia

Sherin Kunhibava
Aishath Muneeza
Maryam Binti Khalid
Zakariya Mustapha
Thong Ming Sen

Acknowledgments

We extend our sincere gratitude to the Faculty of Law, Universiti Malaya, for their generous support through the Breaking the Silo Fund, grant number UMG001M-2022. The funding provided by the Faculty has been instrumental in the successful realization of this project. We acknowledge their commitment to fostering academic research and innovation.

Our sincere gratitude is extended to the esteemed interviewees who generously shared their insights, enriching the content of this book. Dr. Abideen Adewale, Head of Research, Statistics, and Publications at the Islamic Financial Services Board (IFSB); Dr. Ahcene Lahsasna, Chief Executive Officer of SALIHIN Shariah Advisory; Dr. Ayaz Ismail, Director of Wholesale Banking at CIMB Islamic in Malaysia; Associate Professor Dr. Mohamed Eskandar, Associate Dean at Hamdan bin Khalifa University, Doha; Ahmad Hafiz Abdul Aziz, Financial Sector Specialist with the World Bank Group Global Knowledge and Research Hub in Malaysia; Mr. Johnny Moi, a self-employed individual; and Tan Sri Andrew Sheng, a former central banker and financial regulator in Asia, as well as a commentator on global finance, all played pivotal roles in providing valuable perspectives and contributing to the depth of our discussions.

Additionally, we express our appreciation to the Research Office of Universiti Malaya's Law for their unwavering support and assistance throughout the research process. Their commitment to facilitating academic endeavors has been indispensable.

These collective efforts and support from individuals and organizations alike have significantly contributed to the completion of this book. Their expertise and dedication have not only enriched the content but also played a crucial role in elevating the overall quality of the work.

Book Blurb

Discover the intricate tapestry of Islamic social finance through *Islamic Social Finance—Law and Practice in Malaysia.* Delving into the rich teachings of the Quran and Sunnah, this comprehensive textbook provides a profound exploration of Zakat, Sadaqah, Waqf, Qard Hassan, Islamic Microfinance, Social Sukuk, and Social Takaful.

Unraveling the legal foundations and practical applications, each chapter unveils case studies, offering a real-world perspective on the transformative impact of technology. From the historical emergence to contemporary integration with blended finance and the circular economy, this book navigates the dynamic landscape of Islamic social finance in Malaysia.

Whether you are an academic, practitioner, policymaker, or student aspiring to delve into the emerging discipline of Islamic social finance, this textbook serves as an indispensable guide. Authored by experts in the field, it not only fills a crucial gap in literature but also propels the understanding of Islamic social finance into the digital era.

Embark on a journey that explores the intersection of tradition and innovation, shedding light on the profound role Islamic social finance plays in shaping inclusive financial landscapes. *Islamic Social Finance—Law and Practice in Malaysia* is your gateway to a deeper comprehension of this dynamic and impactful field within Islamic finance.

Contents

About the Authors

Dr. Sherin Kunhibava is a Senior Lecturer at the University Malaya Law faculty. Her area of expertise is in commercial law, fintech regulation, and Islamic finance law. Apart from her fifteen years of teaching experience in academia, she has also worked at Pacific Bank Bhd., International Shariah Research Academy (ISRA), and Wisdom Management Consultancy Sdn. Bhd. She is an Associate Editor of ISRA journal from 2023, and she is on the editorial board of the *Journal of Malaysian and Comparative Law* as a Subject Editor and is the Academic Advisor to the Student *Journal of UMLR* of the faculty of Law. Since 2018, she has worked on research projects funded by external grants researching on regulatory issues for digital solutions pertaining blockchain technology for the financial industry. She was part of a team of researchers who were first to report on regulatory issues in the blockchain space in Malaysia. Currently, she is researching on Islamic social finance.

Professor Dr. Aishath Muneeza is a Professor and the Associate Dean for Students and Internationalization at INCEIF University in Malaysia, renowned as the global University of Islamic Finance. She has an extensive career, having served as the first female Deputy Minister of the Ministry of Islamic Affairs in the Maldives, Deputy Minister of the Ministry of Finance and Treasury in the Maldives, and Head of Islamic Finance at the Capital Market Development Authority of the Maldives.

She has also been a member of the Islamic Fiqh Academy (National Fatwa Council of the Maldives), the first chairman of the Hajj pilgrimage fund at Maldives Hajj Corporation Limited, and the chairman of Maldives Center for Islamic Finance Limited. The latter was established by the government of the Maldives to position the country as the hub of Islamic finance in South Asia. She has played key roles as an Islamic finance consultant, contributing to the development of the first Shariah-compliant Islamic microfinance scheme in the Maldives.

Furthermore, she has served as the Shariah Advisor for structuring all corporate sukuk offerings in the Maldives, as well as private sukuk and Islamic treasury instruments for the Maldivian government. She was a consultant involved in drafting the Islamic capital market legal framework for the country. Since 2013, she has been a registered Shariah Adviser with the Capital Market Development Authority of the

Maldives, specializing in structuring Islamic capital market products. She is also a registered Shariah Adviser at the Securities Commission Malaysia.

From 2011 to 2022, she chaired the apex Shariah Advisory Council of the Capital Market Development Authority of the Maldives. She currently serves as the chairperson of various in-house Shariah advisory committees and is a member of the Board Shariah Committee of CIMB Islamic, Malaysia, and Munich Re. Additionally, she is a member of the Public Interest Monitoring Consultative Committee (PIMCC) of the Accounting and Auditing Organization for Islamic Financial Institutions (AAOIFI). She is an elected executive committee member of the Bar Council of the Maldives.

Dr. Maryam Binti Khalid is currently a Senior Lecturer at the University Malaya Law faculty. Previously, she practiced as an Islamic financial corporate lawyer and has experience in advising clients on banking product developments and financial regulatory reforms. She has also worked as a legal executive to a public trustee company and a private company advising on the companies' compliance regarding their commercial operations. Her area of interest is mostly in financial and fintech regulatory developments.

Dr. Zakariya Mustapha is a Researcher at the Faculty of Law, University of Malaya. He is as an Advocate and Solicitor of Nigeria's Supreme Court since 2008. He specializes in legal and Shariah issues in Islamic finance and offers legal and Islamic advisory services regarding regulatory framework, dispute resolution, and Shariah-compliant product development in Islamic finance. He is an aspiring Researcher who published in academic journals and presented research papers in national and international conferences. He holds LL.M., LL.B. (with Shariah specialization), and membership of professional bodies including the Nigerian Bar Association.

Thong Ming Sen is a Ph.D. student at University of Malaya (UM), Law faculty. His thesis revolves around the use of blockchain for financial regulatory compliance, Islamic finance, and financial inclusion. His area of expertise is in capital markets law, blockchain technology, and fintech regulation. He was part of a team of researchers who were first to report on regulatory issues in the blockchain space in Malaysia. He holds a LL.B. (Hons.) from the University of London, Master of Laws (LL.M.) (Distinction) from UM, and is an Advocate & Solicitor of the High Court of Malaya.

Acronyms

ACE Market	'Access, Certainty, Efficiency' market of Bursa
AIBIM	Association of Islamic Banking and Financial Institutions
AIM	Amana Ikhtiar Malaysia
AMLA	Administration of Muslim Law Act
ASEAN	Association of Southeast Asian Nations
ATMs	Automated Teller Machines
BAZNAS	The National Board of Zakat for the Republic of Indonesia
BBA	bai' bithaman ajil
BNM	Bank Negara Malaysia
BRN	Business Registration Numbers
BSH	Bantuan Sara Hidup
BWI	Badan Wakaf Indonesia
CVI	Corporate Value Intent
CWLS	Cash Waqaf Link Sukuk
DITOs	Digital Insurers and Takaful Operators
ETBS	Exchange traded Bond and Sukuk
FAST	Fully Automated System for Issuing and Tendering
FPX	Financial Process Exchange
GLCs	Government-Linked Companies
ICMIF	International Cooperative and Mutual Insurance Federation
ICT	Information and Communication Technology
IFPRI	International Food Policy Research Institute
IFSA	Islamic Financial Services Act
IRCIEF	International Research Centre for Islamic Economics and Finance
IsDB	Islamic Development Bank
JAWHAR	Department of Awqaf, Zakat dan Haji
JAWI	The Federal Territories Islamic Religious Department
KKR	People's Credit Cooperation
KPIs	Key Performance Indicators
LEAP Market	Leading Entrepreneur Accelerator Platform market of Bursa
LFSA	Labuan Financial Services Authority

LZNK	Kedah Zakat Agency
MAIS	Selangor State Religious Council
MAIWP	Wilayah State Religious Council
MFIs	Microfinance Institutions
MOU	Memorandum of Understanding
MSMEs	Micro, Small and Medium Enterprises
MUIS	Majlis Ugama Islam Singapore
NGOs	Non-Governmental Organizations
NPL	Non-Performing Loan
NRD	National Registration Department
OKU	Orang Kurang Upaya
OTC	Over-the-Counter
PENJANA	*Pelan Jana Semula Ekonomi Negara*
PV	Photovoltaic
REIT	Real Estate Investment Trust
RENTAS	Real-Time Electronic Transfer of Funds and Securities System
SAC	Shariah Advisory Council
SAW	Sallallahu álaihi wasallam which is translated in English as peace and blessing be upon him.
SC	Securities Commission of Malaysia
SC	Shariah Committee
SDGs	Sustainable Development Goals
SMEs	Small and Medium Enterprises
SPM	Skim Pembiayaan Mikro
SPV	Special Purpose Vehicle
SRI	Sustainable and Responsible Investment
SSF	Sustainable Social Finance
TH	Tabung Haji
TKJHM	Tabung Kebajikan Jemaah Haji Malaysia
TOs	Takaful Operators
TWT	Tabung Was'ul Khair Tetamu Allah
VBIT	Value-Based Intermediation for Takaful
YUM	Yayasan Usaha Maju

List of Figures

List of Tables

Chapter 1
Islamic Social Finance from the Quran and Sunnah

Abstract This chapter provides a comprehensive exploration of the principles of Islamic social finance rooted in the Quran and Sunnah. Readers will gain insights into the various dimensions of Islamic social finance, understanding its core concepts and principles without compromising the ethical and legal frameworks defined by Shariah. The chapter outlines the Shariah injunctions that govern Islamic social finance institutions and instruments, offering a deep dive into the ethical and legal foundations that guide these financial practices. It also examines the historical context and emergence of Islamic social finance in contemporary development discourse, shedding light on its evolution over time. A significant focus of the chapter is on illustrating the impact of Islamic social finance on sustainability. By showcasing how these financial practices align with principles of social responsibility and ethical investing, the chapter emphasizes the positive contributions of Islamic social finance to broader societal and environmental goals. Additionally, the chapter explores the interconnections between Islamic social finance and blended finance, alternate finance, and the circular economy. Readers will gain a nuanced understanding of how Islamic social finance can seamlessly integrate with diverse financial models, contributing to a more holistic perspective on its role in the global economic landscape. Upon completing this chapter, readers will have a solid foundation in Islamic social finance, enabling them to appreciate its theological origins, legal frameworks, contemporary relevance, and its potential synergy with various financial paradigms.

Keywords Islamic Social Finance · Shariah Injunctions · Sustainability · Blended Finance · Circular Economy

Learning Outcomes
At the end of this chapter, readers will be able to:

- Understand Islamic social finance and its dimension
- Identify Shariah injunctions on Islamic social finance institutions and instrument
- Explain emergence of Islamic social finance in contemporary development discourse

S. Kunhibava et al., *Islamic Social Finance*,
https://doi.org/10.1007/978-981-97-1410-0_1

- Demonstrate impact of Islamic social finance towards sustainability
- Correlate Islamic social finance with blended finance, alternate finance and circular economy

1.1 Islamic Social Finance: A Background

Islamic social finance is the provision of resources to enhance attainment of socio-economic justice by means of wealth redistribution and just financial dealings. In other word, it is a component of Islamic finance used for furtherance of philanthropic, community/charitable and social purposes. Islamic social finance channels funds into these causes via zakat (religious wealth tax/obligatory charity), waqf (perpetual endowment/charitable trust), sadaqah (voluntary charity) and qard hasan (benevolent loan). These are instruments that are distinct from contracts used in Islamic finance for commercial or for-profit transactions. However, financial gains via Islamic finance can be channelled to zakat, sadaqah and waqf investments to further social, charitable and humanitarian causes in an effort to promote some *maqasid al-Shariah*, i.e., the Islamic legal doctrine that signifies the overarching objectives or goals of *Shariah* (the Islamic law). Thus, Islamic finance helps in this regard whereby part of capital earned from its for-profit aspect is allocated for and utilized towards charitable and social causes using zakat, waqf, sadaqah and qard hasan. Islamic social finance furthers the Islamic notion of humans as God's vicegerents on earth (Quran 2:30), guarding the well-being of society and environment, preventing harm and destruction (Quran 6:165), ensuring sustainability of resources by engaging in sustainable practices to enable future generations enjoy the same resources, environment and conditions on earth. This in essence ensures social justice through the fair distribution of wealth and a just economy.[1]

The idea of a just economy in Islam presupposes a fair distribution whereby everyone is morally responsible to consider and share with each other. This is because Islam considers it as everyone's moral right to be basically satisfied in terms of socio-economic needs.[2] Today, while the world witnesses unprecedented upsurge in population, there are people in almost every corner of the world that are experiencing rising

[1] Hasan, S. (2007). Islamic concept of social justice: its possible contribution to ensuring harmony and peaceful coexistence in a globalised world. *Macquarie Law Journal*, *7*, 167; Tripp, C. (2006). *Islam and the Moral Economy: The Challenge of Capitalism*. Cambridge University Press, p. 229; Qutb, Sayyid. (2000). *Social Justice in Islam*. New York: Islamic Publications International, p. 327.

[2] Mehmood, F., & Ur Rehman, Z. (2023). Islamic teachings on socio-economic justice for a sustainable human society: an evaluation. *INKISHAF*, *3*(7), 1–19; Askari, H., Iqbal, Z., & Mirakhor, A. (2014). Economic and social justice: the policy objective in islam. *Challenges in Economic and Financial Policy Formulation: An Islamic Perspective*, 31–46; Chapra, M. U. (2008). Socio-economic justice and the Muslim world. *Policy Perspectives*, *5*(1), 47–67. http://www.jstor.org/stable/42909186.

poverty and struggling but unable to make a living with requisite economic satisfaction.[3] This is said to be resulting from unsustainable economic practices mainly associated with development choices that warrants persistence of the people being made vulnerable to poverty which jeopardizes the lives of a sizable percentage of the global population.[4] It is obvious that the economic world today is largely dominated by the spirit of capitalism as led by the idea of profit before people and with little or no regard to its exploitative tendencies of people and resources. This is among disquieting facts have led to a globally growing concern among both public authorities and private actors on the need to ensure sustaining the world's resources, the poor and destitute so that all can enjoy basic socio-economic rights. Moreover, the reality of the current global economy based only on unbound profitability drive of enterprises coupled with unsustainable and unethical practices has remarkably demonstrates that sustainability cannot be satisfactorily attained. This informs the need for a paradigm shift in economic and policy decisions towards social and environmental considerations for a people-centred and resource-led development.

Furthermore, this idea of sustainability is the basis of consideration in contemporary mainstream economy for such innovative measures as social finance, alternative finance, blended finance, circular economy, ethical funds, trust funds among other related socio-humanitarian economic tasks and inclinations. These tasks and inclination are considered sacrosanct to and interwoven with the overarching objectives of the Shariah whereupon any permissible dealing sanctioned by the holy Quran and Sunnah shall be based.[5] The holy Quran according to Islamic belief is the word of Allah revealed to Prophet Muhammad (peace be upon him) and it constitutes an impeccable authority that establishes law and legal system for muslims. Meanwhile, the Sunnah encompasses the practices and traditions of the Prophet Muhammad (peace be upon him) which are ordained to serve as exemplary conducts for muslims to model themselves on. Regarded as second only to the Quran in authoritative significance, the sunnah is conveyed by *hadith* which means a report of the actions, sayings and tacit approvals of the Prophet Muhammad (peace be upon him).[6] Muslim jurists are unanimous that both the holy Quran and Hadith are the main sources of Shariah as the divine commandment from which the legal basis of Islamic social finance is sought and established. Thus, from the Quranic and Sunnah standpoint, the notion of social finance conceptualises a communal and collaborative agency

---

[3] UNDP. (2022). *Human Development Report 2021–22: Uncertain Times, Unsettled Lives: Shaping our Future in a Transforming World.* New York. Available at https://hdr.undp.org/system/files/documents/global-report-document/hdr2021-22pdf_1.pdf.

[4] World Bank. (2022). *Poverty and Shared Prosperity 2022—Correcting Course.* Available at https://elibrary.worldbank.org/doi/epdf/10.1596/978-1-4648-1893-6.

[5] Habibullah, M., Al Faruque, A., Faruque, M. O., & Atiullah, M. (2023). Islamic economic framework for the exercise of Islamic financial activities: its conformity with Maqasid Shariah. *Al-Burhān: Journal of Qurān and Sunnah Studies*, 7(1), 81–92.

[6] Kamali, M. H. (2003). *Principles of Islamic Jurisprudence.* Cambridge: Islamic Texts Society, pp. 14–15; Dogan, R. (2015). *Usul al-fiqh: Methodology of Islamic Jurisprudence.* Clifton: Tughra Books, pp. 31, 54; Nyazee, I. A. K. (2016). *Islamic Jurisprudence: Usul al-Fiqh*, 3rd Edition. Scotts Valley: CreateSpace, pp. 22–23, 47.

of individuals, business ventures, enterprises and every economic actor, severally or together, to foster community welfare in both their profitability drive and spiritual pursuit to pave way for socio-economic support and sustainability. Accordingly, this is an important objective of the Shariah that encompasses charitable, philanthropic and humanitarian concerns in enterprises practiced by caring for and sharing with the poor, destitute, underprivileged and helpless attained through instruments such as include Zakat, Waqf, Sadaqah as well as Qard Hasan being instruments for channelling resources to serve a higher purpose.

1.2 Emergence of Islamic Social Finance

Islamic social finance was designed and established at the birth of Islam with view to balancing wealth in society and prevent economic exploitation. It is part of an extensive economic system that exists in Islam only. Although it is ordained and practiced since the advent of Islam, the prominence of Islamic social finance today follows the emergence of contemporary Islamic commercial finance and banking practice.[7] Nonetheless, Islamic social finance instruments such as zakat and waqf have been practiced for centuries and served an important socio-economic roles in the development of muslim societies. These roles include enabling inclusive economic growth coupled with the development of a robust economic model that established an interconnected community with bigger impact that sustainably empowered the people. However, certain interferences in the management of muslim societies as occasioned by the European colonisations of those societies, the espousal of secular society and the advent of nation-states have drastically diminished the roles of those instruments in many muslim societies.[8]

A potential game changer, Islamic social finance, like other comparable modern sustainability-based financings, has drawn policymakers' attention to consider its proposition as well as implication to the economy.[9] The proposition and implication in terms of shared prosperity and sustainability are too obvious to neglect by the modern economy. Thus, though largely on conceptual and theoretical bases, some scholars even attributed some of the past global financial crises to the neglect of this

[7] See Asutay, M. (2007). Conceptualisation of the second best solution in overcoming the social failure of Islamic banking and finance: examining the overpowering of homoislamicus by homoeconomicus. *IIUM Journal of Economics and Management, 15*, 167–195; Dusuki, A. W. (2008). Banking for the poor: the role of Islamic banking in microfinance initiatives. *Humanomics, 24*, 49–66.

[8] Dallh, M. (2023). Accumulate but distribute: Islamic emphasis on the establishment of Waqf (Pious Endowment). *Religion and Development*, 2(1), 21–40; Tamanni, L., Indra, I., Syamlan, Y. T., & Priantina, A. (2022). Islamic social finance and commercial finance: a marriage made in heaven? *Journal of Islamic Accounting and Business Research*, 13(8), 1216–1233; Kuanova, L. A., Sagiyeva, R., & Shirazi, N. S. (2021). Islamic social finance: a literature review and future research directions. *Journal of Islamic Accounting and Business Research, 12*(5), 707–728.

[9] Nicholls, A., Paton, R., & Emerson, J. (2015). *Social Finance*. Oxford: Oxford University Press.

kind of financing by the mainstream conventional economy.[10] Therefore, although existing since the advent of Islam, Islamic social finance has regained a level of significance today that makes it to relatively feature in contemporary financial economic literature from a peripheral into mainstream subject of discussion.[11]

1.3 Islamic Social Finance Instruments/Institutions

This section provides preliminary discussion that briefly explains specific Islamic social finance instruments and products/services by drawing authority for them from the Quran and Sunnah or juristic viewpoints. It is noteworthy that redistribution of wealth in the Islamic framework is subsumed in the concept of *infaq* i.e., spending, which can be voluntary or involuntary (obligatory). Therefore, the instruments and products/services of Islamic social finance instruments are discussed under two categories: philanthropy-based and cooperation-based instruments/products and services. The former involves benevolent bestowment, i.e., zakat, sadaqah, qard hasan and waqf, and it is wholly charitable while the latter involves some form of business collaboration among people for mutual help, i.e., Islamic microfinance, sukuk social investments and social takaful as for-profit social enterprises.

1.3.1 Philanthropy-Based Social Finance Instruments/ Products and Services

Zakat

Zakat is the foremost instrument of Islamic social finance under the philanthropy-based category. As a pillar of Islam upon which the Islamic economic framework is built, zakat is a form of an obligatory charity levied on people (muslims) that possess a certain threshold of qualified wealth. Leaving aside animals and agricultural yields which have a different taxable minimum, zakat is set at 2.5% or or 1/40 of eligible person's net earned income, specifically cash, as well as valuables such as gold and silver that reach a *nisab*, i.e., the threshold of a taxable minimum wealth. The nisab differs with different kinds of zakatable property. Zakat is paid annually, and it is ordained to be given out of one's *nisab* which is accumulated over the passage of one year. The amount due to be given out of a property as zakat is determined by a precise procedure of calculation. The calculation to determine payable amount is

[10] Tamanni, L., Indra, I., Syamlan, Y. T., & Priantina, A. (2022). Islamic social finance and commercial finance: a marriage made in heaven? *Journal of Islamic Accounting and Business Research, 13*(8), 1216–1233.

[11] Diaw, A. (2015). The global financial crisis and Islamic finance: a review of selected literature. *Journal of Islamic Accounting and Business Research*, *6*(1), 94–106.

as important as the obligation of giving out the zakat. So much is the importance of zakat that the holy Quran in several verses proclaims the giving out of zakat as an obligatory charity in close connection with *salat*, i.e., prayer, for instance:

Quran 2:43: 'You shall observe the Contact Prayers (Salat) and give the obligatory charity (Zakat) and bow down with those who bow down.'

Quran 2:110: 'You shall observe the Contact Prayers (Salat) and give the obligatory charity (Zakat). Any good you send forth on behalf of your souls, you will find it at Allah. Allah is seer of everything you do.'

Quran 2:277: 'Those who believe and lead a righteous life, and observe the Contact Prayers (Salat), and give the obligatory charity (Zakat), they receive their recompense from their Lord; they will have nothing to fear, nor will they grieve.'

Quran 24:56: 'You shall observe the Contact Prayers (Salat) and give the obligatory charity (Zakat), and obey the messenger, that you may attain mercy.'

Quran 70:24: 'And those in whose wealth there is a known right'.

Wealth that qualifies for zakat includes cash money, livestock, farm produce, gold, silver and incomes generated from assets among others. The instrument of zakat, being an obligation upon the privileged and wealthy that is paid annually, ensures redistribution of wealth among the underprivileged, poor and deserving people/ entities, known collectively as *asnaf*, i.e., a category eight eligible zakat recipients, as stated in the following Quranic verse:

Quran 9:60: 'Zakat is for the *poor* and the *needy*, the *amil* (those employed to administer Zakat funds), and the *muallaf* (those who have embraced Islam), for those *in bondage* and *in debt*, for *those who strive in the cause of Allah* and for the *wayfarer* – (it is thus) ordained by Allah and Allah is All-Knowing and Wise.'

In terms of agricultural produce, it was reported in a hadith of the Prophet Muhammad (SAW) in Sahih Muslim, *Hadith Number 2139:*

Abu Sa'id al-Khudri reported Allah's Messenger (may peace be upon him) as saying: No zakat is payable on the grains and dates till it (comes to the weight) of five *wasqs* (measure of weight), or less than five heads of camels, or less than five *uqiyas* (ounce) (of silver).

In another hadith from Sahih Muslim, *Hadith Number 2143,* according to Jabir b. Abdullah, the prophet (may peace be upon him) is reported to have decreed that:

A *tenth* is payable on what is watered by rivers, or rains, and a *twentieth* on what is watered by camels.

Sadaqah

Sadaqah is a voluntary Islamic charity and philanthropy recommended by the Shariah for muslims to attain piety and spiritual upliftment. For sadaqah, there is no set criterion to be eligible to pay or receive it. Sadaqah can be made of everything from monetary donation and material well-being to an act of kindness. Thus, sadaqah comprises feeding others; donating to someone or people in need; protect people from harm; making *du'a* (prayers) for others; being kind to nature; visiting and providing for the sick among other good deeds. By the unequivocal injunctions of several Quranic verses, sadaqah is a voluntary charity that constitute an important Islamic instrument of social finance for promoting societal welfare and devoutness. These Quranic verses provide:

> Quran 2:262: 'Those who spend their wealth in the cause of Allah and do not follow their charity with reminders of their generosity or hurtful words – they will get their reward from their Lord, and there will be no fear for them, nor will they grieve.'
>
> Quran 2:265: 'And the example of those who spend their wealth seeking means to the approval of Allah and assuring [reward for] themselves is like a garden on high ground which is hit by a downpour - so it yields its fruits in double.'
>
> Quran 2:271: 'If you disclose your charitable expenditures, they are good; but if you conceal them and give them to the poor, it is better for you, and He will remove from you some of your misdeeds [thereby]...'
>
> Quran 2:274: 'Those who spend their wealth [in Allah's way] by night and by day, secretly and publicly - they will have their reward with their Lord. And no fear will there be concerning them, nor will they grieve.'

In the sunnah, according to hadith 2202 of Sahih Muslim, the holy prophet Muhammad (peace be upon him) was reported to have enjoined giving *sadaqah* as essential for every muslim. The Prophet Muhammad (SAW) introduced and ordained sadaqah as a source of income for use in a predefined purpose as an Islamic institution of welfare when he proclaimed in *Hadith No. 1378* of *Al-Tirmidhi*:

> When a person dies, his deeds are cut off except for three: *sadaqah jariyah* (continuing charity), knowledge that others benefitted from, and a righteous son (or daughter) who supplicates for him.

A continuing charity (*sadaqah jariyah)*, in accordance with the above hadith, includes teaching people/someone a valuable knowledge and skills; endowing or donating religious, educational and health institutions; endowing/donating shelter for people; planting a tree etc. Accordingly, sadaqah is highly regarded both as an institution and a singular transaction of voluntary giving that plays a vital socio-economic purpose.

Waqf

Waqf is an Islamic endowment. Waqf is a form of Islamic charitable instrument for social finance to support and promote welfare of society generally.[12] Even though the

[12] Omar, K., & Marwa, A. (2022). Waqf Contributions for sustainable development goals: a critical appraisal. In Toseef, A., Murniati, M., & Othman, A. (eds.). *Wealth Management and Investment in Islamic Settings*, (pp 367–391), New York: Springer; Khusaeri, K. (2015). Productive endowments. *Al-A'raf: Journal of Islamic Thought and Philosophy*, *12*(1), 77–95; Khan, N.A., Jareen, S. (2015). The *Waqf* and Human Security in Muslim Majority Countries: Traditions, Modern Practices, and Challenges. In: Hasan, S. (Eds.). *Human Security and Philanthropy. Nonprofit and Civil Society Studies.* New York, NY: Springer. https://doi.org/10.1007/978-1-4939-2525-4_7.

word 'waqf' is not specifically used in the Quran, there are verses that are the basic drivers for establishing waqf. Also, in accordance with *Sunan Abi Dawud Book 18, Hadith 17* (Sunan Abi Dawud 2878), it was encouraged by the Prophet Muhammad (peace be upon him) for Muslims to dedicate their wealth or property in perpetuity and offer proceeds therefrom to charity. The hadith was narrated as follows:

> Narrated Ibn 'Umar: 'Umar got some land in Khaibar, and went to the Prophet (peace be upon him) and said: I have acquired land in Khaibar which I consider to be more valuable than any I have acquired; so what do you command me to do with it? He replied: If you wish, you may make the property as inalienable possession, and give its produce as sadaqah (charity). So 'Umar gave it as a sadaqah declaring that the property must not be sold, given away, or inherited (and gave its produce as sadaqah to be devoted) to poor, relatives, the emancipation of slaves, Allah's path, travellers.

The prophet had also enjoined waqf, as narrated in *Sahih Muslim Book 25, Hadith 20* (Sahih Muslim 1631), when he advised Muslims to engage in *sadaqah jariyah*, i.e., a continuing, flowing and ongoing charity, as one of the things that survive and ensure rewards for a muslim after death. The hadith was narrated thus:

> Abu Huraira (Allah be pleased with him) reported Allah's Messenger (peace be upon him) as saying: "When a man dies, his acts come to an end, but three, recurring charity (*sadaqah jariyah*), or knowledge (by which people) benefit, or a pious son, who prays for him (for the deceased)."

As a form of *sadaqah jariyah*, waqf is an endowment that enduringly gives as opposed to one-off kind of charity. Therefore, while it continuously benefits its recipients, it equally serves as an instrument for the donor to keep on earning rewards even after death.

Qard Hasan

In place of interest, which is forbidden, Shariah enjoins a benevolent, interest-free loan, knowns as qard hasan. Qard hasan is a loan granted mainly for welfare purposes and on the basis of goodwill. Qur'an encourages giving of qard hasan to those that need them and in the event a borrower encounters difficulty, the lender is required to extend repayment time and can voluntarily waive the debt, or part of it. Qard Hasan is sanctioned and ordained by the following Quranic verses:

> Quran 73:20: 'Establish regular prayer and give regular charity and give Allah Qard Hasan.'
>
> Quran 2:245: 'Who is it that would loan Allah a goodly loan (Qard Hasan) so He may multiply it for him many times over? And it is Allah who withholds and grants abundance, and to Him you will be returned.'
>
> Quran 57:18: 'For those who give in charity men and women, and loan to Allah a Beautiful Loan (Qardan hasana), it shall be increased manifold (to their credit) and they shall have (besides) a liberal reward.'
>
> Quran 64:17 'If ye loan to Allah a beautiful loan (Qardan hasana) He will double it to your (credit) and He will grant you Forgiveness: for Allah is most Ready to appreciate (service) Most Forbearing.'

On the authority of the above Quranic verses, any amount one spends in the cause of Allah or advances the same to help someone out of benevolence without seeking any reward or worldly benefit in return but as an act of charity to seek God's grace, then God almighty takes it as a loan in His cause which He promise to repay and reward the creditor in manifold in the Hereafter.

Qard hasan is a prescribed loan that is critical in supporting communities and societies on a voluntary basis. As an interest-free loan, qard hasan is regarded as a form of assistant to the needy and the poor. The benevolent nature of qard hasan, for example, facilitates financial help to the deserving individuals and entities by not encumbering them with the burden of collateral or interest.[13]

1.3.2 Cooperation-Based Islamic Social Finance Instruments/Products and Services

Islamic Microfinance

Islamic Microfinance is the provision of financial services in tiny amounts to poor and low-income segments of the population according to Islamic values underpinned by Shariah principles. Recipients of such financial services are mostly of low economic standing and thus unable to provide collateral for their financing. This fact excludes them from formal financial systems, and they are thus financially unserved or under-served. Islamic microfinance enables financial services offerings for this category of people in conformity with Shariah.[14]

The Islamic social finance model for microfinance works as a charity aimed at poverty alleviation among affected members of the society. In Islam, poverty is a condition in which one cannot afford to fulfil one's basic requirements of life which include wealth, religion, knowledge or intellect and physical self. Therefore, poverty alleviation is a major thrust of Islamic social finance which seeks to provide leverage that enables people in need to attain the basic requirements of life.[15] Poverty alleviation in Islam is considered indispensable to the public duty to render social justice. Accordingly, institutional approach has been promoted by contemporary muslim scholars for effective role of the public sector and market towards alleviating poverty

---

[13] Selim, M. (2019). The effectiveness of Qard-al-Hasan (interest free loan) as a Tool of Monetary Policy. *International Journal of Islamic and Middle Eastern Finance and Management*, *12*(1), 130–151.

[14] Alkhan, A. M., & Hassan, M. K. (2021). Does Islamic microfinance serve maqāsid al-shari'a?. *Borsa Istanbul Review*, *21*(1), 57–68; Mohamed, E. F., & Fauziyyah, N. E. (2020). Islamic microfinance for poverty alleviation: a systematic literature review. *International Journal of Economics, Management & Accounting*, *28*(1), 141–163.

[15] Salleh, M. S. (2017). Contemporary vision of poverty and Islamic strategy for poverty alleviation. *SAGE Open*, *7*(2), 1–8. https://doi.org/10.1177/2158244017697153; Mansori, S., Kim, C. S., & Safari, M. (2015). A Shariah perspective review on Islamic microfinance. *Asian Social Science*, *11*(9). https://doi.org/10.5539/ass.v11n9p273.

and redistribution of wealth.[16] Islamic microfinance services as such are notably provided by Islamic microfinance institutions. Islam instructs mutual cooperation and community-based activities to assist one another in accordance with Qur'an 5:2. The mutual cooperation extends to community welfare by alleviating poverty via the instrument of Islamic microfinance. For this purpose, several Shariah-based contracts such as Ijarah, musharakah, mudarabah, murabahah and qard al-hasan are used to model Islamic microfinancing. Similarly, Islamic microfinance models have been developed and operated based on zakat, waqf, qard hasan and sadaqah funds which underpin the nature and approach of certain Islamic microfinance institutions and entities in providing relevant services.[17]

Thus, in contrast with conventional system that gives rise to and perpetuate debt, Islamic microfinance seeks to provides basic conditions for a successful and sustainable poverty alleviation through market-based as well as mission-based plans that advance cooperation using financing models based on equity, lease, sale among others that blend wealth creation with empathy for the poor.[18] In this regard, Islamic approach to poverty alleviation is an inclusive one which provides not only financial inclusion but financial development and independence.

Social Sukuk

The word "sukuk" is a plural form of the Arabic word "*sakk*" which literally means a certificate or written document or official record showing ownership, commercial agreement or a financial right.[19] In this regard, it was reported that around the end of the first century after Hijra [AH] (seventh century AD), the Umayyad dynasty administration paid army personnel using sukuk (documents) that showed and conferred the right to purchase a certain amount of foodstuffs from the government grain warehouses after harvest.[20] It is also on record that that the sukuk issued in the form of commodity coupons during the reigns of Caliph Umar and Marwan bin Hakam (b. 623–624—d. 685) were sold by some holders for cash in the market before the maturity date written on them.[21] As a financial instrument in Islamic

[16] Iqbal, M. (2002). Introduction. In Iqbal, M. (Ed.). *Islamic Economic Institutions and the Elimination of Poverty* (pp. 1–24). Leicester: The Islamic Foundation, p. 13.

[17] El-Komi, M., & Croson, R. (2013). Experiments in Islamic microfinance. *Journal of Economic Behavior & Organization, 95*, 252–269; Obaidullah, M. (2008). *Introduction to Islamic Microfinance*. New Delhi: International Institute of Islamic Business and Finance.

[18] Riwajanti, N. I. (2013). Islamic Microfinance as an Alternative for Poverty Alleviation: A Survey. *Afro Eurasian Studies*, 2(1–2), 254–271; Obaidullah, M., & Khan, T. (2008). *Islamic Microfinance Development: Challenges and Initiatives*. Jeddah: IRTI, Islamic Development Bank.

[19] Ismail, E. (2021). Historical origins of sukuk as a popular instrument in modern Islamic finance. *Islam Hukuku Araştirmalari Dergisi*, (38), 103–127; Manzur, Ibn. (2000). *Lisan al-Arab*, 3rd edition. Beirut: Dar Sader, pp. 2474–2475.

[20] Hassan, A. A. H. (2007). *Sales and Contracts in Early Islamic Commercial Law* (No. 92). Petaling Jaya: The Other Press, p. 119.

[21] Coulson, N. J., (1984). *Commercial Law in the Gulf States*. London: Graham-Trotman, p. 112.

history, however, sukuk has served as a legal, commercial and financial tool that was used in different ways, particularly during the Ottoman period, which include ration certificate, payment order and debt note.[22]

In the contemporary sense of the word, though used commonly as it were singular in English works, sukuk has been defined by the Securities Commission Malaysia as "certificates of equal value evidencing undivided ownership or investment in the assets using Shariah principles and structures endorsed by the Shariah Advisory Council (SAC)."[23] Similarly, according to the Accounting and Auditing Organisation for Islamic Financial Institutions (AAOIFI), sukuk are defined as "certificates of equal value representing undivided shares in the ownership of tangible assets, usufructs and services or (in the ownership of) the assets of particular projects or special investment activities."[24] Thus, as an Islamic capital market instrument, sukuk is often referred to as an investment certificate which is developed as a sharia-compliant alternative to bonds. Sukuk as such is based on Shariah compliant contracts such as such as *ijarah, mudarabah, musharakah, murabahah, bai' bithaman ajil* (BBA), *musharakah* among other others and an underlying asset is essential for sukuk transaction. Sukuk can be debt or equity type of financial instrument which is used to raise funds in the Islamic capital market.

The process of sukuk involves issuer and holders (of the sukuk). The holders constitute undivided beneficial owners of the underlying assets and receive profits generated from the sukuk assets or an obligor as proceeds obtained from leasing or selling of the assets. In practice however, Sukuk are largely structured as debt instrument using appropriate Shariah contracts while some structured with an equity or hybrid feature.[25]

Social sukuk is an investment instrument that furthers the objective of social justice with green and socially responsible investing in its fold for societal well-being in accordance with the Shariah. Social sukuk is a way to enable private and not for profit organisations to partner in delivering better social outcomes for the society. The main goal of social sukuk main is to facilitate investment opportunities that focus on and deal with societal and environmental issues.[26] As a relatively recent innovation, social sukuk has been used in time of national crisis to raise

---

[22] Ismail, E. (2021). Historical origins of sukuk as a popular instrument in modern Islamic finance. *Islam Hukuku Araştirmalari Dergisi*, (38), 103–127; Manzur, Ibn. (2000). *Lisan al-Arab* (pp. 2474–2775), 3rd edition. Beirut: Dar Sader.

[23] Securities Commission, Malaysia. (2018). *Guidelines on Issuance of Corporate Bonds and Sukuk to Retail Investors.* Available at https://www.sc.com.my/api/documentms/download.ashx?id=7be24ad9-1846-4de9-8897-d5ed58ec0011 (accessed 19 November 2023).

[24] Accounting and Auditing Organisation for Islamic Financial Institutions [AAOIFI]. (2017). *Shari'ah Standard No. 17: Investment Sukuk.* Manama, Kingdom of Bahrain: AAOIFI, p. 468.

[25] Kunhibava, S., Mustapha, Z., Muneeza, A., Sa'ad, A. A., & Karim, M. E. (2021). Ṣukuk on Blockchain: a legal, regulatory and Sharī'ah review. *ISRA International Journal of Islamic Finance, 13*(1), pp. 119–120.

[26] Mohamed, S., Othman, J., Lehner, O., & Muda, R. (2017). Social sukuk: a new mechanism to fund social services. *Journal of Emerging Economies and Islamic Research, 5*(1), 69–81.

funds for society's needs, for example Sukuk Prihatin in Malaysia[27] and Cash Waqf-linked Sukuk in Indonesia.[28] Proceeds realised from the issuance and subscriptions of these kind of sukuk were was channelled into and expended on socio-economic and socio-environmental programmes that provide not only financial gains but addresses societal and environmental issues through, for instance, funding of development projects that border around small/micro enterprises (targeting women entrepreneurs), housing, rural schools connectivity, as well as grants for educational or health-related research. The goal is to develop social benefits for people and eliminate such social menace as poverty and unemployment while building maintainable environment for the society.

Social Takaful

Takaful (Islamic insurance) is not a recent development but has its historical roots in an Arab custom of 'aqilah' which predated Islam. *Aqilah* was a practice whereby a clan or tribe members collectively compensated legal heirs of a deceased on behalf of their killer tribesman (in cases other than premeditated murder) as a form of *diyya* (blood money).[29] Based on this custom, a rough model of takaful was practiced by merchants of Mecca who pooled funds for a victim of natural disasters and as a form of assistance. This form of compensation was known as '*maaqil'* and upheld by the Prophet Muhammad (peace be upon him) and incorporated, in its earliest form as social insurance, in the constitution of Medina.[30] It is an application of a form of assurance to provide for one another through a takaful-like arrangement.

Takaful, in its contemporary practice, is an Islamic version of insurance where members pool money into a common fund to guarantee one another based on Shariah to cover life, health and general insurance needs. The contributing members constitute policyholders. It is notable that this coming together of people to pool money and guarantee one another as the main underlying principle of takaful has its origin from the practice of '*aqilah*', a tradition which was transformed from the pre-Islamic tradition to an institution of the Shariah that further evolved through medieval and post medieval Islamic law and society. Moreover, the principles of *kafala,* i.e., guarantee, is an important element of takaful whereby participants in the pool jointly guarantee

---

[27] Bin Mohamed Fisol, W. N., & Bin Saad, M. A. (2021). Rebuilding the National Economy by Issuance of The First Malaysia Digital Sukuk (Sukuk Prihatin) And Its Distribution Through Fintech Services: A View from The Perspective of Maqasid Al-Shari'ah. *Journal of Contemporary Issues in Business and Government, 27*(1).

[28] Fauziah, N. N., Ali, E. R. A. E., & Bacha, A. M. (2021). An analysis of cash waqf linked sukuk for socially impactful sustainable projects in Indonesia. *Journal of Islamic Finance, 10*, 001–010.

[29] Olorogun, L. A. (2013). Critical Evaluation of Fundamental Theoretical Concept of Islamic Insurance "Takaful". *Asian Journal of Research in Banking and Finance, 3*(12), 39–51.

[30] Ismail, A. G., & Possumah, B. T. (2014). Poverty and social security in Islam. In: Hassan, M. K., & Lewis, M. K. (Eds.). *Handbook on Islam and Economic Life* (pp. 437–439); Emon, A. (2001). Reflections on the constitution of medina: an essay on methodology and ideology in Islamic legal history. *UCLA J. Islamic & Near EL, 1*, 103.

each other against loss or injury i.e. to share burden of the loss or injury via the pool of funds. Therefore, in its basic conception, the principal purpose of takaful is not to make profit but to ease pure risk faced by contributors to the fund.[31] Takaful operates as a co-operative system of repayment or reimbursement in an event a calamity befalls any of the contributors to whom a compensation will be paid from the common fund. The members' contributions are regarded as gifts or donations to the fund to help those in need of assistance. Where the fund records loss or incur liability, such are spread among the members in accordance with their pre-agreed contributing system.

The Shariah basis for takaful is *ta'awun* (mutual assistance), contract of *tabarru* (donation) and solidarity in furtherance of the good virtues of mutual indemnity to help those in need in accordance with the following commandment of the holy Quran:

> Quran 5:2 'Help ye one another in righteousness and piety, but help ye not one another in sin and rancour, fear Allah, for Allah is strict in punishment.'

From a sunnah perspective, takaful would be regarded as one of the solutions for unforeseen circumstances such as death of a sole breadwinner, permanent disability, critical ailments and accident/incidents that occasion incapability to work. In a hadith, reported by both *Bukhari and Muslim*, the holy Prophet Muhammad (peace be upon him) was reported to say that:

> Allah blesses those who acquire wealth in a good manner, then the wealth is spent accordingly, and the remaining is saved for future use when hardship occurs.

Takaful is an important option for the protection of one's life and wealth in the light of the hadith reported by Bukhari, *Book 13, Hadith Number 3991*, where the holy Prophet Muhammad (peace be upon him) said:

> Leaving behind one's heirs rich is better than leaving them poor.

Generally, there are a number of models to establish takaful and pursue Islamic social finance ideals. A waqf model for instance compensates members for their loss using irredeemable donations that constitute an endowment fund. Meanwhile, in a commercial model, the fund is established using members' voluntary contributions which an agency can manage for a fee charged from the fund.[32] Alternatively, members can decide to invest/manage the fund by themselves, share profit therefrom or reinvest same in the takaful fund.[33]

Social takaful will be viewed with the foregoing in mind at the level of the whole society. Social takaful is a type of takaful that backs up and bails out each other in the

---

[31] Nasir, N. I. F. M., & Hassan, R. (2021). Delineating the Islamic social elements in takaful. In: *Handbook of Research on Islamic Social Finance and Economic Recovery After a Global Health Crisis* (pp. 348–360). IGI Global.

[32] Bidabad, B. (2015). Rastin social takaful (RST). *Journal of Islamic Economics, Banking and Finance, JIEBF*, *11*(1), 13–23.

[33] Alhammadi, S. (2023). Expanding financial inclusion in Indonesia through Takaful: opportunities, challenges and sustainability. *Journal of Financial Reporting and Accounting*, [Vol. ahead-of-print No. ahead-of-print]. https://doi.org/10.1108/JFRA-05-2023-0256.

society personally and collectively through affirmative actions motivated by sense and conscience of Islamic belief to protect and enhance human lives in the society. The goal is for the society to assist people in such a way that all help one another to establish a better society where poverty, harms/injuries and losses are eliminated from members. In essence, social takaful signifies collective support, patronage and bailment of people in a society by themselves and for themselves.[34] Unlike in takaful where only contributing members to a pool of funds benefit therefrom when the need arises, social takaful provides an avenue for support and means of livelihood to people (poor) who cannot make afford contributions. Consequently, manifest social and economic inequality is assuredly bridged ensuring that no member of the society is socially or economically disadvantaged.

Funding for social takaful is obtained from benevolent depositors in Islamic finance institutions and benefactors (public and private) and deployed through relevant institutions for public charity. The benefactors include all people, institutions, religious entities and authorities, organizations, governments and affiliated agencies and parastatals, non-governmental organizations who can allocate their own funds and resources that comprise donations, subsidies, sadaqah (alms), zakat (obligatory tax), waqf (endowment), will (wasiyyah), kaffarah (redemption), diyya (blood money), ghanimah (spoils of war), nazr (vows), gift (hadiyah), poll tax (jizyah), tribute (kharaj), inheritance with no inheritor, fines of convict, confiscated properties among others.[35]

Social takaful is an evolving concept and its practice is so far not widespread, but it has very strong potential of financial inclusion for all in society and wider community-led initiatives for Islamic-based development and sustainability. Social takaful facilities significantly increase the chances for poor people to be self-reliant and consequently benefit their families and the communities.

1.4 Impact of Islamic Social Finance

Islamic social finance has a potentially significant positive contribution to poverty alleviation, economic empowerment and sustainability, thus, its impact in the global development agenda is potentially huge. Despite lack of reliable data, figures from the World Bank and World Economic Forum indicate an estimated 2.5–3 trillion dollars of funding gap annually towards the global sustainability agenda, i.e., the Sustainable Development Goals (SDGs).[36] To that effect, Islamic social finance is

[34] Bidabad, B. (2015). Rastin social takaful (RST). *Journal of Islamic Economics, Banking and Finance, JIEBF*, *11*(1), 13–23.

[35] Hassan, M. K., Muneeza, A., & Sarea, A. M. (Eds.). (2021). *Towards a Post-Covid Global Financial System - Lesson in Social Responsibility From Islamic Finance*. Bingley: Emerald Publishing Limited.

[36] UN. (n.d.). *2030 Agenda and the Sustainable Development Goals: Financing and Funding*. Available at https://unsdg.un.org/2030-agenda/financing.

considered an alternative source of funding. Thus, in 2020, the World Bank and IRTI-IsDB projected that the Islamic social finance instrument of zakat could mobilize an estimated 200 billion to 1 trillion dollar per year to be expended for the same purpose.[37] This can have an impact in boosting efforts towards poverty alleviation and achieving better living with view to sustainability.

Moreover, according to available estimates with the relevant stakeholders, global waqf assets today range between USD 100 billion and 1 trillion, comprising of land and landed properties across muslim countries, of which more than one-third is cultivable.[38] Moreover, as statistics and the estimates have established, majority of these assets, from as high as 70% and 80% of total assets in the sector, are real estate.[39] Cash waqf, an innovative waqf instrument separate from the traditional landed asset waqf, has been estimated to be worth USD 35 billion, invested in regional Islamic money markets.[40]

Practically, Islamic social finance takes on an important public role in the development of contemporary muslim societies. The instruments of zakat, waqf and sadaqah for instance have been very useful in the establishment and management of public utility, health and educational institutions among other charitable endeavours in many countries.[41] Coincidentally, the efficacy of Islamic social finance in social empowerment, poverty alleviation and economic and community well-being has been somewhat observed when zakat and sadaqah were deployed to provide relief during the Covid-19 pandemic and in post Covid-19 recovery measures among several Islamic countries.[42]

---

[37] UNDP. (2020). *Zakat for the SDGS*. Available at https://www.undp.org/blog/zakat-sdgs; UNDP. (2017). *The Role of Zakat in Supporting the Sustainable Development Goals*. Available at https://www.undp.org/indonesia/publications/role-zakat-supporting-sustainable-development-goals.

[38] IDB. (2014). *Waqf and Zakat, Solidarity-Based Financing for Sustainable Development*. Available at https://sustainabledevelopment.un.org/content/documents/10289Mahiridrissipresentation.pdf (accessed 12 October 2023).

[39] Nazim, A. (2010). *Philanthropy to Accelerate Islamic Finance Growth*. Available at https://www.emirates247.com/business/economy-finance/philanthropy-to-accelerate-islamic-finance-growth-2010-12-19-1.331297 (accessed 12 October 2023).

[40] Abdul Aziz, A. H. B., Zhang, W., Hamid, B. A., Mahomed, Z., Bouheraoua, S., Kasri, N. S., & Sano, M. A. A. (2019). *Maximizing Social Impact through Waqf Solutions* (pp. 1–89). The World Bank, INCEIF & ISRA.

[41] Usman, M., & Ab Rahman, A. (2023). Funding higher education through waqf: a lesson from Malaysia. *International Journal of Ethics and Systems, 39*(1), 107–125; Usman, M., & Ab Rahman, A. (2021). Funding higher education through waqf: a lesson from Pakistan. *International Journal of Islamic and Middle Eastern Finance and Management, 14*(2), 409–424; Sowtali, S. N. (2021). Waqf for healthcare: social security of the future. *International Journal of Care Scholars, 4*(2), 89–92; Ascarya, Tanjung, H. (2021). Structures of healthcare Waqf in Indonesia to support SDGs. In: Billah, M.M. (Eds.). *Islamic Wealth and the SDGs*. Cham: Palgrave Macmillan. https://doi.org/10.1007/978-3-030-65313-2_15.

[42] Ascarya, A. (2022). The role of Islamic social finance during Covid-19 pandemic in Indonesia's economic recovery. *International Journal of Islamic and Middle Eastern Finance and Management, 15*(2), 386–405; Purwanto, P., Sari, F. N., Burasukma, M., & Nursolihah, S. (2021). The role of Islamic social finance through Ziswaf and BMT during the COVID-19 pandemic. *MALIA:*

On the whole, Islamic social finance provides funds needed to address the rising social and economic challenges that the world faces—funds that purposefully offset the menace of poverty, end hunger and inequality, address waste and unfair distribution of wealth and curb unsustainable economic exploits.[43] These are commitments enjoined by and encompassed in the objectives of Shariah and incidentally shared with some SDGs.[44] Therefore, speaking in terms of impact and/or contribution to society in general and towards achieving the SDGs in particular, the Islamic social finance provides adaptably powerful instruments that are currently being deployed to facilitate addressing the SDGs funding and financing gap.

1.5 Relationship of Islamic Social Finance to Blended Finance, Alternative Finance and Circular Economy

1.5.1 Blended Finance and Islamic Social Finance

Blended finance is the use of catalytic or incentizing funds from philanthropic or public sources to augment investments from private sector. As emphasis mounts on mobilizing private funds to expedite development progress, blended finance or blended concessional finance becomes prominent, rising from its niche position and features among important underlying tools for development finance.[45] As a result, blended finance is considered as much an activity as it is a subsystem of development financing. Thus, in relation to SDGs financing, being a development finance matter, blended finance is used to combine concession finance from third party donors with a development financial institutions own-account or commercial finance from investors with the aim of mobilizing private resources to develop market and advance progress on the SDGs.[46] Available data suggest progressive increase in using blended for certain aspects of SDG, even though blended finance is yet to leverage private funds

Journal of Islamic Banking and Finance, 5(2), 81–98; Hamed, M. M. (2020). The role of Islamic social finance in mitigating humanitarian crises. *European Journal of Islamic Finance*, (16).

43 Khan, T., & Badjie, F. (2022). Islamic blended finance for circular economy impactful SMEs to achieve SDGs. *The Singapore Economic Review, 67*(1), 219–244; OECD. (2018). *Making Blended Finance Work for the Sustainable Development Goals* (pp. 41–42). Paris: OECD Publishing. https://doi.org/10.1787/9789264288768-en.

44 Laldin, M. A., & Djafri, F. (2021). The role of Islamic finance in achieving sustainable development goals (SDGs). In: Hassan, M. K., Saraç, M., Khan, A. (Eds.). *Islamic Finance and Sustainable Development* (pp. 107–126). Cham: Palgrave Macmillan; World Bank. (2018). *Sustainable Development Goals and the Role of Islamic Finance.* Available at https://blogs.worldbank.org/eastasiapacific/sustainable-development-goals-and-role-islamic-finance (accessed 25 August 2023).

45 Pereira, J. (2017). *Blended Finance: What It Is, How It Works and How It Is Used.* Oxfam International.

46 Mutambatsere, E., & Schellekens, P. (2020). The Why and How of Blended Finance. The World Bank.

at scale.[47] Nonetheless, blended finance is considered an important tool to support implementation of the SDGs. It is noteworthy that Islamic social finance compares to blended finance in that it blends to mobilize and channel social funds such as social sukuk and social takaful for for-profit social enterprises for socio-economic development. It is also the case in the objective of Islamic social finance towards responsible and green investing as well as efficient resource allocation for sustainability.[48]

1.5.2 Alternative Finance and Islamic Social Finance

Alternative finance refers to financing from external sources other than bond or stock markets or banks. In addition, alternative finance underscores the direct relationship between funders and fundraiser, usually through online avenues.[49] The various forms of alternative finance that exist in practice do not fit into discrete, mutually exclusive categories. These evolving tools overlap at times and may combine aspects of each other. For example, the form of alternative financing known as "peer-to-peer lending" can be considered both crowdfunding and marketplace lending. Islamic finance as well uses such tools and platforms and thus form alternative Islamic finance. Moreover, in relation to Islamic social finance, the development of Islamic and its use for zakat, sadaqah, social sukuk, charity and other forms of infaq in the virtual space have collectively pointed at the dynamics of alternative finance for Islamic social financing.

1.5.3 Circular Economy and Islamic Social Finance

A circular economy is an economic system established on regeneration and reuse of materials as a means of production in a sustainable way. It is a model of manufacturing and consumption that builds an economy that centres around and advocates for redesign, reuse, repair, reduction, renovation, recycling and recovery in industry and development. From its theoretical conception, two elements have been precursory for the idea of circular economy as advocated by earlier environmental and conservation experts. One relates to the movement of materials through an economy and the other has to do with the thought regarding the economic conditions that might cause such

---

47 Kenny, Charles. (2019). *Marginal, Not Transformational: Development Finance Institutions and the Sustainable Development Goals*. Center for Global Development.

48 Khan, T., & Badjie, F. (2022). Islamic blended finance for circular economy impactful SMEs to achieve SDGs. *The Singapore Economic Review*, *67*(01), 219–244.

49 Segal, M. (2016). What is alternative finance. *Office of Advocacy*, *1*, 1–4; Baeck, Peter, Collins, Liam, & Zhang, Bryan. (2014). *Understanding Alternative Finance: The UK Alternative Finance Industry Report*. Available at www.jbs.cam.ac.uk/fileadmin/user_upload/research/centres/alternativefinance/downloads/2014-uk-alternative-finance-benchmarking-report.pdf, Cambridge University and Nesta.

flow. These elements underlie an industrial symbiosis that seeks to foster and share mutually profitable dealings through long-term eco-innovative and culture change.[50] The reality of circular economy is built upon "an industrial system that is restorative or regenerative by intention and design. It replaces the 'end-of-life' concept with restoration, shifts towards the use of renewable energy, eliminates the use of toxic chemicals which impair reuse, and aims for the elimination of waste through the superior design of materials, products, systems, and, within this, business models."[51] In practice, an instance of circular economic activity is seen in the way plastic and plastic products are recycled to make pellets to manufacture new products. It is also a circular economic practice for consumers to share, instead of buy new, products they occasionally use like a power drill or vehicles. Circular economy is a direct contrast of linear economy where determinate resources are extracted to manufacture products that are used negligibly, i.e., not to fullest potential, and then discarded.[52]

Comparatively speaking, circular economy has been provided for by the holy Quran and one of the ways its practice is demonstrated is through Islamic social finance practice. The holy Quran calls on muslims to rethink nature and earthly creations. Several Quranic verses declare that sustenance for all earthly creatures is provided, protected and delivered in precise quantities by Allah (the most glorified, the most high). For instance, Quran 15:21 provides "There is not any means of sustenance whose reserves We do not hold, only bringing it forth in precise measure." "Precise measure" is to make mindful consumers of muslims and ordain a curb to waste, restraint in resources use, forestall harm to environment and ensure sustainability. This informs of the Islamic ethics towards community support, moderation and responsibility in all dealings to foster sustainability.[53]

1.6 Conclusion

The Quran and hadith (sunnah) are the primary sources of Islamic law (Shariah) through whose provisions all dealings are mainly validated. From this perspective, Islamic social finance is established with the principal objectives to enhance

---

[50] Agudo, F. L., Bezerra, B. S., & Júnior, J. A. G. (2023). Symbiotic readiness: factors that interfere with the industrial symbiosis implementation. *Journal of Cleaner Production, 387*, 135843.

[51] Ellen MacArthur F. (2019). *Circular Cities: Thriving, Liveable, Resilient*, p. 7. Available online at https://www.ellenmacarthurfoundation.org/our-work/activities/circular-economy-in-cities; Ekins, P., Domenech Aparisi, T., Drummond, P., Bleischwitz, R., Hughes, N., & Lotti, L. (2020). *The Circular Economy: What, Why, How and Where* (p. 82); OECD/EC Workshop "Managing environmental and energy transitions for regions and cities." Paris, 5 July 2019.

[52] Rashid, S., & Malik, S. H. (2023). Transition from a linear to a circular economy. In: *Renewable Energy in Circular Economy* (pp. 1–20). Cham: Springer International Publishing; Neves, S. A., & Marques, A. C. (2022). Drivers and barriers in the transition from a linear economy to a circular economy. *Journal of Cleaner Production, 341*, 130865.

[53] Ali, S. N., & Jumat, Z. H. (2021). Islamic finance and circular economy: an introduction. In: Ali, S. N., & Jumat, Z. H. (Eds.). *Islamic Finance and Circular Economy—Connecting Impact and Value Creation*. Singapore: Springer. https://doi.org/10.1007/978-981-16-6061-0_1.

social welfare, economic empowerment, inclusivity and quality societal growth which collectively create a just economy. By design and intention, the Quran and hadith traditionally provide for Islamic social finance to facilitate the establishment of human community based on shared prosperity. There is no better time for the Islamic shared prosperity in the world than today. Therefore, the contemporary world, by its dynamism in innovative industry and development needs, has made it imperative to expand the Shariah commandment and authoritative recommendations for Islamic social finance. This is to further its relevance alongside blended finance, sharing economy, circular economy among other sustainability appellations subsumed in the SDGs. In this regard, a legal and regulatory framework that ensures the Shariah dictates is a requisite, hence the efforts for strategic implementation and operationalization of Islamic social finance instruments and instruments facilitated by digital legal framework.

Review Questions

1. Question 1: Islamic social finance services can obtain in the form of charitable enterprises and ……

   a. *for-profit enterprises.*
   b. Benevolent enterprises.
   c. Helpful enterprises.
   d. Liberal enterprises.

2. Question 2: Which of the following instrument can be a cooperation-based Islamic social finance product?

   a. Sadaqah jariyah.
   b. Zakat.
   c. *Social sukuk.*
   d. All of the above.

3. Question 3: Islamic social finance comprises of obligatory and …… instruments/institutions.

   a. Compulsory.
   b. *Voluntary.*
   c. Enforceable.
   d. Mandatory.

4. Question 4: Which of the following instrument is an obligatory Islamic social inance institution?

   a. Sadaqah.
   b. Zakat.
   c. Waqf.
   d. Qard.

5. Question 5: Islamic social finance instruments of ……. have been practiced since the advent of Islam and brought important socio-economic development of muslim societies.

   a. Digital Sukuk and bond.
   b. Takaful and social bond.
   c. Zakat and waqf.
   d. Zakat and digital sukuk.

6. Question 6: Islamic social finance is considered …… to contemporary development and sustainability needs.

   a. Crucial.
   b. Trivial.
   c. Inconsequential.
   d. Frivolous.

7. Question 7: Giving to the poor and needy under the Islamic framework of wealth redistribution is subsumed in the concept of ……. which involves spending for charity, both voluntary and obligatory.

   a. Maqasid al-shariah.
   b. *Infaq*.
   c. Sunnah.
   d. None of the above.

8. Question 8: One of the following Quranic verses mentions and ordains zakat as an obligatory act of worship enjoined upon Muslims of means.

   a. Quran 2:56.
   b. Quran 2:282.
   c. Quran 2:271.
   d. *Quran 24:56*.

9. Question 9: Islamic social finance compares to blended finance in that it blends to channel social funds into ……… for socio-economic development.

   a. Capital enterprises.
   b. *For-profit social enterprises*.
   c. Profitable enterprises.
   d. Zero-profit enterprises.

10. Question 10: For circular economic practice according to the Shariah, one of the following Quranic verses calls for mindful consumption, curb waste, exercise restraint in resources use and forestall harm to environment.

    a. Quran 2:282.
    b. Quran 5:22.
    c. *Quran 15:21*.
    d. All of the above.

Answers

1. a
2. c
3. b
4. b
5. c
6. a
7. b
8. d
9. b
10. c

Chapter 2
Sadaqah, Zakat and Qard Hassan: Legal Framework

Abstract In this chapter looks into the intricacies of Islamic charitable practices, namely Sadaqah, Zakat, and Qard Hassan. Providing a nuanced overview, the chapter explores the historical and conceptual dimensions of each form of charity, emphasizing their unique roles within the Islamic social finance framework. Drawing distinctions between Sadaqah, Zakat, and Qard Hassan, the chapter navigates through the legal frameworks governing these practices, shedding light on the Shariah injunctions that guide their implementation. Rich with case studies, the chapter illustrates the real-world applications of these charitable concepts, offering insights into their impact on communities. Additionally, the chapter critically examines the issues and challenges that may arise in the context of Sadaqah, Zakat, and Qard Hassan, contributing to a holistic understanding of these essential elements of Islamic social finance.

Keywords Sadaqah · Zakat · Qard Hassan · Legal Framework · Community Impact

Learning Outcomes
At the end of this chapter, students will be able to understand:

- an overview of Sadaqah, Zakat and Qard Hassan,
- the differences between Sadaqah, Zakat and Qard Hassan,
- legal framework for Sadaqah, Zakat and Qard Hassan,
- case studies,
- issues and challenges.

2.1 What is Sadaqah, Zakat and Qard Hassan

Based on the earlier chapters, it is important to reiterate that social finance is rooted in well-defined and entrenched divine injunctions from the holy Quran and sunnah that underpin Islamic charity, philanthropy, and social justice. Nevertheless, it is

S. Kunhibava et al., *Islamic Social Finance*,
https://doi.org/10.1007/978-981-97-1410-0_2

only recently that social finance has been given more focused and the term Islamic social finance was coined. This is especially after the COVID19 pandemic erupted, contributing to an increase social disparity and enlarging the United Nation's Sustainable Development Goal's funding gap.[1] The focus and traction in the Islamic finance area shifted to social finance as it seemed that such shift would be the answer to bridging the gap.[2] Furthermore, such shift also happened after realizing social finance is a component part of the greater objective of Islam sought to be accomplished by individuals and more formal corporate entities whose aim is to improve social justice through fair dealings and wealth redistribution.

Under this chapter, it focuses on three of the most researched Islamic financial instruments in social finance[3]; sadaqah, zakat and qard hassan.

2.1.1 Sadaqah

Sadaqah signifies a voluntary act of charity extended to others with the intention of aiding those in need, without having any expectation of return. The nature and extent of this charitable contribution are left to the discretion of individuals, as it is a form of assistance that is not obligatory but highly encouraged as a means of alleviating the plight of those in need and fostering societal well-being. Sadaqah takes on diverse forms, which may include offering financial aid, providing food, clothing, or other essential resources to individuals or charitable organizations. This virtuous deed is believed to carry blessings and rewards for the giver.

Notably, Sadaqah assumes a pivotal role in advancing socio-economic equity and financial inclusivity within Muslim communities, serving as a catalyst for wealth redistribution and extending support to the less fortunate. It is crucial to underscore that Sadaqah is not restricted solely to underprivileged members of the Muslim community but can also be extended to others facing adversity. The primary aim of Sadaqah is to promote the ethos of charitable giving, stimulate wealth redistribution, enhance social cohesion, and bolster socio-economic justice.

As the primary sources of the Islamic law are the Al-Quran and Hadith (sayings of Prophet Muhammad s.a.w), Sadaqah is highlighted in various verses and Hadith. Some of which are:

> The example of those who spend their wealth in the cause of Allah is that of a grain that sprouts into seven ears, each bearing one hundred grains (2:261, Qur'an)

> O believers! Donate from what We have provided for you before the arrival of a Day when there will be no bargaining, friendship, or intercession. (2:254, Qur'an)

---

[1] Abubakar, J., & Aysan, A. F. (2022, October). Research trends in the field of Islamic social finance. In *Eurasian Business and Economics Perspectives: Proceedings of the 36th Eurasia Business and Economics Society Conference* (pp. 253–268). Cham: Springer International Publishing.

[2] Ibid.

[3] Ibid.

> Those who spend their wealth by night and by day, secretly and publicly, will find that their reward is secure with their Lord and that there is no reason for them to entertain any fear or grief. (2:274, Qur'an)

The importance of Sadaqah in Islam was highlighted when Prophet Muhammad s.a.w stated:

> When a man dies, his deeds come to an end except for three things: Sadaqah Jariyah (good deeds/charity), the knowledge he attained which is beneficial, and virtuous descendants who prays for him. (Sahih Muslim)

2.1.2 Zakat

Zakat stands as a cornerstone of Islamic faith, representing one of the five pillars of Islam and exemplifying a practice of charitable giving to support the impoverished and those in need. It constitutes a religious duty, compelling adherents of Islam who meet specific wealth criteria to allocate a designated portion of their earnings or assets, usually 2.5%, to assist the less fortunate. Zakat serves a dual purpose: it purifies an individual's wealth and simultaneously advances social equity by providing financial aid to those struggling within the community. Islamic law meticulously delineates the eligible recipients and permissible uses of Zakat, encompassing categories or initiatives aimed at promoting the Islamic faith.[4]

Such categories refer to the selected recipients where the collection of zakat will be given to, as stated in the Qur'an:

> Zakat expenditures are only for the poor and for the needy and for those employed to collect zakat and for bringing hearts together for Islam and for freeing captives or slaves and for those in debt and for the cause of Allah and for the stranded traveler - an obligation imposed by Allah. And Allah is Knowing and Wise. (9:60, Qur'an)

From the verse above, the eligible recipients are poor and needy, the 'Amil (Zakat collector), those who converted to Islam, slaves, those who are in debt, those who are strive in the cause of Allah (jihad) and travellers in need.

There are many other Quranic verses and the sayings of Prophet Muhammad that form the legality of Zakat in Islamic law. Below are some of the verses that can be found in the teachings of Islam:

> And establish prayer and give Zakat, and whatever good you put forward for yourselves, you will find it with Allah. (2:110, Qur'an)

Zakat is the obligatory charity that Muslims must fulfil as it is part of the pillars of religion. This can be further referred to the verse below:

---

[4] Zauro, N. A., Zauro, N. A., Saad, R. A. J., & Sawandi, N. (2020). Enhancing socio-economic justice and financial inclusion in Nigeria: the role of zakat, Sadaqah and Qardhul Hassan. *Journal of Islamic Accounting and Business Research, 11*(3), 555–572.

> Righteousness is not turning your faces towards the east or the west. Righteous are those who believe in God, the Last Day, the angels, the scripture, and the prophets; and they give the money, cheerfully, to the relatives, the orphans, the needy, the traveling alien, the beggars, and to free the slaves; and they observe the prayers (Salat) and give the obligatory charity (Zakat); and they keep their word whenever they make a promise; and they steadfastly persevere in the face of persecution, hardship, and war. These are the truthful; these are the righteous. (2:177, Qur'an)

From the sayings of the Prophet, this hadith resonates well with how Islamic finance works as social finance:

> Zakat is a right that the poor have upon the rich. (Sahih Bukhari)

The societal significance of zakat lies in its function to alleviate poverty and promote a more equitable wealth distribution. It plays a vital role in fostering social stability and solidarity, discouraging the accumulation of wealth, and encouraging the circulation of capital throughout the economy.[5]

2.1.3 Qard and Qard Hassan

Qard and Qard Hasan are distinctive concepts within Islamic finance, both revolving around the lending of money or property. Qard, in its broad sense, entails providing property to a party with the anticipation of receiving an equivalent replacement in the future.[6] Its historical application in Malaysia includes products like Government Investment Certificates and benevolent loans, and it has evolved to encompass various financial instruments, including rahn loans, credit cards, charge cards, and liquidity management tools for Islamic financial institutions. On the other hand, Qard Hasan is a specific type of qard characterized by benevolence and charity, requiring adherence to Shariah principles.

The term "Qard Hassan" holds both a literal and a technical definition. Literally, it translates to "beautiful or benevolent loan." From a technical perspective, it represents a type of loan provided without any anticipation of profit. This loan is entirely interest-free, and the borrower is only bound to repay the principal amount, although they retain the option to make additional contributions as a token of gratitude. In the realm of Islamic finance, "Qard Hassan" carries high significance due to its prioritization of the borrower's needs over the lender's pursuit of profit, actively fostering a culture of generosity and social unity.

> Indeed, the men who practice charity and the women who practice charity and they who have loaned Allah a benevolent loan – it will be multiplied for them, and they will have a noble reward. (57:18, Qur'an)

---

[5] Emara, N. F. (2003). Islam: 'A guide for the perplexed': study and evaluation of an attempt of application: Alleviating poverty in tafahna al-ashraf. (Master's Thesis, American University in Cairo), p. 239.

[6] Shariah Resolution in Islamic Finance, 2nd Edition. https://www.bnm.gov.my/documents/20124/9198675/shariah_resolutions_2nd_edition_EN.pdf (1 October 2023).

> Who is it that will lend Allah a benevolent loan, that He may multiply it for him and [that] there may be a noble reward for him? (57:1, Qur'an)
>
> If you lend Allah a benevolent loan, He shall multiply it for you and forgive you, and Allah is All-Appreciative, All-Forbearing. (64:17, Qur'an)

From the sayings of the Prophet Muhammad, he has stated on benevolent loans as follows:

> There is no Muslim who lends something to another Muslim twice, but it will be like giving charity once. (Sunan Ibn Majah)

In its 51st meeting on July 28, 2005, the Shariah Advisory Council (SAC) determined that financing products grounded in the qard principle are acceptable.[7] However, the resolution includes the removal of the term "hasan" from "qard hasan." This alteration signifies that the borrower is obligated to repay the qard to the lender or financier. Furthermore, this repayment obligation extends to the heirs of the borrower in the event of the borrower's demise before the complete settlement of the loan. Henceforth, the rest of this chapter will make reference to the term "Qard".

2.2 Differences Between Sadaqah, Zakat and Qard

The concepts of Sadaqa, Zakat, and Qard thrive as different forms of Islamic financial instruments, and each has unique parameters that share the same purpose. Nevertheless, there are several differences some of which is further tabulated below in the Table 2.1.

2.3 Legal Framework for Sadaqah, Zakat and Qard

The preceding sections of this discussion have provided valuable insights into the Islamic law that underpins the various Islamic social instruments. These instruments play a pivotal role in the realm of Islamic finance, offering unique financial solutions that adhere to the principles and values of Islamic law. In this section, this chapter will delve deeper into the legal framework that governs each of these instruments, shedding light on how they are integrated into the broader landscape of Islamic finance.

By understanding the legal foundations of these Islamic social instruments and their place within the Islamic finance ecosystem, we gain valuable insights into how they contribute to a financial system that is not only Sharia-compliant but also places a strong emphasis on social responsibility and economic justice. These instruments are not only financially sustainable but also serve as vehicles for philanthropy and social

---

[7] Ibid.

Table 2.1 Differences between Sadaqah, Zakat and Qard

No	Characteristics	Zakat	Sadaqah	Qard
1	Nature of instrument	Compulsory form of charity with the intention to purify the giver's wealth	Voluntary charity that comes in various forms such as financial assistance, food, acts of kindness and other non-material contribution such as volunteer work to help those in need	Involves lending money with the intention of getting the principal amount back without any returns, profits, and interests within a specified period
2	Obligations	Compulsory for eligible Muslims. Those who meet specific wealth criteria are required to give a portion of their wealth to specified categories of recipients	Voluntary and is not mandated by religious law. It is a matter of personal choice	Voluntary
3	Recipients	There is a list of recipients that are eligible for zakat. If the recipients do not come within the list, they are not eligible	Open and flexible in terms of recipients. It can be given to a wide range of individuals or large groups, and there are no specific restrictions or designated categories	A borrower who is in need in receiving an interest-free loan
4	Usage	Designated for helping those in need and purifying the giver's wealth. It promotes social justice and financial assistance to the less fortunate	It is like zakat. However, it provides more flexibility in terms of who can receive it and the forms it can take, extending to various causes	Assist borrowers without the burden of interest payments

Source Authors' own

development, aligning seamlessly with the principles of Islamic law and finance. The legal framework discussed in this section will be primarily centered around the Malaysian jurisdiction.

It is important to understand that under the Malaysian Federal Constitution, the laws pertaining to Shariah matters are under the state based on Article 74 and the 9th Schedule, List II. Where it states that jurisdictional purview of state includes matters of "Islamic law and personal and family law of persons professing the religion of Islam…". Nevertheless, the general financial matters lie on the federal list based on the 9th Schedule, List I. Therefore, the legal framework governing the Islamic social instruments may be covered under both Federal Acts and the State Regulations. The state religious authorities are responsible for laying down the rules, procedures, and guidelines for the collection, distribution, and management of the Shariah matters.

2.3.1 Sadaqah

Within the Malaysian legal framework, there are no specific state regulations pertaining to Sadaqah. Additionally, there are no laws or established guidelines delineating how Sadaqah should be structured within a legal context. Technically, Sadaqah can be perceived as a form of public crowdfunding that carries a charitable element. In general, there are four different models of crowdfunding, namely donation-based crowdfunding, reward-based crowdfunding, equity-based crowdfunding and peer-to-peer (debt-based) crowdfunding.[8] From the discussion above, sadaqah clearly lies under the donation-based crowdfunding.

For the Malaysian government, Sadaqah constitutes a benevolent offering to those in need, undertaken with the intention of drawing closer to Allah.[9] Consequently, when affirming one's faith or commitment to Allah's promises, tangible proof is demonstrated through the act of generously giving one's possessions in the path of Allah. This act of charity may be directed towards the poor, those in need, family members, or in support of jihad fi sabilillah.

In terms of innovation, Tabung Haji (TH) leads the way through its process for performing Sadaqah transactions through the THiJARI portal and THiJARI application by TH depositors.[10] The process starts with the transfer of funds from TH accounts to designated funds, specifically Tabung Kebajikan Jemaah Haji Malaysia (TKJHM) and Tabung Was'ul Khair Tetamu Allah (TWT). Receipts for successful transactions are provided, but Sadaqah donations are not eligible for tax deduction.

In the context of Malaysia, licenses for crowdfunding activities are issued by the Securities Commission under the provisions of the Guidelines of Recognized Market, as stipulated in section 34 of the Capital Markets Services Act 2007. As it stands, the existing Guidelines of Recognized Market do not explicitly encompass Islamic crowdfunding as a distinct category in Malaysia.

Nevertheless, despite the absence of specific regulatory recognition, there are crowdfunding platforms in Malaysia that assert their adherence to Shariah principles and market themselves as Shariah-compliant Crowdfunder. Examples of such

---

[8] Belleflamme, P. Omrani, N., & Peitz, M. (2015). The Economics of Crowdfunding Platforms. *Information Economics and Policy, 3*, 11–28. https://doi.org/10.1016/j.infoecopol.2015.08.003.

[9] MyGovernment, Managing Sadaqah. Available at https://www.malaysia.gov.my/portal/content/27677.

[10] Tabung Haji, Terms and Conditions of Sadaqah. Available at https://www.tabunghaji.gov.my/en/terms-and-conditions-sadaqah.

platforms include Ethis Ventures Sdn Bhd and Launch Good.[11] It is worth noting, however, that these crowdfunding platforms primarily serve businesses seeking to raise capital. They do so by offering equity in return for investment, thereby allowing investors to share in the profits generated by these businesses.[12] Sadaqah, being inherently associated with the spirit of charitable giving, raises an essential concern that is intricately linked to Item 15 of List II in Schedule 9. This item stipulates those charities and charitable endowments, with the notable exception of Wakaf, fall under the purview of the Federal government. Furthermore, the Trustees Act of 1949 extends its authority over any charitable organizations.

Based on the discussion above, the legal situation surrounding donation-based crowdfunding in Malaysia is inherently complicated due to the coexistence of federal regulations overseeing charitable activities and specific laws such as the Trustees Act governing charitable organizations. This mixture of laws raises questions about how to categorize and regulate donation-based crowdfunding platforms, often used for charitable fundraising. The absence of a clear and specific legal framework for crowdfunding adds complexity and the potential for confusion, highlighting the need for a thorough review and resolution to provide clear guidance for those involved in this field.

2.3.2 Zakat

Like sadaqah, the Malaysian legal framework for zakat is an integral part of the country's governance structure, subject to the jurisdiction of state authorities. This arrangement stems from the inclusion of zakat in List II of the State List within the Ninth Schedule of the Federal Constitution. As a result, the responsibility for managing and regulating zakat collection and distribution rests with the individual states and Federal Territories.

Among the fifteen states and Federal Territories in Malaysia, nine of them exercise their autonomy by governing their respective zakat institutions through state enactments and regulations. This legal framework allows these states to tailor their zakat systems to meet the unique needs and demands of their communities. It also empowers them to ensure that the principles and practices of zakat are implemented effectively in line with Islamic law.

Furthermore, within this framework, nine of these states and Federal Territories have passed specific zakat regulations, each designed to address the zakat management and distribution within their jurisdiction. These regulations play a crucial role in maintaining transparency, fairness, and accountability in the zakat process. They also

---

[11] Kamaruddin, M. I. H., Muhamed, N. A., Radzi, R. M., Nazarie, W. N. F. W. M., & Kamarubahrin, A. F. (2023). Financial management practices in Islamic donation-based crowdfunding (DCF) platforms in Malaysia. *Future Business Journal*, *9*(1), 32.

[12] Capital Markets Malaysia. (2023, September 20). Digital Equity Crowdfunding (ECF). Capital Markets Malaysia. https://www.capitalmarketsmalaysia.com/digital-equity-crowdfunding-ecf/.

help in streamlining the collection and allocation of zakat funds to maximize their impact in alleviating poverty and supporting those in need. The states with specific zakat regulations are; Federal Territories (Kaedah Baitul Mal Wilayah Persekutuan - Perbelanjaan dan Penggunaan) 1980, Selangor (Peraturan Kutipan Zakat dan Fitrah Selangor 1973), Malacca (Peraturan-Peraturan Zakat dan Fitrah, Urusan Waqf dan Baitulmal Negeri Melaka 1982), Johor (Peraturan-Peraturan Zakat dan Fitrah Johor 1962), Kedah (Peraturan Zakat Kedah 1982), Pahang (Kaedah Zakat dan Fitrah 1970), Perak (Peraturan Zakat dan Fitrah 1975), Penang (Peraturan Pungutan Zakat dan Fitrah Pulau Pinang 1979), Negeri Sembilan (Kaedah Zakat Negeri Sembilan 1998) and Kelantan (Enakmen Majlis Agama Islam dan Adat Melayu dan Mahkamah Kadi 1953), As the regulations are substantively similar, we can understand their key sections and provisions using the Selangor (Peraturan Kutipan Zakat dan Fitrah Selangor 1973) as a reference example. Table 2.2 provides the key provisions of the Selangor (Peraturan Kutipan Zakat dan Fitrah Selangor 1973).

These regulations are also a testament to Malaysia's commitment to upholding the principles of zakat and ensuring that the wealth distribution mechanism prescribed by Islamic law is executed efficiently and fairly. By doing so, Malaysia aims to provide vital support to those in need, promote social justice, and foster the economic well-being of its citizens while honouring Islam as their official religion.[13]

2.3.3 *Qard*

As the nature of qard is a traditional loan instrument, its legal framework in Malaysia lies under its Central Bank (Bank Negara Malaysia). This is since the Malaysian regulatory architecture is dependent on the division of work scope between financial institutions and financial markets. The Central Bank governs financial institutions[14] while the Securities Commission regulates the financial markets[15] except for offshore markets, which fall under the supervision of Labuan Financial Services Authority (LFSA).[16] For qard, Bank Negara Malaysia has issued a policy document to provide reference on the legal standing, rules applicable to qard and set out key operational requirements for qard implementation to further promote sound Islamic banking and takaful practices and safeguard consumer interests.[17]

The Bank Negara's policy document on qard applies to all Islamic Financial Institutions under the Islamic Financial Services Act 2013 and the Development of Financial Institutions Act 2002. It is important to highlight that the institutions called as Development Financial Institutions are referred to financial institutions established

[13] Article 3 (1) of the Malaysian Federal Constitution.

[14] Central Bank of Malaysia Act 2009.

[15] Securities Commission Act 1993.

[16] Labuan Financial Services Authority Act 1996.

[17] Qard Policy Document. https://www.bnm.gov.my/documents/20124/938039/PD+Qard_2602 2018.pdf/795395cd-aeee-d497-109d-e3af19874a44?t=1592245448584 (1 October 2023).

Table 2.2 Key provisions of the Selangor (Peraturan Kutipan Zakat dan Fitrah Selangor 1973)

Sections	Provisions
Section 2 (definition of zakat)	"*A specified rate of several types of wealth that is obligatory to be given to the asnaf (those eligible to receive zakat) according to Islamic Law*"
Section 3 (powers of Council)	Outlines the authority and responsibilities of the Council in Selangor regarding the collection and distribution of zakat and fitrah to the designated recipients (asnaf) within the time frame of a year from the date of collection for distributing collected funds to eligible recipients (asnaf) and addresses the handling of any remaining funds or portions allocated to asnaf that cannot be distributed in a particular year. The unallocated portions are subject to distribution according to specified regulations namely regulation 40 which provides that excess zakat payments, beyond the amount required by Islamic Law, must be refunded to the payer under two conditions: if determined by the Chief Officer or the Council, or if the Chief Officer identifies an error in the estimation leading to the excess collection. However, any excess amount eligible for refund may also be carried forward as zakat payment for the subsequent year
Section 15 (zakat payment obligations)	Outlines the mandatory conditions for individuals obligated to pay zakat, including being a Muslim, being free, being mature and of sound mind, and having wealth and income subject to zakat. It also specifies the obligation for zakat payment within companies or partnerships, which extends to key roles held by Muslims, such as shareholders, directors, managers, secretaries, or any individuals performing similar functions
Section 21 (zakat payment mechanism)	Provides that individuals obligated to pay zakat can do so through salary deductions or in accordance with the terms set by the Board. If someone refuses to make zakat payments, the Board has the authority to direct the person's employer to deduct zakat from the person's income
Section 41 (zakat contributions recipients)	Lists the categories of individuals who are deemed eligible to receive zakat and fitrah based on Islamic Law. The recipients include the poor, needy, collectors and distributors of zakat, new converts to Islam, those in bondage, individuals in debt, those striving in the path of Allah, and stranded travelers

Source Selangor (Peraturan Kutipan Zakat dan Fitrah Selangor 1973)[18]

by the Government with specific mandate to develop and promote key sectors that are considered of strategic importance to the overall socio-economic development objectives of the country which include agriculture, small and medium enterprises (SMEs), infrastructure, maritime, export-oriented sector as well as capital-intensive and high-technology industries.[19]

[18] Available at https://www.mais.gov.my/wp-content/uploads/2020/10/PERATURAN-PERATURAN-ZAKAT-DAN-FITRAH-NEGERI-SELANGOR-2012.pdf.

[19] Overview of Development Financial Institutions (DFIs) in Malaysia https://www.bnm.gov.my/dfi-overview (1 October 2023).

The policy documents underpin the Shariah governance, prudential matters and the business conduct to the financial institutions that utilize qard. The policy document issued by the Bank Negara Malaysia (BNM) concerning qard outlines a clear definition of this financial arrangement. Qard, in this context, represents an agreement for lending money, involving both a lender and a borrower. Under this agreement, the borrower assumes the responsibility of returning an equivalent sum to the lender.[20] Notably, the subject matter of this agreement, which pertains to money, can encompass various forms, including cash in any currency, gold, or silver.[21] One of the distinctive features of qard, as emphasized by BNM, is its traditional nature. This traditional nature underscores the lender's commitment not to derive any contractual benefits arising from the loan itself. However, an exception is made if these benefits are unrelated to the loan contract, in which case the lender is permitted to enjoy them without restriction.[22]

The primary focus of the policy document regarding qard centers on the repayment terms that financial institutions must clearly stipulate in the contractual agreements. Here, it is crucial for the borrower to fulfil their duty of repaying the loan as specified in the contract. Failure to do so may result in the imposition of late payment charges, which are determined by the relevant authorities.[23]

Other key points in the policy document include the necessity for qard operations to adhere to Shariah requirements, endorsement by the Shariah committee, resolution of Shariah issues through committee deliberation, and consultation with the Shariah Advisory Council in case of unresolved issues. The document emphasizes that qard product structures must align with essential qard features, such as the transfer of ownership, repayment obligations, discretionary benefits, and fees based on direct costs.

It further addresses the purpose of qard lending, roles and responsibilities of contracting parties, obtaining consent for minor customers, and ensuring agent compliance. In transactions involving gold or silver, specific details must be documented. Clear evidence of offer and acceptance is required in qard contracts, and fees and charges should directly relate to transaction costs. Legal documentation should avoid stipulating contractual benefits for lenders.

The policy document also highlights the risk management framework, including identifying, measuring, and mitigating risks associated with qard. IFIs are required to establish sound risk management policies, including those for liquidity management and credit risk. Regular reviews and updates of policies and procedures are essential to ensure consistency with risk appetite.

The business and market conduct principles in the policy document stress on fairness, transparency, responsibility, and professionalism in qard transactions. This involves accurate information provision, disclosure of fees, and suitable advice. Promotional and marketing activities must comply with qard requirements, and

[20] BNM's Qard Policy Document.

[21] Ibid.

[22] Ibid.

[23] Ibid.

historical information on hibah (gift) must be presented with clarity. The use of Arabic terminology in documentation should be clarified for customer understanding.

The financial disclosure requirements in the policy document require IFIs to maintain accurate accounting records for timely reporting of financial performance. A transition period is provided for existing products using wadi'ah yad dhamanah,[24] with a deadline for compliance. Customers must be notified of changes in terms, and IFIs must allow termination without cost if customers reject the changes. New deposit products based on qard should avoid using certain terms.

Finally, an implementation plan is outlined for IFIs to transition existing products to comply with the policy document's requirements, including submitting plans to regulatory bodies, revising documentation and systems, conducting necessary processes, providing training, and undertaking operational adjustments. Independent Shariah review is required to ensure compliance with the policy document during this transition.

Looking at the SAC's resolution that narrows the focus of qard hassan to qard, it establishes a more specific framework for these financial arrangements. This resolution stems from a commitment to ensure the smooth operation of Islamic financial institutions in Malaysia while mitigating potential systemic risks. The oversight of prudential measures and business conduct becomes paramount in maintaining the integrity of the Islamic financial sector and safeguarding against potential disruptions. This resolution, therefore, aligns with the broader goal of upholding the stability and ethical principles of Islamic finance in Malaysia.

2.4 Use of Technology and Innovation in Sadaqah, Zakat and Qard and Case Studies

Today, the technologies that surround us profoundly impact the way we lead our lives, and our dependence on them is substantial. This influence is often referred to as the Fourth Industrial Revolution, a period where human existence is shaped by the principles of automation and digitalization.[25] In such an era, the application of technology is crucial for advancing innovation, particularly in financial matters. The

[24] "Wadi'ah Yad Dhamanah means safe keeping with guarantee. It refers to the transaction between the depositor (Customer) and the custodian (Bank) for the safe keeping of the goods or money. The acceptance and continuance of an account may be granted by the Bank subject to the Shariah principles, and upon compliance with the Rules & Regulations under the concept of Wadi'ah Yad Dhamanah by the depositor. The Bank in this situation is guaranteeing the safe keeping of the goods or money and will return the same to the depositor accordingly, subject to the Bank's procedures." (extracted from https://www.lawinsider.com/dictionary/wadiah-yad-dhamanah).

[25] Davis, N. (2016, January). What is the fourth industrial revolution. In *World Economic Forum* (Vol. 19).

term pertinent to our discussion is 'fintech.' As fintech has evolved in both conventional and Islamic finance,[26] it is prudent to explore the application of technology in Islamic financial instruments.

In terms of innovation, Malaysia has implemented innovative measures through Islamic social finance, exemplified by its iTEKAD program. This program was introduced by Bank Negara Malaysia as part of its initiatives to mitigate the impact caused by COVID-19. iTEKAD serves as an overarching program established by Bank Negara Malaysia with the objective of aiding low-income microentrepreneurs in enhancing their financial management skills and business acumen, ultimately leading to sustainable income generation. Each iTEKAD program combines the provision of business assets financed by social finance instruments, such as donations, social impact investment, zakat, and cash waqf, with microfinance. These resources are complemented by structured financial and business training.[27]

In this section, several case studies will be highlighted to illustrate the use of technology and innovation in Sadaqah, Zakat, and Qard Hassan.

2.4.1 Sadaqah

Sadaqa House

In Sadaqah, the introduction of Sadaqa House in Malaysia was one of the innovative ways in digitalising the instruments. Sadaqa House represents a concept in the realm of social finance that incorporates the practice of 'sadaqah' within the domain of Islamic banking and finance. The concept took shape under the guidance of Dato' Dr. Abdul Halim Ismail, the recipient of the 2014 Royal Award for Islamic Finance.

During his keynote address at the sixth Asia Islamic Banking Conference in 2015, he proposed for the Islamic banking industry to form a new Islamic banking institution of Sadaqah House, or Bayt Al-Sadaqah, as a vehicle to serve the financial requirements and demands of social welfare sector.[28] He emphasized the collaborative role of both the government and the private sector in mobilizing resources for the assistance of impoverished and needy individuals. Dato' Dr. Abdul Halim Ismail also underscored the importance of the Islamic banking and finance sector in developing products and services that facilitate the efficient allocation of these funds. However, he noted that the sector, as it stood, was not giving adequate attention to this

[26] Ali, H., Abdullah, R., & Zaini, M. Z. (2019). Fintech and its potential impact on Islamic banking and finance industry: a case study of Brunei Darussalam and Malaysia. *International Journal of Islamic Economics and Finance (IJIEF)*, *2*(1), 73–108.

[27] https://www.bnm.gov.my/social-finance.

[28] New Strait Times. Form Sadaqah house to narrow gap between poor and rich. https://www.nst.com.my/news/2015/09/form-sadaqah-house-narrow-gap-between-poor-and-rich (August 12, 2015).

aspect. Consequently, he suggested a thorough examination of this idea to explore its potential implementation within the Islamic banking and finance sector.[29]

In response to this call, the International Research Centre for Islamic Economics and Finance (IRCIEF-KUIS) at the International Islamic University College Selangor undertook an extensive study to assess the viability of Sadaqa House within the framework of Islamic banking. This research effort, spanning from 2014 to 2017, encompassed two pivotal phases: a perception study and a feasibility study, addressing key dimensions such as Shariah compliance, legal considerations, taxation implications, and governance. The concept of Sadaqa House ultimately materialized when Bank Islam Malaysia Berhad introduced Sadaqa House Bank Islam in January 2018.[30]

Sadaqa House was proposed as a platform for Islamic financial institutions in Malaysia to collect donations mainly from public and public listed companies. The concept of Sadaqa House emphasizes on preserving the principal amount of the charity or sadaqah eternally, and regularly distributing the income generated from the principal to the needy. The purpose of this establishment is to contribute towards the social-welfare sector, enhancing necessities such as education, and alleviating chronic issues such as poverty, consistent with the requirements of Shariah.[31]

The innovative aspect of Sadaqa House is where it integrates Islamic philanthropy with the corporate structure in a new way. Sadaqa House is proposed to operate like financial institutions like banks, which is unique in the field of Islamic philanthropy. It aims to centralize the collection of donations and their distribution amongst the needy. Furthermore, it enables public listed companies to fulfil their social responsibilities through a trusted and regulated platform. The house is also designed to report their activities and transparency, gaining more credibility and trust for potential contributors. This system promotes corporate governance, religiosity, tax incentives, and transparency. In a way, it brings the practice of sadaqa within a formal, regulated framework, opening opportunities for larger societal impact.[32]

Another important case study that underscores the use of technology for innovative sadaqah is Global Sadaqah.

Founded in 2018, Global Sadaqah has been actively engaged in the administration and distribution of Islamic social finance funds within the charitable sector. A primary goal of the organization is to create a positive influence on Muslim communities by addressing the challenge of ensuring transparency in fund utilization, tracking impact, and providing timely updates. Global Sadaqah holds the distinction of being one of the pioneering platforms in Malaysia, establishing a trustworthy channel through which donors can have confidence that their contributions will directly benefit those

---

[29] Ibid.

[30] Hameed, L. B., dan Nur, A. F. M. S., & Jamaludin, I. (2018). Model SADAQA HOUSE: Menyantuni Kebajikan Ummah. In *Proceedings of the 6th International Seminar on Entrepreneurship and Business. ISEB, UMK. (PDF) Model SADAQA HOUSE: Menyantuni Kebajikan Ummah (researchgate. net).*

[31] Karim, N. A., Ab Aziry, N. A., Ridzuan, N. I. M., Jaafar, M. N., & Muhamat, A. A. (2023). Customers' intention to use digitalized Islamic crowdfunding: the case of Bimb Sadaqa House. *Advances in Social Sciences Research Journal, 10*(6.2).

[32] Ibid.

in need through our verified partners. The organization's emphasis is on maximizing immediate impact and fostering long-term sustainability for the recipients.[33]

The platform functions as a marketplace that connects corporate contributions, Corporate Social Responsibility initiatives, as well as sadaqah, zakat, and waqf with social causes. It accomplishes this by offering comprehensive details about the charitable projects in progress, and donors can make payments through online banking, e-wallets, or Bitcoin. Two types of charges will be deducted from the donated funds: payment gateway fees and platform service fees. The remaining portion will be directed to the charity partner.[34]

Global Sadaqah creates social impact by bringing together a multitude of stakeholders such as individual and institutional donors, corporates, international humanitarian and development agencies, religious authorities, and governments.[35] It is pertinent to note that Global Sadaqah had successfully raised RM450,000 through an issuance on Ethis Malaysia, a recently regulated Shariah-compliant equity crowdfunding platform. This flash-fundraising campaign, which remained open for 72 h, exceeded its minimum target of RM200,000 and attracted investors from ten countries, including strategic angel investors.[36]

2.4.2 Zakat

Paddy Estate Scheme

One notable initiative in innovative Islamic social finance, particularly in the context of zakat, is the provision of financial support to eligible zakat recipients for their involvement in the agricultural sector. In 2021, the Kedah Zakat Agency (LZNK) introduced the Paddy Estate Scheme, where each participant is entrusted with the management of a 0.29-hectare paddy field owned by LZNK. LZNK supplies all essential inputs required for paddy cultivation, spanning from the initial planting to the final harvesting stage.[37] Furthermore, because of a collaboration between LZNK and Bank Islam Malaysia Berhad, participants benefit from an interest-free BangKIT micro-financing program, amounting to RM5,000, twice a year. This soft loan plays a vital role in providing essential financial support, allowing participants to sustain their families during the crucial four months leading up to the paddy harvest. Subsequently, LZNK deducts the loan repayments from the proceeds of paddy sales. In addition, LZNK extends the Paddy Estate Cultivation Scheme to existing small-scale farmers.

---

[33] https://myethis.com/campaigns/global-sadaqah#about.

[34] Eldersevi, S., & Muhammad, M. (2022). Asnaf Care: a case study of the Malaysian-based charity crowdfunding platform to combat the impact of COVID-19.

[35] https://myethis.com/campaigns/global-sadaqah#about.

[36] See https://www.bnm.gov.my/web/mifc/-/malaysian-fintech-global-sadaqah-raises-rm450-000-in-shariah-compliant-crowdfunding.

[37] See https://www.zakatkedah.com.my/sawah-milik-lznk-dijadikan-estet-padi/.

Within the framework of this initiative, LZNK covers all expenses associated with cultivation and harvesting, with loan repayments being deducted from the sales at a later stage. Both of these schemes share a common objective: the transformation of low-income earners into prosperous and skilled paddy farmers.[38]

Rice Automated Teller Machines (ATMs)

In February 2019, it was announced that The Federal Territories Islamic Religious Department (Jawi) announced their intention to install 'rice ATM machines' at 85 mosques in the Federal Territory to facilitate its *zakat* recipients.[39] Furthermore, it has been reported that this machine, priced at RM19,000, is the first of its kind in the country. It serves two primary functions: dispensing rice supplies in desired quantities and functioning as a donation box to collect funds from the public.[40]

Rice ATMs are an innovative solution for providing rice to those in need, eliminating the need for human intermediaries. Much like the way cash is dispensed from bank ATMs, rice is distributed through a similar process. These Rice ATMs serve as the bridge between allocating a portion of Zakat funds to support the poor and needy and ensuring that the distribution is carried out efficiently and cost-effectively through a proper mechanism.[41]

The primary objective of Rice ATMs is to offer support to individuals and families registered as recipients and beneficiaries of zakat due to their impoverished status, allowing them to acquire rice by utilizing a dedicated card issued for this purpose. The operational procedure of these rice ATMs involves users inserting their special purpose card into the machine's sensor. Subsequently, the machine dispenses 2 kg of rice through the designated collection point at its base. Moreover, this specialized rice ATM machine also accommodates individuals interested in contributing monetary donations by depositing cash through a designated slot.[42] Even though Rice ATMs were introduced in Malaysia in 2019, Rice ATMs were first innovated for zakat purpose by The National Board of Zakat, Republic of Indonesia (BAZNAS).[43]

---

[38] See https://www.nst.com.my/news/nation/2021/12/756938/kedah-zakat-agency-transforming-low-income-earners-successful-paddy.

[39] https://www.astroawani.com/berita-malaysia/jawi-jangka-tempatkan-mesin-atm-beras-di-85-masjid-199367.

[40] Ibid.

[41] Muneeza, A., & Nadwi, S. (2019). The potential of application of technology-based innovations for zakat administration in India. *International Journal of Zakat*, *4*(2), 87–100.

[42] Ibid.

[43] Retnowati, M. S., & Aziz, M. A. (2022). Modern philanthropy model as a mosque economic empowerment strategy: in rice ATM program reviewing from Maqasid Sharia. In *Indonesian Conference of Zakat-Proceedings* (pp. 239–249).

2.4.3 *Qard*

I-tekad Bangkit Microfinance

In the year 2020, Bank Islam introduced a novel form of Islamic microfinancing known as "Mikro Bangkit" under the auspices of the Bank Islam Sadaqah House. This financial initiative is primarily funded by contributions from the public and is designed to cater to individuals who typically fall outside the purview of traditional banking services, particularly those seeking to initiate or expand their entrepreneurial endeavours. The financial support provided encompasses working capital and capital expenditure requirements.[44]

Bank Islam engages in collaborative arrangements with designated partners, such as Amanah Ikhtiar Malaysia, tasked with the responsibility of identifying prospective micro-entrepreneurs from their respective memberships, beneficiaries, or affiliated stakeholders. An essential prerequisite for obtaining financing entails the mandatory participation of these identified micro-entrepreneurs in a comprehensive business training and coaching program organized by the partner.[45]

The financial framework employed in this endeavour operates under a Qard contract structure, characterized by a 0% financing rate.[46] The range of financing amounts extends from as modest as RM500 to RM3,000 for those embarking on new business ventures, while those seeking to expand their existing enterprises may access funding ranging from RM3,000 to RM20,000. The duration of the repayment period is flexible, spanning from 6 months to a maximum of 3 years.[47]

This initiative undertaken by Bank Islam represents a noteworthy endeavour to align with the principles of value-based intermediation and to facilitate financial assistance to individuals who might otherwise encounter impediments in accessing capital for their entrepreneurial pursuits.[48]

2.5 Issues and Challenges

In this chapter, a comprehensive discussion and various examples have been provided regarding Islamic social finance instruments. As mentioned earlier, the fundamental objectives of Islamic social finance are straightforward: to facilitate wealth redistribution and enhance socio-economic justice. The case studies presented here serve as excellent illustrations of the opportunities that Islamic social finance offers to

[44] Nawai, N. (2021). The implementation of Islamic microfinancing for poverty alleviation in Malaysia.

[45] Frequently Asked Question Bangkit Microfinance. https://www.bankislam.com/wp-content/uploads/BangKIT-FAQs_web.pdf (1 October 2023).

[46] Ibid.

[47] Ibid.

[48] Nawai, N. (2021).

both the market and the public. Nevertheless, it's important to acknowledge that the application of Islamic social finance instruments also comes with several issues and challenges.

There are several common challenges in the implementation of Islamic Social Finance instruments, which include zakat, and sadaqah. In the previous section, the discussion had outlined the legal framework for Shariah matters fall within the jurisdictional purview of the states by virtue of List II of the Ninth Schedule under the Federal Constitution. As matters such as zakat and sadaqa are under states matter, the governance provision lies under the State Islamic Religious Council. The primary challenge we encounter in this context pertains to ensuring uniformity in the application of these laws. Given that different states may have distinct legal provisions, this diversity can lead to varying interpretations and understandings of the subject matter.

Prior research has shown a range of challenges in the governance of State Islamic Religious Councils. These challenges encompass a dearth of qualified human resources, a lack of transparency and disclosure practices, and an inadequately structured funding framework.[49] Ensuring robust governance standards, particularly regarding transparency and the disclosure of financial information, plays a pivotal role in fostering public trust.[50]

In terms of zakat management and administration, there is a lack of coordination in distributing the zakat.[51] Such issue of coordination is not unique to Malaysia; other countries, including Egypt, also grapple with similar coordination challenges.[52] Despite the vital role zakat plays in reducing poverty, a notable issue has arisen in the coordination of activities among the different zakat committees and organizations responsible for collecting and distributing funds. This lack of coordination results in funds being scattered, ultimately reducing the practice's effectiveness within the legal framework.[53] Another obstacle concerning zakat lies in its underutilization for addressing contemporary issues like poverty, refugee crises, healthcare, and microfinance debt. Despite its significant potential, zakat is not being fully leveraged to effectively address these modern challenges.[54]

As discussed in the previous section, crowdfunding relies on digital platforms. One of the foremost challenges associated with crowdfunding is the demand for advanced technology. Its success is most evident in areas with reliable and widespread internet access, which may be lacking in certain regions, especially in developing countries. Furthermore, there is a notable need for stricter regulations and government policies

[49] Razak, D. A., & Dawami, Q. (2020). Achieving Islamic social finance goals through Zakat, Waqf, and Sadaqa in selected countries: issues and challenges.

[50] Ibid.

[51] Atia, M. (2011, December). Islamic approaches to development: a case study of Zakat, Sadaqa and Qard al Hassan in Contemporary Egypt. In: *8th International Conference on Islamic Economics and Finance, Center for Islamic Economics and Finance, Qatar Faculty of Islamic Studies, Qatar Foundation.*

[52] Ibid.

[53] Ibid.

[54] Ibid.

to mitigate substantial risks to this sector. Given that crowdfunding operates primarily online, it is susceptible to cybercrimes.[55]

For qard, the challenge lies in the adoption of such product although there are many potentialities in qard to advance the corporate social responsibility of Islamic banks and fulfilling socio-economic objectives. There are only a few of Islamic banks offer such product.[56] From a profitability standpoint, the absence of returns generated by qard can discourage banks from providing this service. Additionally, previous study highlighted a concerning trend of increasing non-performing loans associated with the expansion of funds loaned through qard, posing another challenge for financial institutions to adopt the product.[57] Apart from that, operational costs and administrative fees present a practical hurdle, raising questions about how such charges can be applied without contravening the core principles of the loan. Finally, the bulk of the problem lies on repayment issues.[58] Some borrowers run into repayment problems partly due to the utilization of loans in non-income generating activities.[59] This increases the likelihood of encountering repayment issues and potentially leading to clients leaving the program or becoming inactive borrowers.[60]

Review Questions

1. What is the main difference between Sadaqah, Zakat and Qard ?
   a. the rewards subscribed to it
   b. the level of obligation
   c. the nature of the instruments
   d. the social objectives
2. How are donation-based crowdfunding platforms, like sadaqah, categorized in the discussion?
   a. As equity-based crowdfunding
   b. As reward-based crowdfunding
   c. As peer-to-peer (debt-based) crowdfunding
   d. As donation-based crowdfunding

---

[55] Nordin, N., & Zainuddin, Z. (2023). A review of a fintech financing platform: potential and challenges of Islamic crowdfunding to entrepreneurs. *International Journal of Islamic Business, 8*(1), 79–90.

[56] Abidin, A. Z., Alwi, N. M., & Ariffin, N. M. (2011). A case study on the implementation of Qardhul Hasan concept as a financing product in Islamic banks in Malaysia. *International Journal of Economics, Management and Accounting, 19*(3).

[57] Ibid.

[58] Satar, N., & Kassim, S. (2020). Issues and challenges in financing the poor: lessons learned from Islamic microfinance institutions. *European Journal of Islamic Finance*, (15).

[59] Ibid.

[60] Ibid.

3. Under the Malaysian Federal Constitution, which jurisdiction primarily oversees matters related to Islamic law and personal law for individuals professing Islam?

   a. Federal government
   b. Local municipalities
   c. State authorities
   d. Non-governmental organizations

4. What distinguishes qard from other loans, according to the discussion?

   a. The interest rate applied
   b. The lack of a repayment obligation
   c. The lender's ability to derive contractual benefits from the loan
   d. The traditional nature of the loan

5. What is the primary legal authority responsible for regulating and governing qard in Malaysia?

   a. The Securities Commission
   b. The Central Bank (Bank Negara Malaysia)
   c. The Labuan Financial Services Authority (LFSA)
   d. The Islamic Financial Services Act 2013

6. Which Malaysian states exercise autonomy in governing their zakat institutions through state enactments and regulations?

   a. All fifteen states and Federal Territories
   b. Nine out of the fifteen states and Federal Territories
   c. Only the Federal Territories
   d. None of the states; it's governed by federal regulations

7. In the context of Qard, as mentioned in the text, what key characteristic distinguishes the financing structure used in the "Mikro Bangkit" initiative introduced by Bank Islam?

   a. It requires a high-interest rate.
   b. It involves a mandatory repayment period of one year.
   c. It operates under a 0% financing rate.
   d. It is exclusively available for established business owners.

8. In the context of the 'Rice ATMs' mentioned in the text, what is the primary purpose of the specialized card that users insert into the machine's sensor?

   a. To dispense cash to the user
   b. To collect donations for zakat recipients
   c. To record the user's personal information
   d. To allow the user to collect rice supplies

9. What is the underlying factor contributing to the lack of uniformity in the application of laws related to zakat and sadaqa in different states?

    a. Varying interpretations by State Islamic Religious Councils
    b. Differences in the legal provisions of various states
    c. The absence of a legal framework for zakat and sadaqa
    d. Insufficient public trust in the governance of State Islamic Religious Councils

10. What is one of the challenges related to qard ?

    a. A high rate of return on investment
    b. A surplus of available Islamic banks offering this product
    c. Increasing non-performing loans with its expansion
    d. Low operational costs and administrative fees

Answers

1. b
2. b
3. c
4. d
5. b
6. b
7. b
8. d
9. b
10. c

Chapter 3
Legal Framework for Waqf

Abstract In this chapter, the focus shifts to the institution of Waqf in Islamic social finance. The chapter provides a comprehensive understanding of Waqf, elucidating its nature, purpose, and distinctions from other forms of charitable giving such as Sadaqah and Zakat. With a specific emphasis on the legal framework governing Waqf in Malaysia, readers gain insights into the regulatory landscape that shapes and guides these endowments. Real-world applications are explored through the presentation of use-case studies, showcasing the diverse and impactful ways in which Waqf has been employed. The chapter also addresses the inherent issues and challenges associated with Waqf, offering a critical examination of its implementation within the context of Islamic social finance.

Keywords Waqf · Endowment · Cash waqf · Innovation

Learning Outcomes

At the end of this chapter, readers will be able to:

- describe what waqf is,
- explain the differences between sadaqah, zakat, waqf,
- apply the legal framework for waqf in Malaysia,
- understand the use-case studies on waqf,
- and access the issues and challenges on waqf.

S. Kunhibava et al., *Islamic Social Finance*,
https://doi.org/10.1007/978-981-97-1410-0_3

3.1 What is Waqf?

Globally, waqf is a trillion dollar market with the global value of waqf assets estimated to range from USD 100 billion (equivalent to RM 455 billion) to as much as USD1 trillion.[1] Waqf, also known as "waqaf" or "awqaf" in its plural form, is an important concept in Islamic finance and law.[2] It refers to an endowment or charitable donation of a specific asset, property, or wealth by an individual, with the intention that its benefits and revenues are used for specified charitable or religious purposes. The concept of waqf has historical and religious significance in Islam and serves as a means of promoting social welfare, supporting religious institutions, and assisting the needy.[3]

The concept of waqf has its roots in the early Islamic period and draws inspiration from the teachings and practices of Prophet Muhammad (peace be upon him) and his companions (see Table 3.1).[4]

It was developed as a way to ensure the perpetual availability of resources for charitable and religious purposes. Over time, waqf became an integral part of the Islamic economic system and played a significant role in supporting educational institutions, healthcare facilities, mosques, and other public goods.

One of the most compelling aspects of waqf is its potential to enhance financial inclusion, particularly for marginalized and underserved populations. The concept aligns with the principles of Sustainable Social Finance (SSF), championing the equitable distribution of resources for societal well-being. Waqf-based microfinance models, for instance, have emerged as mechanisms to provide accessible financial services to those who are excluded from traditional banking systems.[5] This approach not only empowers individuals economically but also reinforces a sense of communal solidarity. This waqf-based sustainable economy is shown in the Fig. 3.1.

---

[1] New Straits Times. (2023, August 6). Economist: Waqf Can Complement Fiscal Policy Gap. Retrieved from https://www.nst.com.my/news/nation/2023/08/939596/economist-waqf-can-complement-fiscal-policy-gap.

[2] Siddiqi, M. N. (2005). Islamic banking and finance in theory and practice: a survey of state of the art. *Islamic Economic Studies, 13*(2), 1–48. Retrieved from https://iaif.ir/images/khareji/articles/bank/15.pdf.

[3] Chapra, M. U. (1992). *Islam and Economic Development*. Islamic Research and Training Institute.

[4] Ibid.

[5] Khan, M. F. (2015). Waqf-based microfinance: realizing the social role of Islamic finance. *International Journal of Islamic and Middle Eastern Finance and Management, 8*(2), 229–245. Retrieved from https://www.isfin.net/sites/isfin.com/files/waqf-based_microfinance-_realizing_the_social_role_of_islamic_finance.pdf.

Table 3.1 Validity of Quran from the Hadith

Hadith	Provision
Book 13, Number 4006	*Ibn Umar reported: Umar acquired a land at Khaibar. He came to Allah's Apostle (may peace be upon him) and sought his advice in regard to it. He said: Allah's Messenger, I have acquired land in Khaibar. I have never acquired property more valuable for me than this, so what do you command me to do with it? Thereupon he (Allah's Apostle) said: If you like, you may keep the corpus intact and give its produce as Sadaqa. So 'Umar gave it as Sadaqa declaring that property must not be sold or inherited or given away as gift. And Umar devoted it to the poor, to the nearest kin, and to the emancipation of slaves, aired in the way of Allah and guests. There is no sin for one, who administers it if he eats something from it in a reasonable manner, or if he feeds his friends and does not hoard up goods (for himself). He (the narrator) said: I narrated this hadith to Muhammad, but as I reached the (words) "without hoarding (for himself) out of it." he (Muhammad' said: "without storing the property with a view to becoming rich." Ibn 'Aun said: He who read this book (pertaining to Waqf) informed me that in it (the words are) "without storing the property with a view to becoming rich."*
Book 13, Number 4007	*This hadith has been narrated on the authority of Ibn 'Aun with the same chain of transmitters up to the words: "Or he may feed the friend withoiut hoarding from it" and he made no mention of what follows.*
Book 13, Number 4008	*'Umar reported: I acquired land from the lands of Khaibar. I came to Allah's Messenger (may peace be upon him) and said: I have acquired a piece of land. Never have I acquired land more loved by me and more cherished by me than this. The rest of the hadith is the same, but he made no mention of this: "I narrated it to Muhammad" and what follows.*

Source Kitab Al-Wasiyya[6]

[6] International Islamic University Malaysia, Translation of Sahih Muslim, Book 13. Retrieved from https://www.iium.edu.my/deed/hadith/muslim/013_smt.html.

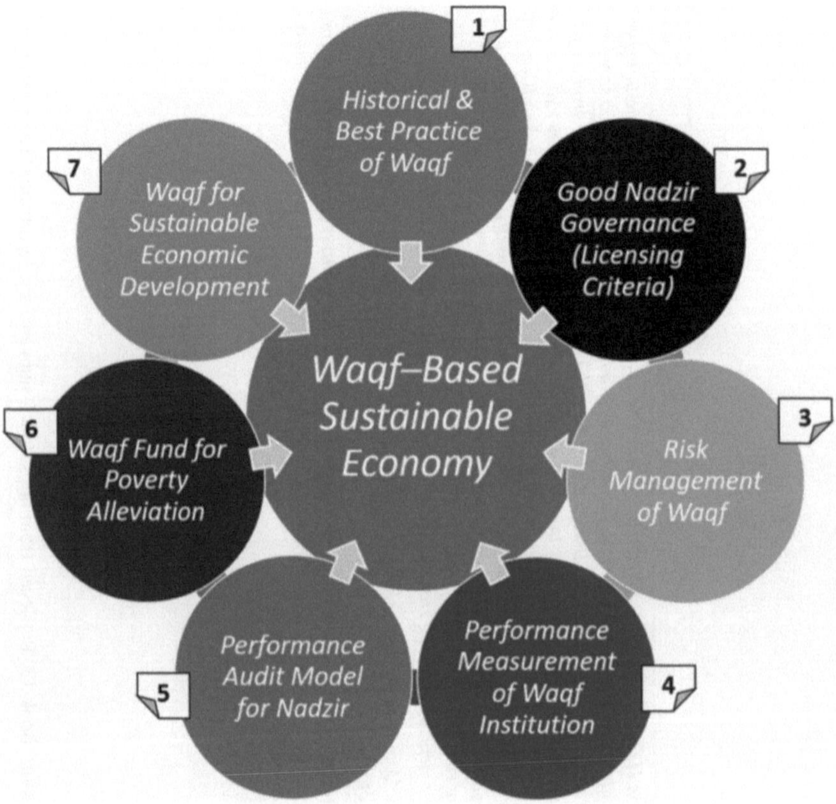

Fig. 3.1 Waqf-based sustainable economy (*Source* International Center for Awqaf Studies [ICAST])[7]

Waqf embodies a unique structure that reflects its role as a charitable endowment aimed at serving religious, social, and communal needs.[8] The primary components in the financing structure of waqf are as below.[9]

1. Waqif (Founder)

The individual who initiates the waqf by donating assets, properties, or wealth for specific purposes. The waqif's intentions and conditions guide the use of the endowed resources.

[7] ICAST. Research and Publication. Retrieved from https://icast.unida.gontor.ac.id/research-and-publication/.

[8] El-Gamal, M. A. (2006). *Islamic Finance: Law, Economics, and Practice*. Cambridge University Press.

[9] Ibid.

2. Mawquf (Beneficiary)

The recipient of the endowed assets, properties, or wealth that are set aside by the waqif. These resources generate income or benefits that are allocated for charitable and religious purposes.

3. Mutawalli (Supervisor)

The individual or entity entrusted with the day-to-day management of the waqf's operations, including financial management, distribution of benefits, and maintenance of assets.

4. Nazir (Administrator) (optional)

The trustee or administrator responsible for managing the endowed assets, ensuring they are utilized according to the waqif's intentions and in compliance with Islamic principles.
Waqf operates through well-defined mechanisms that ensure the fulfillment of its intended purposes. The operational aspects of waqf are as below.[10]

1. Income Generation

The endowed assets generate income through rent, profits, or other means. This income is directed towards the specified charitable objectives, which may include supporting education, healthcare, and social welfare.

2. Beneficiary Identification

The beneficiaries of a waqf's income are defined by the waqif. These beneficiaries typically include individuals in need, institutions, and specific social causes.

3. Distribution of Benefits

The generated income is distributed periodically among the beneficiaries, aligning with the principles of equity and social justice.

4. Accountability and Transparency

Waqf administrators, including the nazir and mutawalli, are responsible for transparently managing and utilizing the waqf's resources. Accountability mechanisms ensure that the endowed assets are utilized for their intended charitable and social purposes as below.[11]

---

[10] Shaikh, S. A., Ismail, A. G., & Mohd Shafiai, M. H. (2017). Application of waqf for social and development finance. *ISRA International Journal of Islamic Finance, 9*(1), 5–14. Retrieved from https://www.emerald.com/insight/content/doi/10.1108/IJIF-07-2017-002/full/html.

[11] Abdul-Rahman, Y. (2017). Waqf-based institutions and socio-economic development: the case of Malaysia. *International Journal of Islamic and Middle Eastern Finance and Management, 10*(3), 331–346.

1. Educational Waqf *(Waqf al-Ilmi)*

Educational waqf structures involve endowing assets to establish and maintain schools, colleges, and universities. The generated income is used to cover expenses such as teacher salaries, infrastructure maintenance, and providing scholarships to students from underprivileged backgrounds as shown in the Table 3.2. This type of waqf has historical significance in the Islamic world and continues to play a vital role in promoting education.

2. Healthcare Waqf *(Waqf al-Sihah)*

Healthcare waqf involves dedicating assets to support medical facilities, hospitals, clinics, and healthcare services as shown in the Table 3.3. The income generated can be used to provide free or subsidized medical care to those in need, ensuring that quality healthcare services are accessible to all members of the community, irrespective of their financial means.

3. Orphanage Waqf *(Waqf al-Yatim)*

Orphanage waqf structures involve setting aside assets to establish and maintain orphanages. The income generated is utilized to provide housing, education, healthcare, and emotional support to orphaned children, ensuring their well-being and development as shown in the Table 3.4.

4. Green Waqf *(Waqf al-Hijra)*

Green waqf is a modern adaptation that focuses on environmental sustainability. Assets are endowed for ecological purposes, such as reforestation, water conservation, and renewable energy projects as shown in the Table 3.5. The generated income is used to fund initiatives that contribute to environmental protection and conservation.

5. Microfinance and entrepreneurship waqf *(Waqf al-Tijara)*

Microfinance and entrepreneurship waqf involve providing financial resources to empower individuals with limited access to traditional banking systems as shown in the Table 3.6. The income generated can be used to offer micro-loans to entrepreneurs, supporting small businesses and income-generating activities.

6. Cemetery Waqf *(Waqf al-Maqbara)*

Cemetery waqf structures dedicate assets to maintaining cemeteries, burial grounds, and related facilities. The income generated ensures that proper burial services are available to all members of the community, regardless of their financial circumstances as shown in the Table 3.7.

Table 3.2 Examples of educational waqf

Educational waqf (country)	Description
Al-Qarawiyyin University (Turkey)[12]	Founded in 859 CE by Fatima al-Fihri, this university in Fez, Morocco, is often considered the oldest existing degree-granting educational institution in the world. It was established as a waqf, providing free education to students for centuries
Madrasa al-Firdaws (Egypt)[13]	This modern educational waqf in Egypt was established by a philanthropist to fund the education of underprivileged students. It covers the expenses of students attending universities and vocational training institutes
Qatar Foundation for Education, Science, and Community Development (Qatar)[14]	Founded by the Qatar royal family, the Qatar Foundation is a prominent example of a contemporary educational waqf. It supports education and research initiatives, including the renowned Education City in Doha, which hosts various international universities

Source Authors' own

[12] Abdullah, A. (2023). Re-examination of selected waqf and western university endowments. *Journal of King Abdulaziz University-Islamic Economics, 36*(1), 3–26. Retrieved from https://www.researchgate.net/profile/Adam-Abdullah-3/publication/368755856_Re-Examination_of_Selected_Waqf_and_Western_University_Endowments/links/63f84ebfb1704f343f79f8c8/Re-Examination-of-Selected-Waqf-and-Western-University-Endowments.pdf.

[13] Rusydiana, A. S., Laila, N., & Sukmana, R. (2021). Waqf on education: a bibliometric review based on scopus. *Library Philosophy and Practice (e-journal)*. 5537. Retrieved from https://digitalcommons.unl.edu/cgi/viewcontent.cgi?article=10234&context=libphilprac.

[14] Qatar Foundation. Education City in Qatar. Retrieved from https://www.qf.org.qa/education/education-city.

Table 3.3 Examples of healthcare waqf

Healthcare waqf (country)	Description
Sultan Qaboos University Hospital (SQUH) (Oman)[15]	Established in Muscat, Oman, SQUH is a prominent healthcare institution funded through a waqf established by Sultan Qaboos bin Said al Said. It provides advanced medical services and healthcare education
King Fahd Medical City (Saudi Arabia)[16]	This major healthcare complex in Riyadh, Saudi Arabia, is funded by a waqf. It comprises several specialized medical facilities and hospitals, including the King Fahd Hospital, which offers comprehensive healthcare services
Hospital Baiturrahmah, Indonesia[17]	Located in Aceh, Indonesia, Hospital Baiturrahmah is a charitable healthcare institution funded through a waqf. It offers healthcare services to the local community, including medical treatment and surgeries

Source Authors' own

[15] Bouzenita, A. I, & al-Salimi, M. (2020). Teacher formation for Islamic education: the experience of Sultan Qaboos University. *The Malaysian Journal of Islamic Sciences*, 32. Retrieved from https://uijournal.usim.edu.my/index.php/uij/article/download/133/136/848.

[16] The World Folio. (2016, December 7). Medical City at the Forefront of Saudi Healthcare Revolution. Retrieved from https://www.theworldfolio.com/interviews/medical-city-at-the-/4264/.

[17] Ascarya, A., & Tanjung, H. (2021). Structures of healthcare waqf in Indonesia to support SDGs. *Islamic Wealth and the SDGs, Global Strategies for Socio-economic Impact*, pp. 305–324. Retrieved from https://www.researchgate.net/publication/351040398_Structures_of_Healthcare_Waqf_in_Indonesia_to_Support_SDGs.

Table 3.4 Examples of orphanage waqf

Orphanage waqf (country)	Description
Zakat House Orphanage (Kuwait)[18]	The Zakat House in Kuwait manages several orphanages and childcare centers funded through waqf. These facilities provide shelter, education, healthcare, and support to orphaned children
Bait al-Ansar Orphanage (Palestine)[19]	This orphanage in Palestine is funded through a waqf and provides care, education, and support to orphaned Palestinian children who have been affected by conflict
Dar Al-Bir Orphanage (Lebanon)[20]	Dar Al-Bir operates an orphanage in Lebanon that offers a nurturing environment, education, and healthcare services to orphaned children, funded through charitable waqf

Source Authors' own

[18] Ahmad, M., Rashid, S. K., Ibrahim, U., & Oseni, U. A. (2015). The legal and regulatory framework for zakah and waqf administration in Kuwait: lessons for Nigerian zakah and waqf institution. *International Journal of Business, Economics and Law, 7*(4), 9–21. Retrieved from https://www.ijbel.com/wp-content/uploads/2015/09/KLIBEL7_Law-3.pdf.

[19] IESCO. Waqf Al-Qu'ran for Palestinian. Retrieved from https://www.iesco.my/donations/waqf-al-quran-for-palestinian-students/.

[20] The National News. (2015, August 3). Dar Al Ber Society: A Charity Built on Tradition. Retrieved from https://www.thenationalnews.com/uae/dar-al-ber-society-a-charity-built-on-tradition-1.78340.

Table 3.5 Examples of green waqf

Green waqf (country)	Description
Al-Azhar Park (Egypt)[21]	Al-Azhar Park in Cairo, Egypt, is an example of a green waqf project. Aga Khan Trust for Culture (AKTC) initiated the restoration and development of this park through a waqf endowment. The park not only serves as a green space but also includes historic restoration and sustainable development, contributing to environmental preservation
Environmental Science Center (Qatar)[22]	Qatar Foundation has established a waqf-funded environmental education center known as the "Environmental Science Center." This center focuses on environmental research, education, and sustainability initiatives
Green Waqf Framework (Indonesia)[23]	The Indonesia Waqf Board (BWI), in partnership with the United Nations Development Programme (UNDP-Indonesia), the Waqf Center for Indonesian Development and Studies (WaCIDS), and the Green Waqf Organization, has put forth a Green Waqf Framework. This comprehensive framework encompasses the concept, stages, key success indicators, stakeholder identification, and policy recommendations for the future advancement of Green Waqf initiatives in Indonesia. This framework draws upon the valuable experiences and insights of various stakeholders within Indonesia

Source Authors' own

[21] Kasdi, A. (2018). The empowerment of productive waqf in Egyptian al-azhar for education and its relevance to be implemented in Indonesia. *International Journal of Mechanical Engineering and Technology (IJMET), 9*(11), 1839–1851. Retrieved from https://iaeme.com/MasterAdmin/Journal_uploads/IJMET/VOLUME_9_ISSUE_11/IJMET_09_11_191.pdf.

[22] Olawuyi, D. S., & Athwal, E. I. (2022). *Law and Governance Innovations on Sustainability in Qatar: Current Approaches and Future Directions, Gulf Studies*, vol. 9, p. 3802. Retrieved from https://link.springer.com/chapter/10.1007/978-981-19-7398-7_3.

[23] UNDP. (2022, September 20). Green Waqf Framework. Retrieved from https://www.undp.org/indonesia/publications/green-waqf-framework.

Table 3.6 Examples of microfinance and entrepreneurship waqf

Microfinance and entrepreneurship waqf (country)	Description
Bait Al-Mashura Finance House (Bahrain)[24]	The historic Al-Qarawiyyin Cemetery in Fez, Morocco, is one of the world's oldest waqf cemeteries. It was established as part of the Al-Qarawiyyin Mosque and University complex. Income generated from the waqf endowment is used for the maintenance and preservation of the cemetery
Waqf Foundation (Bangladesh)[25]	Waqf Foundation Bangladesh utilizes the concept of waqf-based microfinance to provide interest-free microloans to disadvantaged individuals to help them start or expand small businesses
Islamic Development Bank (IsDB) (Tunisia)[26]	IsDB has established a youth entrepreneurship waqf fund which provides financial support, training, and mentorship to young entrepreneurs to help them launch and grow their businesses

Source Authors' own

[24] Ali, S. N., & Oseni, U. A. (2022). *Waqf Development and Innovation: Socio-Economic and Legal Perspectives*. Routledge. Retrieved from https://books.google.com.my/books?hl=en&lr=&id=_vtNEAAAQBAJ&oi=fnd&pg=PT9&dq=Bait+Al-Mashura+Finance+House+(Bahrain)+waqf&ots=LGcKk-zjR_&sig=2f6MJOYkzTEQcBx1TK_Jmlhcp2E#v=onepage&q&f=false.

[25] Alpay, S., & and Haneef, M. P. (2015). Integration of Waqf and Islamic Microfinance for Poverty Reduction: Case Studies of Malaysia, Indonesia and Bangladesh, Statistical, Economic and Social Research and Training Centre for Islamic Countries. Retrieved from https://sesricdiag.blob.core.windows.net/sesric-site-blob/files/article/501.pdf.

[26] IsDB. Youth Development. Retrieved from https://www.isdb.org/youth-development.

Table 3.7 Examples of cemetery waqf

Cemetery waqf (country)	Description
Maqbarat Al-Baqi' (Saudi Arabia)[27]	The Al-Baqi' Cemetery, located in Medina, Saudi Arabia, is one of the most famous Islamic cemeteries globally. It contains the graves of numerous companions of the Prophet Muhammad (peace be upon him) and family members. The maintenance and preservation of this historic cemetery are supported through waqf funds and charitable donations
Al-Qarawiyyin Cemetery (Morocco)[28]	The historic Al-Qarawiyyin Cemetery in Fez, Morocco, is one of the world's oldest waqf cemeteries. It was established as part of the Al-Qarawiyyin Mosque and University complex. Income generated from the waqf endowment is used for the maintenance and preservation of the cemetery
Jannat al-Mu'alla (Saudi Arabia)[29]	Jannat al-Mu'alla is a historic cemetery located in Mecca, Saudi Arabia. It is the final resting place of several prominent figures in Islamic history. Waqf initiatives help ensure the proper upkeep and preservation of this cemetery

Source Authors' own

[27] Komalasari, R. (2020). The Waqf Cemetery Information System. *IOP Conference Series,* p. 879.

[28] Perry, C. F. (2018). A Geniza for Mamluk studies? Charitable trust (waqf) documents as a source for economic and social history. *Mamluk Studies Review,* 2. Retrieved from https://knowledge.uchicago.edu/record/993/files/MSR_II_1998-Petry.pdf.

[29] Fauzia, A. (2018). Waqf Making and Commercial Cemeteries: Religious Circulation and Commodification of the Economy of Giving. *The Muslim World,* pp. 676–701. Retrieved from https://www.researchgate.net/profile/Amelia-Fauzia/publication/329845935_Waqf_Making_and_Commercial_Cemeteries_Religious_Circulation_and_Commodification_of_the_Economy_of_Giving_Waqf_Making_and_Commercial_Cemeteries/links/6344bd42ff870c55ce166371/Waqf-Making-and-Commercial-Cemeteries-Religious-Circulation-and-Commodification-of-the-Economy-of-Giving-Waqf-Making-and-Commercial-Cemeteries.pdf.

7. Community Development Waqf *(Waqf al-Khair)*

Community development waqf encompasses a wide range of initiatives aimed at improving the overall well-being of a community. This can include funding infrastructure projects, recreational facilities, and social programs that enhance the quality of life for residents as shown in the Table 3.8.

In a nutshell, Waqf is an embodiment of Islamic principles rooted in the pursuit of social utility and financial justice. Its historical legacy, enriched by the teachings of Prophet Muhammad (peace be upon him), has transitioned seamlessly into contemporary contexts. From its role in establishing vital community assets to its potential for fostering financial inclusion, waqf stands as a testament to the enduring relevance of Islamic economic philosophy in addressing societal challenges.

As the world grapples with issues of inequality and economic disparity, the utility principles embedded within waqf continue to offer a beacon of hope, urging societies to channel resources towards the common good. In the tapestry of Islamic finance, waqf remains an enduring thread that binds generations, echoing the essence of compassion, justice, and community stewardship.

Having explained and understood what is waqf, next this chapter will explain the differences between sadaqah, zakat, waqf, and then move on to explain the regulatory framework of waqf in Malaysia.

3.2 Differences Between Sadaqah, Zakat and Waqf

Sadaqah, zakat, and waqf are integral concepts within Islamic social finance but each has their distinct purposes and mechanisms as below.

3.2.1 Sadaqah[30]

The word "Sadaqah" which is derived from the Arabic root "sidq," meaning truth, refers to voluntary acts of charity or giving. It involves offering assistance, financial support, or resources to individuals, communities, or causes, driven by compassion and goodwill.

In terms of its purpose, Sadaqah is not bound by specific rules or calculations and is considered a means of earning spiritual rewards. It is a selfless act of kindness that can be offered at any time and in any amount, depending on one's willingness and ability.

The collection mechanism of Sadaqah can take various forms, including monetary donations, giving away possessions, providing services, or offering one's time and

[30] Hassan, A. (2015). *Islamic Philanthropy*. Palgrave Macmillan.

Table 3.8 Examples of community development waqf

Community development waqf (country)	Description
Mawhiba Foundation for Community Development (Saudi Arabia)[31]	The Mawhiba Foundation is a prominent waqf-based organization in Saudi Arabia that focuses on community development by providing educational and talent development programs for gifted and talented students
Central Waqf Council (India)[32]	The Central Waqf Council is a statutory body responsible for the implementation of waqf education and empowerment programs through skill development and training for the poor, especially women
National Awqaf Foundation of South Africa (Awqaf SA) (South Africa)[33]	Awqaf SA undertakes various community development projects, such as the construction and renovation of schools, mosques, community centers, and other essential infrastructure to enhance the quality of life for residents

Source Authors' own

[31] Saad, N. M., Kassim, S., & Hamid, Z. (2016). Best practices of waqf: experiences of Malaysia and Saudi Arabia. *Journal of Islamic Economics Lariba, 2*(2), 57–74. Retrieved from https://journal.uii.ac.id/JIELariba/article/download/9685/7849.

[32] Central Waqf Council. Functions. Retrieved from https://centralwaqfcouncil.gov.in/content/function.

[33] National Awqaf Foundation of South Africa. Rebuilding Our Community. Retrieved from https://awqafsa.org.za/.

expertise. It is often given to alleviate immediate needs or to support projects that contribute to the betterment of society.

3.2.2 *Zakat*[34]

The word "Zakat" which is derived from the Arabic root "z-k-w," meaning to purify or grow, refers to the obligatory almsgiving ordained in Islam. It involves giving a specific portion of one's wealth to eligible recipients, ensuring the purification of one's wealth and the upliftment of the less fortunate.

In terms of its purpose, Zakat serves both spiritual and social purposes. It aims to purify the giver's wealth, cultivate humility, and foster a sense of responsibility towards the marginalized. It also functions as a mechanism to redistribute wealth and address economic inequalities.

The calculation mechanism of Zakat is based on specific guidelines, typically a percentage of one's accumulated wealth, including savings, investments, and income. It is distributed to specific categories of recipients, such as the poor, the needy, those in debt, travelers, and others in accordance with Islamic principles.

3.2.3 *Waqf*[35]

The word "Waqf" which is derived from the Arabic root "waqafa," meaning to stop or immobilize, refers to an endowment of assets, properties, or wealth for charitable or religious purposes. The endowed resources generate income that is dedicated to specific social, educational, or religious objectives.

In terms of its purpose, waqf aims to provide sustained benefits to the community by establishing a perpetual source of funding for essential services and causes. It embodies the spirit of giving while ensuring the longevity of its impact over generations.

The management mechanism of waqf involves dedicating assets to specific purposes, often with detailed instructions from the donor. The income generated is directed towards the intended beneficiaries and causes, such as supporting education, healthcare, or community development.

The key differences between sadaqah, zakat and waqf are summarized below in the Table 3.9.

---

[34] Ahmad, M. U., & Mahmood, A. (2009). Zakat fund-concept and perspective. *International Journal of Monetary Economics and Finance, 2*(¾). Retrieved from https://www.researchgate.net/profile/Moid-U-Ahmad/publication/46514893_Zakat_fund_--_concept_and_perspective/links/58119d0608aea04bbcbd575a/Zakat-fund--concept-and-perspective.pdf.

[35] Mar Iman, A. H., & Sabit Mohamad, M. T. (2014). *Waqf Property: Concept, Management, Development, and Financing*. UTM Press.

Table 3.9 Summary of key differences between sadaqah, zakat and waqf

Aspect	Key differences
Nature	Sadaqah is voluntary and can be given in various forms without specific obligations or calculations. Zakat is obligatory and has precise guidelines for its calculation and distribution. Waqf involves endowing assets for specific purposes to generate sustained income
Purpose	Sadaqah is a gesture of goodwill and kindness, often used to address immediate needs. Zakat aims to purify wealth and promote socio-economic justice by redistributing resources. Waqf establishes a long-term mechanism to support charitable, educational, or religious initiatives
Calculation	Sadaqah has no fixed amount or percentage and is given based on individual willingness. Zakat is calculated based on specific criteria and typically requires giving a fixed percentage (usually 2.5%) of one's eligible wealth. Waqf's calculation involves dedicating specific assets or resources for charitable purposes
Recipients	Sadaqah can be given to anyone in need. Zakat has predefined categories of recipients, ensuring it reaches those specified by Islamic teachings. Waqf's recipients are determined by the purpose for which the endowment was created

Source Authors' own

In a summary, sadaqah, zakat, and waqf collectively embody the principles of compassion, social justice, and community welfare within the framework of Islamic social finance. While each has its unique characteristics, they all contribute to creating a more equitable and compassionate society.

3.3 Legal Framework for Waqf in Malaysia

The legal framework for waqf in Malaysia is established through a combination of state Islamic laws, regulations, and bodies which outlines the establishment, administration, and management of waqf properties that play a crucial role in promoting social welfare and religious objectives.[36] At the national level, the legal framework for waqf in Malaysia is administered by the Securities Commission of Malaysia (SC) and the Department of Awqaf, Zakat dan Haji (JAWHAR).

The SC had in November 2020 introduced a Waqf-Featured Fund Framework to expand Islamic capital market products for Islamic social and impact investing. The Framework aims to integrate commercial and social objectives by enabling investors to contribute to waqf initiatives while earning income from their investments by allowing the creation of Islamic unit trusts and wholesale funds with a specific purpose of directing a portion or all of their income towards prescribed purposes.[37] The key requirements of the Framework include specifying the fund's investment

[36] Zakaria, Z., Noh, M. N. M., & Mohamad, A. A. (2019). Exploring waqf enactments and their implications on waqf management in Malaysia. *Journal of Critical Reviews, 6*(7), 257–263.

[37] SC. Waqf-Featured Fund Framework. Retrieved from https://www.sc.com.my/development/icm/developmental-initiatives/waqf-featured-fund-framework.

objective, identifying eligible waqf recipients, and disclosing this information in offering documents and periodic reports. The Framework aims to integrate commercial and social objectives by enabling investors to contribute to waqf initiatives while earning income from their investments.[38]

As for (JAWHAR), it is the federal governing body for Islamic social financing that plays a significant role in harmonizing the development of waqf institutions across the country.[39] JAWHAR works to establish a consistent legal framework that underpins the growth and evolution of waqf institutions, ensuring their integrity alongside other Islamic financial instruments like zakat and hajj.[40] They also collaborate with state religious authorities, government-linked companies (GLCs), and private entities to expand and enhance waqf, zakat, and other Islamic social financing mechanisms.[41] A summary of JAWHAR's role is as below.[42]

- To strategically plan, execute, oversee, and harmonize the advancement of waqf institutions, aiming to bolster their effectiveness in contributing to the socio-economic progress of the ummah (Muslim community) in Malaysia.
- To strategize and synchronize the establishment of a consistent legal framework that underpins the growth and evolution of waqf institutions, ensuring their integrity alongside zakat, mal (Islamic taxation), and Hajj/Umrah establishments.
- To foster innovative partnerships with governmental bodies, as well as GLCs and private entities, fostering cooperative ventures for the expansion and enhancement of waqf, zakat, mal, and hajj/umrah institutions.
- To engage in comprehensive research, studies, and publications while facilitating coordination on pertinent matters and initiatives concerning the enhancement of Muslim wealth, with the goal of optimizing its utilization for the betterment of the ummah.
- To provide valuable aid and support services encompassing human resources, financial management, and information and communication technology (ICT) to State Religious Authorities and affiliated agencies, ensuring the efficient functioning of waqf-related operations.

With regard to the administration of waqf, List II of the State List in Schedule Nine of the Federal Constitution provides that this falls under the state jurisdiction as stated below.[43]

> Islamic law and personal and family law of persons professing the religion of Islam, including the Islamic law relating to succession, testate and intestate, betrothal, marriage, divorce, dower, maintenance, adoption, legitimacy, guardianship, gifts, partitions and non-charitable

[38] Ibid.

[39] JAWHAR. Vision, Mission and Objective. Retrieved from https://www.jawhar.gov.my/en/corporate-info/vision-mission-and-objective/.

[40] Ibid.

[41] Ibid.

[42] Ibid.

[43] Federal Constitution, Schedule Nine, State List, List II.

Table 3.10 Waqf specific state legislations

State	Regulation
Perak	ENAKMEN WAKAF (PERAK) 2015
Johor	KAEDAH-KAEDAH WAKAF 1983
Selangor	ENAKMEN WAKAF (SELANGOR) 2015
Negeri Sembilan	ENAKMEN WAKAF (NEGERI SEMBILAN) 2005
Terengganu	ENAKMEN WAKAF (TERENGGANU) 2016
Melaka	ENAKMEN WAKAF (MELAKA) 2005

Source Authors' own

> trusts; Wakafs and the definition and regulation of charitable and religious trusts, the appointment of trustees and the incorporation of persons in respect of Islamic religious and charitable endowments, institutions, trusts, charities and charitable institutions operating wholly within the State.

The exclusive powers of the State Legislature to enact laws on Islamic matters were affirmed in the Federal Court decision of *Mamat bin Daud v Government of Malaysia.*[44] The central issue in this case was whether the refusal by the National Registration Department (NRD) to change Mamat bin Daud's name to Muhammad bin Abdullah was justified under Malaysian law. The Federal Court, in a unanimous decision, held in favor of Mamat bin Daud and ruled that the NRD's refusal to allow the name change was not justified as the enforcement of laws on Islamic matters are under the purview of State Legislatures.

Thirteen of the states in Malaysia govern their waqf institutions independently under their respective state enactments with six of the states namely Perak, Johor, Selangor, Negeri Sembilan, Terengganu, and Malacca having enacted waqf specific legislations whereas the remaining states and federal territories have provisions on waqf in their general administrative legislations as shown in the Table 3.10 (below).[45] These legislations provide the legal basis for the establishment, management, and administration of waqf properties in Malaysia.

As the enactments are *pari materia*, their provisions are quite similar in nature though the enactments differ slightly in terms of the scope of their provisions. Using the Enakmen Wakaf (Negeri Melaka) 2005[46] ("the Enakmen") which provisions has the most comprehensive scope as reference, the Enakmen provides for the definitions and classifications of waqf assets, including real properties, monetary assets, and other assets dedicated for specific religious, educational, or social purposes. The Enakmen outlines the procedures for establishing and registering waqf properties and assets by setting out the responsibilities of waqf administrators, including their

[44] [1988] 1 MLJ 119 (SC).

[45] Ali, N. S., Kamaruddin, N. H., Mohamed, Z., & Baharum, N. S. (2021). Strengthening waqf legal framework in Malaysia. *Pertanika Journal of Social Sciences & Humanities, 29*(3).

[46] Enakmen Wakaf (Melaka) 2005. Retrieved from http://www2.esyariah.gov.my/esyariah/mal/portalv1/enakmen2011/State_Enact_Ori.nsf/b3ac9c218c8efdc4482568310022d8b3/33b9289a6c1f2eed4825715e000788b0?OpenDocument.

duties in managing, maintaining, and generating income from waqf assets. In this regard, the Enakmen specifies the permissible purposes for which waqf assets can be utilized, such as education, healthcare, poverty alleviation, and religious activities subject to the prior identification of the eligible beneficiaries who may benefit from the permitted use of waqf assets.

In terms of the management of waqf assets, the Enakmen requires waqf administrators to maintain proper records and accounts of waqf assets, income, and expenditures and make regular reporting to relevant authorities and beneficiaries to ensure transparency and accountability. Additionally, the Enakmen also sets out the procedures for the making of amendments to the governing conditions and permitted uses of waqf assets and provides mechanisms for the termination of waqf arrangements in specific circumstances in line with legal procedures. Lastly, the Enakmen outlines enforcement mechanisms and penalties for violations, including unauthorized use of waqf assets or failure to fulfill administrative duties.

In sum, the legal framework for waqf in Malaysia which is collectively administered by both national bodies and state religious authorities ensures the proper establishment, management, and utilization of waqf properties for charitable and religious purposes, in alignment with Islamic principles and the intentions of the waqif.

3.4 Use-Case Study on Waqf

3.4.1 Finterra's Waqfchain

Finterra's WaqfChain platform uses blockchain to address critical challenges within Malaysia's waqf management and governance landscape.[47] The platform aims to revolutionize waqf management via blockchain technology through the following ways.[48] The purpose of Finterra's Waqfchain is to support the growth and development of Islamic social finance, in particular the waqf mechanism through the benefits arising from blockchain integration such as global accessibility through the use of smart contracts, enhanced transparency and accountability through the use of blockchain-based ledger records, lower barriers to entry through the use of assets tokenization for fractional ownership and improved security through the use of cryptographic protocols.

1. Smart Contracts

[47] Finterra. Reviving the Power of Waqf through Blockchain Technology. Retrieved from https://mywaqf.com/.

[48] Ibid.

Finterra's Waqfchain's use of smart contracts renders the platform to have global accessibility, unbound by geographical constraints. This attribute not only accommodates international stakeholders but also augments the potential for widespread participation and support, extending the reach and influence of waqf undertakings.

2. Cause Management

Finterra's WaqfChain's transparency mechanism guarantees that every waqf transaction, spanning contributions to the management of assets, is meticulously recorded and accessible to authorized participants. This transparency serves to mitigate the potential for disputes, allowing for a cause management system that is grounded in mutual trust and openness.

3. Reporting

Finterra's Waqfchain uses unalterable blockchain ledgers to establish an auditable trail of its waqf transactions and operations. This equips administrators and stakeholders with an effortless means to scrutinize the historical records of transactions and actions. The upshot of Finterra's Waqfchain's blockchain-based reporting function is a strengthened culture of accountability pervading waqf management practices.

4. In-Built Security

Finterra's WaqfChain uses in-built cryptographic security protocols to provide an impregnable layer of protection against unauthorized manipulation. Transactions recorded on the platform's blockchain are rendered immutably secure, safeguarding sensitive waqf data and ensuring the preservation of data integrity.

5. Fund Accounting

Finterra's WaqfChain undertakes the digitization and automation of diverse administrative processes, thereby diminishing dependence on manual documentation for fund accounting purposes. By doing so, the platform orchestrates a streamlined and efficient management of waqf assets. This newfound efficiency allows for optimal resource allocation and expeditious decision-making when it comes to the accounting management of waqf fund assets.

6. Crowdsourcing

Finterra's WaqfChain crowdsourcing framework establishes a direct channel between donors and beneficiaries. This avenue empowers donors to interact directly with those impacted by their contributions, creating a personalized connection. Such engagement not only enriches the donor experience but also acts as an incentive for sustained support toward waqf endeavors.

In a short, Finterra's WaqfChain harnesses the decentralized and immutable nature of blockchain to construct a robust foundation for transparent record-keeping pertaining to waqf transactions and donations. Each transaction finds its indelible place within a distributed ledger that withstands tampering and alteration. This inherent transparency fosters a climate of trust among stakeholders, be they donors, beneficiaries, or custodians, engendering an environment characterized by integrity and heightened responsibility within the waqf domain.

3.4.2 *Bank BJB Syariah's Wakaf Ikhlas*

Indonesia's Bank BJB Syariah's Wakaf Ikhlas mobile application allows users to make waqf contributions using their mobile phones.[49] After downloading the Wakaf Ikhlas app from Google Play Store, users can directly register using their mobile phone number, Google account, or Facebook account.

Donors (wakif) can select the amount they wish to contribute. They will then receive a virtual account number to continue their endowment transactions using any delivery channel from any bank. Donors can also participate in projects managed by trustees (nazir), including projects for building public facilities, schools, and various other initiatives.

The funds contributed by the donors will be distributed to various institutions. There are 10 trustees (nazir) or organizations that manage the endowments, collaborating with Bank BJB Syariah. These include Wakaf Salman ITB, Dompet Dhuafa, Badan Wakaf Indonesia, Yayasan Wakaf Bangun Nurani Bangsa, Rumah Wakaf, Wakaf Daarut Tauhid, Wakaf Al Azhar, Sinergi Foundation, Global Wakaf, and Wakaf Daqu.[50]

3.5 Issues and Challenges

One of the persistent challenges facing the realm of waqf is the presence of ambiguities or an absence of clear regulatory frameworks governing waqf properties.[51] This deficiency can engender disputes and complexities in determining the rightful beneficiaries and the effective administration of these endowed assets.[52] In cases where regulations are inadequately defined, the intended purposes of waqf can be compromised, inhibiting its potential contribution to the well-being of society.[53]

In order to address the legal and regulatory challenges of waqf properties, the establishment of robust governance structures is pivotal to the successful management of these properties. The appointment of competent administrators, or mutawallis, is integral to ensuring the efficient management and utilization of these endowed assets. The absence of proper governance measures can lead to various predicaments, such as mismanagement, inappropriate utilization of resources, and

---

[49] Google Play Store. Wakaf Ikhlas. Retrieved from https://play.google.com/store/apps/details?id=com.module.wakafmaslahah&hl=en&gl=US.

[50] AyuPurWarkata. (2019). Wakaf Ikhlas Bersama Bank BJB Syariah. Retrieved from https://www.ayopurwakarta.com/nasional/pr-32877730/Wakaf-Ikhlas-bersama-bank-bjb-syariah.

[51] Abubakar, A. M., & Mydin, R. (2017). Challenges and potential of Waqf as a socially responsible investment in Malaysia. *Journal of Islamic Accounting and Business Research, 8*(1), 2–17.

[52] Mohd, A. S. (2018). Legal and administrative challenges in the distribution of waqf property in Malaysia. *International Journal of Law, Government and Communication, 3*(13), 94–106.

[53] Abulhasan, M. J., & Ahmad, N. A. (2019). Exploring the challenges of implementing the waqf governance framework in Malaysia. *Journal of Islamic Accounting and Business Research, 10*(3), 434–450.

conflicts of interest. Strengthening accountability mechanisms and implementing sound governance practices is vital to safeguarding the integrity and impact of waqf assets.

Sound governance frameworks provide a solid foundation for the management and utilization of waqf assets which despite their inherent potential often remain underutilized or generate suboptimal income.[54] In Malaysia for example, about 92.8% of waqf land with the size of about 11,000 hectares are undeveloped.[55] This can be attributed to a range of factors including outdated infrastructure, lack of strategic investment, or inadequate marketing strategies. The untapped potential of these assets underscores the need for innovative approaches to rejuvenate their utility and maximize their socioeconomic benefits.

Poor management and utilization of waqf assets may be exacerbated by the division of these assets among multiple beneficiaries which can culminate in fragmented ownership structures.[56] The dispersion of ownership can pose challenges in decision-making processes and coordination efforts. The resulting complexity can impede effective strategic planning and the implementation of development initiatives, thereby hindering the holistic advancement of waqf assets.

The harnessing of the full potential of waqf assets under a fragmented ownership structure is made more challenging by the inherent vulnerability of waqf assets to economic fluctuations, inflation, and market volatility which underscores the significance of prudent financial planning.[57] These assets' value and the income derived from them can be adversely affected by macroeconomic shifts. The insufficiency of comprehensive financial strategies can potentially undermine the sustainability of waqf initiatives and their long-term contributions.

In order to address these issues and challenges, it is important to put in place effective management frameworks for waqf assets which demand a multifaceted skill set encompassing property management, legal expertise, and financial acumen. By fostering a cadre of skilled professionals, the efficacy of waqf management can be significantly elevated. These professionals can ensure the establishment of watertight documentation which is of paramount importance in elucidating the intentions of the

---

[54] Abdullah, M. A., & Ibrahim, D. H. (2016). Waqf real estate management in Malaysia: issues and challenges. *3rd Advances in Business Research International Conference*, pp. 153–162.

[55] Ali, N. M., Rahman, M. M., Ahmad, R., & Mahdzan, N. S. Necessity of effective and efficient business model for development of Waqf lands in Malaysia. *Conference: Muktamar Waqf IQLIMI II 2015: Enhancing Social Enterprise and Islamic Philanthropy Through Ijtima'i and Waqf*. Retrieved from https://www.researchgate.net/publication/283352648_NECESSITY_OF_EFFECTIVE_AND_EFFICIENT_BUSINESS_MODEL_FOR_DEVELOPMENT_OF_WAQF_LANDS_IN_MALAYSIA.

[56] El-Bdour, R., & Arslan, A. (2018). Developing a new model for the administration of waqf properties in Jordan. *International Journal of Islamic and Middle Eastern Finance and Management, 11*(3), 345–364.

[57] Hasan, Z. (2016). Developing a sustainable framework for waqf management in Malaysia: a proposal. *Journal of King Abdulaziz University: Islamic Economics, 29*(1), 3–24. Retrieved from https://oarep.usim.edu.my/jspui/handle/123456789/15858?mode=full.

waqif (donor) and ensuring transparent administration of waqf assets. Documentation gaps or inaccuracies can precipitate disputes and legal complexities, thereby impinging on the seamless management and optimal utilization of waqf assets.

For the general public, a significant challenge pertains to the limited awareness and understanding of the potential benefits and transformative impact of waqf as an Islamic social financing mechanism. Elevating public awareness and fostering education about the concept and manifold advantages of waqf are pivotal to its expansion and meaningful societal integration.[58] Waqf public education initiatives can be undertaken through industry-academia collaboration.

Review Questions

1. How is the concept of waqf related to social welfare and charitable activities?
   a. It involves investing in profitable businesses
   b. It generates income for the waqif's family
   c. It allocates benefits and revenues for specific charitable or religious goals
   d. It supports government initiatives for economic growth
2. What is the key principle underlying waqf's potential for enhancing financial inclusion?
   a. Encouraging individual savings
   b. Providing interest-based loans
   c. Championing equitable distribution of resources
   d. Promoting consumerism
3. What core principle does sadaqah, zakat, and waqf collectively embody?
   a. Economic growth
   b. Community welfare
   c. Political power
   d. Individual wealth accumulation
4. How do the recipients of sadaqah, zakat, and waqf differ?
   a. They are all determined by the donor's preferences
   b. They are selected by a centralized Islamic authority
   c. Sadaqah recipients must be eligible for zakat as well
   d. Each has distinct predefined categories specified by Islamic teachings
5. Which list in the State List in Schedule Nine of the Federal Constitution in Malaysia outlines matters pertaining to the administration of waqf falling under state jurisdiction?
   a. List I
   b. List II

[58] Salleh, M. N., & Abdullah, M. A. (2018). Enhancing the socio-economic impact of waqf through awareness and education: the case of Malaysia. *Journal of Islamic Monetary Economics and Finance, 4*(2), 409–424.

c. List III
d. List IV

6. At the national level in Malaysia, which department administers the legal framework for waqf?
   a. Department of Islamic Affairs
   b. Department of Awqaf, Zakat dan Haji
   c. Department of Charity Organizations
   d. Department of Financial Regulation
7. How does Finterra's WaqfChain empower donors in the waqf process?
   a. By limiting their interaction with beneficiaries
   b. By anonymizing their contributions
   c. By creating a personalized connection with beneficiaries
   d. By centralizing their donations through intermediaries
8. How does Finterra's WaqfChain platform aim to address geographical constraints in waqf management?
   a. Through traditional documentation methods
   b. By limiting participation to local stakeholders
   c. By using cryptographic security
   d. By offering global accessibility via smart contracts
9. Why do waqf assets often remain underutilized or generate suboptimal income?
   a. Lack of skilled professionals in the field
   b. Limited documentation of waqf assets
   c. Outdated infrastructure and inadequate marketing
   d. Excessive regulatory restrictions
10. What can adversely affect the value and income of waqf assets?
   a. Economic fluctuations and inflation
   b. Overutilization of resources
   c. Lack of public awareness
   d. Fragmented ownership structures

Answers

1. c
2. c
3. b
4. d
5. b
6. b
7. c
8. d
9. c
10. a

Chapter 4
Lessons Learned from the Zakat and Waqaf Frameworks in Indonesia and Singapore for Application in Malaysia

Abstract In this chapter makes a comparative analysis of the Zakat and Waqaf frameworks in Indonesia and Singapore, offering valuable insights for their application in Malaysia within the Islamic Social Finance context. The chapter provides an in-depth examination of the legal and regulatory frameworks governing Zakat and Waqaf in Indonesia and Singapore, shedding light on the respective practices in these jurisdictions. Through a meticulous comparison, the chapter aims to establish benchmarks, facilitating a nuanced understanding of the strengths and areas for improvement in each framework. By drawing lessons from the experiences of Indonesia and Singapore, the chapter presents a framework for Malaysia to enhance its Zakat and Waqaf systems, contributing to the broader field of Islamic Social Finance.

Keywords Zakat · Waqf · Indonesia · Singapore · Malaysia

Learning Outcomes
At the end of this chapter, students will be able to understand:

- General legal, regulatory framework and practice of Zakat and waqaf in Indonesia and Singapore.
- Compare and assess the chosen jurisdictions' frameworks, aiming to establish benchmarks for Zakat and waqaf framework within the context of Islamic Social Finance.
- How Malaysia can learn from Indonesia and Singapore based on the benchmarks that have been set by the two countries.

4.1 Introduction

When defining Islamic Social Finance, it encompasses a broad spectrum of financial instruments and services that adhere to Islamic principles. As discussed in the previous chapters, Islamic Social Finance traditionally encompasses philanthropic

S. Kunhibava et al., *Islamic Social Finance*,
https://doi.org/10.1007/978-981-97-1410-0_4

tools like Zakat (almsgiving), Sadaqah (voluntary charity), Waqaf (endowments), and Qard (interest-free loans). However, Islamic Social Finance is not confined solely to these traditional tools. It also extends to modern Islamic financial services such as Islamic microfinance, Sukuk (Islamic bonds), and Takaful (Islamic insurance),[1] all of which share the common goal of addressing societal challenges.In elaborating Islamic social finance framework comprehensively, each financial instrument must be examined individually, as they entail different elements and transactions tailored to their specific objectives.

This chapter focuses on examining two jurisdictions and their implementation of Islamic Social Finance. The application of zakat and waqaf will be the social finance tools that will be emphasized throughout this chapter. A comparative analysis approach is adopted to analyse how Islamic Social Finance is applied, serving as a valuable lesson for Malaysia in its financial system. The selected jurisdictions for benchmarking this application are Indonesia and Singapore. These two countries were chosen due to their tremendous works on Zakat and waqaf within the context of Islamic social finance. Furthermore, it is prudent to compare Indonesia, and Singapore with Malaysia to benchmark Malaysia's approach and administration of zakat and waqf. This chapter shall show how different countries with varying Muslim population percentages have developed unique models for Islamic Social Finance. Indonesia's extensive Muslim majority offers a robust platform for exploring and implementing Islamic financial practices, while Singapore's minority Muslim population has led to innovative approaches within a smaller demographic context.

Malaysia, with a 63.5% of Muslim population,[2] can indeed gain valuable insights from both Indonesia and Singapore. Indonesia, with an impressive 86.7% of its population identifying as Muslim,[3] provides a substantial case study for the application of Islamic Social Finance. The high Muslim population would indicate that their participation in the Islamic social finance would increase the nation's social economic status. Indonesia's initiatives like Dompet Dua'fa and Badan Wakaf Indonesia showcase the potential for impactful Zakat and waqaf practices, potentially inspiring Malaysia to enhance its existing systems. Although Singapore is a small country that has 15.6% of Muslim population,[4] which makes up less than 1 million Muslims, the country's per capita income is the highest in the South East Asian region.[5] This means, the per capita income of Singaporean Muslims are much more than Malaysia and Indonesia. Other than that, Singapore's religious council's investment arm; Warees Investment, exemplifies how even within a minority Muslim population, creative approaches to

[1] Zain, N. R. M., & Ali, E. R. A. E. (2017). An analysis on Islamic social finance for protection and preservation of Maqāṣid Al-Sharia. *Journal of Islamic Finance, 176*(5872), 1–9.

[2] The Royal Islamic Strategic Studies Centre [RISSC]. (2023). *The Muslim 500: The World's 500 Most Influential Muslims– 2023*. Amman, Jordan: Author. Retrieved from https://themuslim500.com/wp-content/uploads/2023/10/The-Muslim-500-2024-Free.pdf.

[3] Ibid.

[4] Ibid.

[5] Riyanto, S., Nizar, M., & Herningtyas, R. (2021). Muslim's philanthropy in Singapore and the role of government. *Sociología y tecnociencia, 11*(2), 194–214.

Islamic finance can thrive, offering Malaysia alternative perspectives on investment and financial management in the context of social finance.

Islamic Social Finance is considered crucial in generating positive impacts on society, such as alleviating poverty, providing essential infrastructure like schools and hospitals, and preserving human life and dignity.[6] This type of investment is not solely rooted in charitable and social donations; instead, it represents a form of cooperative investment that not only yields financial returns but also fosters social benefits.[7] Therefore, it is essential to explore and analyse the development of these positive impacts on society, particularly in regions with a significant Muslim population that are directly or indirectly linked to Islamic social finance.

Learning from these varied models, Malaysia can potentially combine the strengths of both approaches, leveraging its Muslim population for scale while integrating innovative strategies tailored to its socio-economic landscape. From this comparative analysis, this chapter shall contribute to a growing body of literature that enriches the global understanding of Islamic Social Finance, fostering collaboration and mutual learning among diverse Muslim-majority and minority communities.

Its important to highlight that at a later part of this chapter, an analysis will be made in terms of comparing the selected jurisdictions to Malaysia. By comparing the experiences of these two countries to Malaysia, this chapter aims to gain valuable insights into the challenges, successes, and best practices in implementing Islamic Social Finance within the selected jurisdictions. This knowledge will not only benefit these specific jurisdictions but also serve as a valuable reference for other nations considering the adoption of Islamic Social Finance as a means of promoting financial inclusion and social development within their Muslim-majority populations.

4.2 Legal, Regulatory Framework and Practices on Islamic Social Finance in Indonesia

4.2.1 Zakat

As mentioned earlier, Indonesia stands out as the most populous country in South-East Asia and boasts a substantial Muslim population. Notably, Indonesia's approach to social finance, particularly in the realm of zakat, serves as a model for other nations. The concept of zakat is intricately woven into the fabric of Indonesia's Islamic Banking Act, officially designated as Act No. 21 of 2008. This legislation enables Islamic banks to establish Baitul Mal, which translates to the "House of Wealth." This institution is pivotal for Islamic banks as it allows them to fulfil their crucial social responsibilities within the community.[8] Baitul Mal takes charge of overseeing funds

[6] Zain, N. R. M., & Ali, E. R. A. E. (2017).

[7] Ibid.

[8] Act of the Republic ff Indonesia No. 21 of 2008 concerning Sharia (Islamic) Banking.

gathered from various sources, including zakat (obligatory alms), infaq (charitable giving), sadaqah (voluntary contributions), and waqaf (endowments established by Muslims for religious, educational, or charitable purposes).[9] The disbursement of these funds is strictly governed by Shari'a law, with zakat required to be distributed among eight designated categories of beneficiaries, either through consumptive or productive programs. Other funds can be directed toward various social initiatives and investments in the real sector. Shari'a law identifies specific types of wealth, including assets, livestock, gold, silver, agricultural produce, and even bonds and stocks, as subject to zakat.[10]

Institutionally, the Law of the Republic of Indonesia, number 23 of 2011, concerning zakat management, is designed to establish a comprehensive national framework for the efficient and effective administration of zakat services. The primary goal of this framework is to enhance the management of zakat, maximize its benefits for public welfare, and contribute significantly to poverty alleviation.[11] The apex body in this infrastructure is the Badan Amil Zakat Nasional (BAZNAS) created by the government for the sole objective of zakat management at national level.[12] It is an independent body responsible to the President through the Minister of Religious affairs. Its functions include planning, implementation, controlling the process of collection, distribution and utilization of zakat and reporting the operational performance of zakat management. Its executive committee includes members who are non-political, responsible and competent members from the community. It is supported by a secretariat and has a network of offices in provinces, districts and cities where it forms zakat collecting units (UPZ) to assist the process of zakat collection.

The second tier in the zakat management infrastructure involves private community initiative and comprises Lembaga Amil Zakat (LAZ). It carries the task of assisting in the collection, distribution, and utilization of zakat.[13] Such community organizations must be registered not-for-profit legal entities with adequate competencies and programs of social welfare. These institutions additionally must have Shariah supervisory boards and must undergo periodical Sariah and financial audit. These must be duly authorized by the government based on BAZNAS recommendation. Further, these are required to report their audited performance to BAZNAS. The administration of Zakat, Infaq, and Sadaqa (ZIS) in Indonesia operates through a dual institutional structure, with ZIS being overseen by both government bodies like Badan Amil Zakat Nasional, a Shariah social financial institution (BAZNAS)

[9] Ibid, Article 4.

[10] Widodo, A. (2019). The role of integrated Islamic commercial and social finance in reducing income inequality in Indonesia. *Journal of Islamic Monetary Economics and Finance*, *5*(2), 263–286.

[11] Ibid.

[12] Government Regulation of The Republic Of Indonesia No. 14 of 2014 Regarding Implementation of Law No. 23 of 2011 Concerning the Management of Zakat Chapter 1, Article 1(3).

[13] Ibid, Article 1(4).

and private organizations such as Lembaga Amil Zakat (LAZ), Dompet Dhuafa Republika, and Rumah Zakat Indonesia.[14]

In Indonesia, an intriguing advancement in its Zakat management involves the country's strategy in adopting technology. The traditional method for Zakat payment is usually through payments at Zakat institutional counters or representatives appointed by relevant authorities at mosques.[15] However, in response to the fourth industrial revolution that are focused on technological advancements and high increased reliance on innovation, zakat institutions in various Muslim-majority countries are changing their business models.[16] The rapid technological advancement in this era encompasses the usage of technology and digitization. Therefore, in aiming to benefit both the Zakat institutions and Zakat payers, the Zakat institutions created a web-based platform seeking to establish a comprehensive Zakat ecosystem that connects all stakeholders, including Zakat payers, institutions, and Zakat beneficiaries.[17] For BAZNAS, in order for it to stay relevant, it has planned carefully in entering the digitization era since 2017.[18] BAZNAS has established extensive collaborations with various partners, fostering the collection of Zakat through pioneering digital payment platforms and specialized Zakat applications such as M-Cash, Gojek and GoZakat.[19] These strategic partnerships showcase BAZNAS's commitment to leveraging cutting-edge technology to streamline and enhance the accessibility of Zakat collections for a wider audience, ensuring a more seamless and efficient means of fulfilling this religious obligation.

Another approached that BAZNAS adopted in transforming its Zakat management is known as ZakaTech. This innovative approach combines Zakat and technology, introducing a novel online payment model pioneered by BAZNAS. It was first introduced in 2020 due to the outbreak of the Covid19 pandemic.[20] BAZNAS formulated the technology-based zakat strategy by strengthening zakat institutions and nationally implementing the use of information technology with a view towards improving operational performance in the collection and distribution of zakat in Indonesia.[21] ZakaTech aims to streamline the processes of outreach, service, and zakat fundraising, specifically tailored to meet the needs of muzaki (zakat payers). Utilizing ZakaTech, BAZNAS has modernized the zakat collection process, offering simpler access and more efficient procedures for those fulfilling their zakat obligations. This technological integration enables BAZNAS to expand its outreach

[14] Razak, D. A., & Dawami, Q. (2020).

[15] Bin-Nashwan, S. A., Ismaiel, A. E. A., Muneeza, A., & Isa, M. Y. (2023). Adoption of ZakaTech in the time of COVID-19: cross-country and gender differences. *Journal of Islamic Marketing.*

[16] Ibid.

[17] Ibid.

[18] Zubaidah, S., & Afifah, A. (2020, December). Development of zakat management digitalization in Indonesia. In *Indonesian Conference of Zakat-Proceedings* (pp. 459–468).

[19] Ibid.

[20] Bin-Nashwan, S. A., Ismaiel, A. E. A., Muneeza, A., & Isa, M. Y. (2023).

[21] Syahbudi, M., & Moertiono, R. J. (2021, February). Zakatech: The Readiness of Islamic Economic Development in New Normal Era. In Proceeding International Seminar of Islamic Studies, Vol. 2, No. 1, pp. 314–323.

and simplify zakat payments, not just facilitating collection but also enhancing distribution.

Through the data gathered on this platform, BAZNAS can effectively identify eligible zakat recipients, enabling a more efficient, direct, and transparent allocation of funds. The utilization of ZakaTech proved particularly impactful during the COVID-19 pandemic, facilitating the efficient distribution of zakat funds and supporting mustahiq (zakat beneficiaries), especially those economically affected by the crisis. This strategy of implementing ZakaTech integrates human resources, data management, and analytical skills within the realm of big data and digital services.[22] Employing this technology-centric approach, BAZNAS aims to strengthen zakat institutions and implement nationwide information technology to improve operational efficiency in zakat collection and distribution throughout Indonesia.

To highlight such practice, BAZNAS utilizes comprehensive data analysis to identify the distribution and presence of muzaki and mustahiq across Indonesia's diverse landscape, encompassing Indonesian citizens living abroad. Through its subsidiary organization, Puskas, BAZNAS is able to assess Zakat potentials within the country. Apart from collaborating with other zakat institutions, BAZNAS also engages with the National Shariah Finance Committee (KNKS) for information exchange regarding muzaki, mustahiq, and 'amil (those responsible for zakat distribution) in Indonesia. Since 2019, this collaborative data-sharing initiative has been a primary focus for KNKS's operations.

In addition to disbursing Zakat funds among the eight mentioned beneficiaries in the Qur'an—namely, the poor and needy, Zakat administrators, converts, slaves, debtors, those striving in the cause of Allah, and needy travellers,[23] BAZNAS also extends its distributions to various domains such as health, education, social welfare, humanitarian aid, da'wah (act oof inviting people to Islam) and advocacy, and economics.[24] It's noteworthy that BAZNAS spearheads programs and enters into Memorandums of Understanding with various entities to guarantee the efficient and fruitful distribution of its Zakat funds to the those responsible for zakat distribution.[25]

The revised Zakat management laws in Indonesia now entail oversight for each institution from government, religious, and community leaders.[26] This legal shift has raised awareness about the pivotal role of Zakat in Indonesia's socioeconomic development.[27] BAZNAS has also gained the trust from the public when it digitalized its management to show transparency and accountability. The public can easily access

---

[22] Budi, M. S. (2022). ZakaTech strategy in developing inclusive Islamic social finance (ISF) in Indonesia. *At-tijaroh: Jurnal Ilmu Manajemen dan Bisnis Islam, 8*(1), 35–45.

[23] Al-Quran, 9:60.

[24] Santo Hartono, H. (2022). Indonesia's National Zakat Agency (BAZNAS): digital transformation in managing zakat, infaq and shadaqah (ZIS). *Muslim Business and Economic Review, 1*(2), 183–204.

[25] Ibid.

[26] Zubaidah, S., & Afifah, A. (2020, December).

[27] Ibid.

information on Zakat funds and its distribution with the use of technology. As the information is disseminated and disclosed to the stakeholders, BAZNAS has proven itself to be transparent to the public.[28]

4.2.2 Waqaf

Indonesia presents a recent and noteworthy instance of substantial regulatory changes within the domain of waqaf through the enactment of Republic of Indonesia Act No. 41 on Waqaf in 2004. Previously, the regulatory framework for waqaf in Indonesia was so convoluted and fragmented before its consolidation through a new law that it was beyond the comprehension of both citizens and bureaucrats. This complexity gave rise to significant systemic corruption in the administration of waqaf.[29] The new legislation established the Badan Wakaf Indonesia (Indonesian Waqaf Agency, BWI) as an autonomous institution with the explicit goal of enhancing and advancing the national waqaf.[30] In its operations, the agency takes into account the recommendations and insights of the Minister and the Indonesian Ulama Council.

The establishment of BWI under Article 47 of the Waqaf Act marks a momentous milestone in the history of waqaf in Indonesia, representing the first concentrated endeavour to foster waqaf development. The BWI is entrusted with a substantial responsibility to rejuvenate waqaf institutions on a national scale, assuming diverse roles as motivator, facilitator, regulator, and providing various support functions.[31] Although the BWI's extensive mandate and overlapping functions have garnered both proponents and detractors, it is imperative to afford the benefit of doubt, given the prolonged neglect of the majority of waqaf properties over the years.[32]

As BWI is established in managing Indonesia's waqaf, it lines up a new era of Indonesia waqafship.[33] BWI has pinpointed various stakeholders and approaches that could enhance the nation's waqaf system. These identified stakeholders and methods are thoroughly elaborated upon, aiming to revolutionize Indonesia's waqaf for the betterment of its socioeconomic status. Firstly, is the Waqif, or donors that span across various age groups, encompassing both the youth and the elderly. This diverse group includes individuals from different social statuses, ranging from affluent members of

[28] Ibid.

[29] Lindsey, T. (2008). Constitutional reform in Indonesia: muddling towards democracy. In: *Indonesia: Law and Society* (pp. 23–47).

[30] Article 47 of Republic of Indonesia Act No. 41 on Waqaf in 2004.

[31] Manaf, Z. I. A., Mohamad, N. A., Ali, Z., Kadir, S. Z. S. A., & Nasir, F. M. (2017). Waqf Governance in Malaysia and Indonesia: a comparative analysis. In: *Contemporary Issues on Zakat, Waqf and Islamic Philanthropy* (pp. 219–228).

[32] Ibid.

[33] Presentation by Mohammad Nuh, Chairman of Badan Wakaf Indonesia 'New Era: Waqaf Ecosystem Development in Indonesia', Global Waqf Conference 2023, Istanbul Sabahattin Zaim University and Ibn Haldun University, 7–8 September 2023 Istanbul Turkey.

society to those with more limited financial means. Regardless of age or wealth, they contribute to the waqf system, driven by a shared commitment to philanthropy and social development. Secondly, the waqaf assets. These assets extend beyond mere monetary donations, encompassing diverse forms such as land, currency, precious metals like gold, intellectual property rights, and even shares in various ventures. This variety enriches the waqf pool, enabling multifaceted contributions that address different societal needs.[34]

Thirdly, BWI looks at its Nazirs, or administrators, to operate within a professional framework. The Nazirs are needed to be a certified experts equipped with the knowledge and skills to manage waqaf assets efficiently. Embracing an ecosystem approach, the Nazir will foster collaboration among stakeholders, adopt entrepreneurial strategies, and ensure strict adherence to waqaf core principles. Additionally, the administrators will leverage e-services to streamline waqaf management, ensuring transparency and accountability.[35]

As for the Mauquf alaih or beneficiaries, BWI looks at individuals on a personal level, institutions such as educational or healthcare facilities, and entities dedicated to public services and social businesses. By supporting these diverse beneficiaries, waqaf initiatives aim to create a broader impact across communities, fostering societal welfare and sustainable development. By meticulously outlining the stakeholders involved, BWI charts the course for the nation's waqaf transformation.[36]Another important effort made by BWI in transforming the nation's waqaf institution is where it also leveraged on technology akin to BAZNAS. By utilizing digital transactions and mobile applications, Waqif or donors can easily make pledges and formalize their commitments to the waqaf system. This digital transformation facilitates seamless and secure transactions, enhancing the accessibility and convenience of donating to waqaf initiatives.[37]

There are several main agenda in the digital transformation of the national waqaf system in Indonesia. Firstly, is to build the public trust through implementation of waqaf core principles to establish the BWI's credibility and reliability in managing waqaf assets. Apart from that, BWI introduces digital platforms and services enhancing accessibility for stakeholders, making information readily available and transactions more efficient. BWI also ensured that the beneficiaries of waqaf initiatives experience significant and meaningful improvements, aligning with the purpose of the waqaf contributions.

Secondly, BWI wanted to increase the capacity and professionalism, of the Nazirs. This was done through continuous competency upskilling by providing ongoing training and skill development programs so that nazirs are up-to-date with the best practices, ensuring proficient management of waqaf assets. BWI also recognizes and certifies competent Nazirs to reinforce professionalism and accountability within the management structure. In September 2023, BWI proudly presented that there are

[34] Ibid.

[35] Ibid.

[36] Ibid.

[37] Ibid.

3,101 certified Nazirs in Indonesia, which was achieved through BWI's concerted efforts. These Nazirs underwent certification, enhancing the professionalism and proficiency of the waqaf administration. BWI partnered with organizations such as Wakaf Warrior, Wakaf Cendekia, Wakafa, and many more to achieve this milestone, reflecting a collaborative approach to bolstering waqaf expertise and capacity. Other collaborations were also made with University Centers to promote knowledge exchange and research, further enhancing the expertise of Nazirs.[38]

Thirdly, BWI conducted educational campaigns and disseminating information about waqaf, especially in educational institutions like schools and campuses to raise awareness and understanding of the significance of waqaf contributions. Other than that, BWI revises and updates existing waqaf laws to align them with contemporary needs and practices, facilitating a more effective and robust legal framework.[39] All the efforts made by BWI was in full support from other various institutions such as Bank Indonesia, Ministry of Religion, Ministry of Finance. BWI streamlines the coordination among various institutions involved in waqf management ensures smoother operations and reduced bureaucratic hurdles.

It is important to highlight that the revolution that brought about by BWI and place Indonesia on the world map for Islamic Finance innovation was the concept of Cash Waqaf Link Sukuk (CWLS).[40] To date, there are numerous literature regarding Cash Waqaf Link Sukuk.[41] Essentially, the process entails BWI as the waqaf manager to invest waqaf funds in CWLS, in the form of cash waqaf through Shariah Banks which are members of the Shariah Financial Institution Receiving Cash Waqf (LKSPWU) on Sovereign Sukuk.[42] CWLS rewards or coupons are distributed by BWI to finance social activities, including the development of social infrastructure which can become waqaf assets. When the CWLS matures, the CWLS settlements are received by the BWI and all are returned to the waqafs (temporary waqf) or further managed by BWI (perpetual waqf). More on CWLS is explained in Chapter 6.

The initiatives made by BWI and other stakeholders collectively, drove the digital transformation of Indonesia's national waqaf system, achieving the objective of enhancing its system's efficiency, reach, and impact on society.[43]

---

[38] Ibid.

[39] Ibid.

[40] Further details on CWLS will be further explained in the Social Sukuk chapter.

[41] Mufidah, K. (2022). Systematic Literature Review Cash Wakaf Linked Sukuk Tahun 2018–2022. https://dspace.uii.ac.id/handle/123456789/41824.

[42] Mohammad Nuh, Chairman of Badan Wakaf Indonesia New Era: Waqf Ecosystem Development in Indonesia.

[43] Ibid.

4.3 Legal, Regulatory Framework and Practices on Islamic Social Finance in Singapore

4.3.1 *Zakat*

The regulations concerning zakat are explicit in section 68(3) of the Administration of Muslim Law Act.[44] Under such provision, it is mandatory for all Muslims in Singapore to fulfil their Zakat obligations as outlined in the Act. Additionally, the Act stipulates the procedures for the collection and distribution of zakat, delegating full authority for to the Singapore's Religious Council-Majlis Ugama Islam Singapura (MUIS).[45]

The zakat collection tabulated in the MUIS Annual Report for 2022, highlighted a remarkable and staggering growth in the nation's economic contributions from year 2018 to 2022.[46] This growth is particularly noteworthy considering that Muslims constitute a minority in Singapore and the country has a smaller population compared to other nations in the ASEAN region. In 2018, the Zakat collection was (in Singapore dollars) $43 million, in 2019 it was $46.5 million, in 2020 it was $51.8 million. In 2021, the Zakat collection was $59.5 million and in 2022, MUIS hit the $65 million mark of Zakat collection.[47] Like Indonesia and Malaysia, Singapore also adopts online payments for its Zakat collection. The zakat payer can make payments via eNETS, PayNOW, AXS Islandwide, DBS/POSB iBanking, ATM transfers, and CIMB Clicks banking app.[48]

Regarding Zakat disbursements, the 2022 report outlined a progression in figures (in Singapore dollars): $42.9 million in 2018, $45.4 million in 2019, $50.1 million in 2020, $56.3 million in 2021, and a notable increase to $60.9 million in 2022. The 2022 Zakat disbursement, as outlined in the report, delineates four primary categories: Religious Guidance, Islamic Education & Youth Engagement Programs, Mosque & Amil Management, and Madrasah & Asatizah Development & Assistance, alongside Social Development & Assistance for the Poor & Needy. Of particular note, MUIS allocated a substantial sum of (in Singapore dollars) $28.1 million to support the poor and needy.[49]

It is important to note that when comparing the figures between Zakat collection and disbursements, the surplus after deductions didn't exhibit a significant variance. This indicates that MUIS effectively and professionally managed Zakat

---

[44] (Original Enactment: Act 27 of 1966) REVISED EDITION 2009.

[45] Athief, F. H. N., Rachman, M. A., Rizki, D., Hakim, L., & Noh, M. S. B. M. (2022). Taxation policy and regulation efficiency on increasing zakat collection: countries comparison analysis. *Journal of Islamic Accounting and Finance Research, 4*(2), 301–326.

[46] MUIS Annual Report 2022. https://www.muis.gov.sg/-/media/Files/Corporate-Site/Annual-Reports/Muis-Annual-Report-2022.ashx.

[47] Ibid.

[48] Riyanto, S., Nizar, M., & Herningtyas, R. (2021).

[49] MUIS Annual Report 2022.

disbursements, maintaining a well-handled balance between the funds collected and distributed.[50] Such professional and effective management also highlights the success of Singapore's government strategy, which entrusted MUIS as the only institution with full responsibility for Zakat collection and distribution.[51]

4.3.2 *Waqaf*

In Singapore, critical success factors revolve around robust governance and legislation, recognizing the distinct needs of Muslims that differ from Common Law in various aspects like Zakat, Wakaf, Estate Matters, Marriages, Madrasah, and Halal practices. This understanding led to the passage of the Administration of Muslim Law Act (AMLA). The establishment of institutions like the Majlis Ugama Islam Singapura (MUIS) was a product of the AMLA. The legal provisions for waqaf in Singapore is provided under Sections 57(3) and 59 of AMLA. The provisions state that all waqaf property in Singapore shall be under the regulation and supervision of the Islamic Religious Council (MUIS) which holds the power to administer all such money and property in accordance with the rules made under the Act. Before the current provisions came into place, not all waqaf properties fell under MUIS's supervision.

Some of the properties were privately managed, leading to subpar systems and instances of mismanagement. This included scenarios where guardians sold waqaf lands or properties without MUIS's knowledge. Other than that, there were lack of coordination between the guardians and MUIS and absence of adherence to reporting protocols where the guardians made decisions regarding waqaf properties without informing or seeking permission from MUIS. Such instances further complicates the administration and management of these assets.[52] Following the legal reforms, a pivotal change was instituted whereby all waqaf properties were required to undergo registration. This transformative adjustment centralized the control and decision-making authority over these properties exclusively within MUIS.[53] Consequently, all waqaf properties must be registered under MUIS to prevent irresponsible parties from selling the properties without MUIS' prior approval and proper oversight. This serves as a safeguard, deterring dishonest parties from selling the properties and embezzling the proceeds. The process of converting the waqaf properties has been completed, and now MUIS holds all converted assets under its name in the waqaf registration records.[54]

[50] Riyanto, S., Nizar, M., & Herningtyas, R. (2021).

[51] Ibid.

[52] Pertiwi, R. S., Ryandono, M. N. H., & Rofiah, K. (2019). Regulations and management of waqf institutions in Indonesia and Singapore: a comparative study. *KnE Social Sciences*, 766–783.

[53] Singapore Administration of Muslim Law Act 1966, section 64.

[54] Abdul-Karim, S. (2010). Contemporary shari'ah structuring for the development and management of waqf assets in Singapore (Doctoral dissertation, Durham University).

Thereafter, MUIS needed to strategize in revitalising and maintaining the waqaf properties.[55] In doing so, MUIS faced several challenges in terms of financing. The first challenge was due to many of these properties were pre-war shophouses that required major renovation works beyond what the waqaf could afford. A pivotal moment occurred in 1985 with the transformation of Duku Road into terrace residential housing, significantly increasing its annual rental income. Legislative amendments allowed for the creation of a sinking fund, enabling waqaf entities to allocate a portion of their income for future maintenance and redevelopment requirements. These legislative adaptations paved the way for the future sustainability and growth of waqaf properties and gave waqaf a better position in the future in Singapore.[56]

Legislative practices involve managing waqaf properties collectively, appointing effective mutawallis(custodians), and proposing legislative changes to the Minister of Muslim Affairs in consultation with the Office of Mufti.[57] To further enhance the management of waqaf assets, MUIS appoints mutawalli to oversee the administration and hold managerial responsibilities. These mutawallis are required to report to and seek approval from MUIS for any transactions involving the sale or purchase of waqaf assets.[58] It is important to highlight that Singapore has crafted a unique model for waqaf management by harmonizing philanthropic endeavours with commercial activities.[59] To achieve this integration, MUIS established its wholly owned subsidiary, Warees Investments Pte Ltd. Warees is a niche asset management company which focuses on unlocking and maximizing the value of real estate waqaf and institutional properties for the betterment of Muslim community in Singapore.[60] It serves as a corporate mutawalli responsible for managing and developing waqaf assets.[61] Warees Investments Pte Ltd undertakes nearly all waqaf functions, including tenancy concerns, property development, sales, purchases, and maintenance.[62] By separating commercial functions, MUIS can center its focus on regulatory responsibilities, ultimately enhancing corporate governance within the waqaf framework.[63] Furthermore, the advantages of having a corporate mutawalli include the ability

---

[55] Presentation by Mr. Masagoes Muhammad Isyak, Chief Executive Officer, Warees Investments, Singapore 'Waqf Development and Management—The Singapore Experience'. In: *Global Waqf Conference 2023, Istanbul Sabahattin Zaim University, and Ibn Haldun University 7–8 September 2023 Istanbul Turkey.*

[56] Ibid.

[57] Ibid.

[58] Abdul-Karim, S. (2010).

[59] Mohammed Nasar, A. J., Hasan Saleh, A. O., Alhajri, F. M. F. S., & Taoufiq, E. A. Methods of Financing Waqf Development in Singapore. *International Journal of Business Ethics and Governance, 3*(1), 25–42.

[60] Mr. Masagoes Muhammad Isyak, Chief Executive Officer, Warees Investments, Singapore 'Waqf Development and Management—The Singapore Experience'.

[61] Abdul-Karim, S. (2010).

[62] Ibid.

[63] Ibid.

to cultivate and retain internal proficiency in property development and management.[64] This setup also amplifies speed, efficiency, and adaptability by tapping into the dynamism of the private sector. It shields MUIS from potential commercial risks, augments profits for the betterment of the waqaf's interests, and enables a more agile response to market demands.[65]

One of the success stories of the collaboration between MUIS and Warees Investment Pte Ltd was MUIS application of Real Estate Investment Trust (REIT) in its waqaf funds. The REIT structure was appealing to MUIS as the underlying assets for investors are real estates. Hence, MUIS advanced the REIT framework by proposing the divestment of underperforming waqaf properties situated in less desirable areas. The resulting proceeds would then be utilized to procure higher-quality properties through an asset migration strategy.[66] Nevertheless, the proposal was not immediately accepted and some controversial issues arose. Among these issues was the traditional perspective that waqaf properties are not permissible to be sold. This belief stemmed from the premise that waqaf properties are divinely owned by Allah, given that the waqif has relinquished their ownership rights over the property.

Nevertheless, MUIS clarified that the underlying intent was not the sale of the properties, rather, it focused on exchanging underperforming assets for better ones that would benefit the intended beneficiaries.[67] In 1985, the Singapore Fatwa Committee convened for a fatwa meeting to deliberate the question regarding waqaf properties which are no longer earning income.[68] They resolved that the waqaf properties need to be presentable or prepared for redevelopment. Failing which, these properties may be seized or acquired. The Fatwa Committee decided that the waqaf property's sale is permitted under the condition that its original value remains unchanged, enabling the acquisition of other properties for higher income while upholding the intentions of the donor.[69] The waqaf administrator holds complete responsibility for managing the property and is relieved of religious responsibility if an investment fails despite thorough diligence. Relying on the fatwa decision, MUIS proceeded with the purchase of 11 Beach Road, a six-story commercial property, using the combined sales proceeds from 43 waqaf assets in the early 2000s. Such property generates a stable income from renting out commercial spaces and the earnings are then distributed among the 43 waqaf based on their individual shareholdings.[70]

---

[64] Mr. Masagoes Muhammad Isyak, Chief Executive Officer, Warees Investments, Singapore 'Waqf Development and Management—The Singapore Experience'.

[65] Ibid.

[66] Isyak, M. M. (2018). Enhancing community assets: sustaining the wakaf legacy. In: *Fulfilling the Trust* (pp. 165–177).

[67] Ibid.

[68] Majlis Ugama Islam Singapore, Asset Migration https://www.muis.gov.sg/officeofthemufti/Fatwa/Fatwa-on-Wakaf-Properties-English (accessed 16 November 2023).

[69] Majlis Ugama Islam Singapore, Fatwa on Wakaf Properties. https://www.muis.gov.sg/officeofthemufti/Fatwa/Fatwa-on-Wakaf-Properties-English (accessed 22 November 2023).

[70] Majlis Ugama Islam Singapore, Asset Migration.

Other waqaf funds initiated by MUIS that other jurisdiction may learn upon was The Mosque Building Fund. This fund originated in 1975 to address the pressing need for raising finances to construct mosques in newly developed housing estates and for the maintenance of the mosques' wear and tear. It mandated that every employed Muslim in Singapore contribute a small portion of their monthly salary.[71] Upon completion, mosques underwent waqaf consecration. Employers facilitated contributions on behalf of employees through the Central Provident Fund Board, akin to a pension fund system. This initiative resulted in the construction of 26 mosques and the upgrading of 25 others.[72] These funds significantly alleviated challenges such as overcrowding during Friday prayers, heightened demand for prayer spaces in specific areas, the necessity to enhance facilities in older mosques to cater to congregants' needs, and the opportunity to maximize the development potential, particularly in well-established housing estates.[73]

4.4 Comparative Analysis and Lessons Learned for Malaysia

Based on the preceding discussion and earlier chapters in this book, the comparison of Zakat and waqaf frameworks and practices among Indonesia, Singapore, and Malaysia reveals both commonalities and distinctive elements. There are valuable lessons for Malaysia to glean from both Indonesia and Singapore. Indonesia's substantial Muslim population within the ASEAN region presents a model for Malaysia in terms of managing Islamic social finance on a larger scale. Meanwhile, Singapore's ability to adapt its laws to accommodate Islamic finance despite a smaller Muslim population offers insights into uniformity, efficient management, and progressiveness. Notably, the legal transformations in Indonesia and Singapore have empowered regulators and administrators in the realm of Islamic finance. Conversely, Malaysia faces challenges due to the lack of uniformity in Zakat and waqaf regulations across different state laws.[74]

Each country boasts its respective Zakat and waqaf regulatory bodies, with specific legal provisions and varying degrees of integration of technology and digitalization into their practices. The Table 4.1 below highlights the similarities discussed.

Meanwhile, the Table 4.2 below highlights the different features of each country's Zakat and waqaf frameworks:

Based on the Table 4.2 presented above, in the realm of managing Zakat, BAZNAS and LAZ are appointed by law in Indonesia, while BWI takes charge of waqaf

---

[71] Majlis Ugama Islam Singapura. https://www.muis.gov.sg/mosque/Mosque-Infrastructure/About-MBMF/About (accessed 22 November 2023).

[72] Mr. Masagoes Muhammad Isyak, Chief Executive Officer, Warees Investments, Singapore 'Waqf Development and Management—The Singapore Experience'.

[73] Ibid.

[74] Malaysia Federal Constitution, Article 74 (2) Ninth Schedule.

Table 4.1 Comparison on Zakat and waqaf framework and practices between Indonesia, Singapore, and Malaysia

Country	Zakat regulator	Waqaf regulator	Provision of Zakat in a legal instrument	Provision of waqaf in a legal instrument	Practice of Zakat and waqaf incorporating technology and digitalization
Indonesia	BAZNAS, LAZ	BWI	√	√	√
Singapore	MUIS	MUIS	√	√	√
Malaysia	State Islamic Religious Council	State Islamic Religious Council	√	√	√

Source Authors' own

Table 4.2 Cross-country comparison on Zakat and waqaf features

Country Features	Malaysia	Indonesia	Singapore
Regulatory framework for Zakat and waqaf	State Enactments	Law Regarding Zakat Management No.23 2011	Administration of Muslim Law Act 1966
Authority/administrator for Zakat and waqaf	SIRC	BAZNAS, LAZ BWI	MUIS
Form of Zakat payment	Voluntary	Voluntary	Voluntary
Form of waqaf	Voluntary	Voluntary	Both voluntary and involuntary (deduction from salary for Mosque Building Fund Mosque)
Innovative application	Zakat: Online payments Waqaf: waqaf shares, cash waqaf	Zakat: Online payments Dompet Du'afa ZakaTech Waqaf: waqaf shares, cash waqaf and CWLS	Zakat: Online payments Waqaf: waqaf shares, cash waqaf and Waqaf REITS (Real Estate Investment Trust)

Source Authors' own

affairs. In Singapore, MUIS oversees both Zakat and waqaf matters. This stark contrast reveals a crucial lesson for Malaysia: the need for streamlining Zakat and waqaf management to ensure uniformity. One potential model worth exploring for Malaysia is JAWHAR, offering a potential framework for consistent management across these domains.[75] While some argue that JAWHAR merely functions as a coordinator without direct authority over Zakat and waqaf funds,[76] it's imperative to harness and empower JAWHAR to revolutionize Zakat and waqaf management and administration in Malaysia.

It is pertinent to note that in terms of Zakat, Malaysian Zakat institutions continue to depend on traditional approaches to collect and distribute Zakat funds. Such

[75] Official Portal of Department of Awqaf, Zakat and Hajj. (n.d.). Accessed November 20, 2023, from https://www.jawhar.gov.my/en/corporate-info/vision-mission-and-objective/.

[76] Kamaruddin, M. I. H., Masruki, R., & Hanefah, M. M. (2018). Waqf management practices: case study in a Malaysian Waqf institution. *World Journal of Social Sciences, 8*(3), 1–12.

approach demonstrates the institutions hesitation in adopting technological innovations.[77] Other than that, the Zakat institutions often lack transparency, as detailed information about their activities is not readily available on their websites,[78] unlike what can be easily accessed in Indonesia and Singapore. Additionally, these institutions have shown limited interest in using mobile platforms to engage both contributors and recipients, with only a few embracing such technology to connect with the public.[79] Only few of the institutions, such as The Lembaga Zakat Selangor, Pusat Kutipan Zakat Pahang and Majlis Agama Islam Wilayah Persekutuan provided several ways for Zakat payment that are coupled with technology; internet banking, swiping credit card or debit card, My Clear Financial Process Exchange (FPX), salary deduction scheme, postage and others.[80] Furthermore, Zakat institutions in Malaysia face limitations in adopting technology due to constraints in both financial resources and human capital.[81]

Emulating Indonesia's advancements in Zakat management, Malaysia would benefit from embracing technological progress and preparing its religious institutions for a similar shift. Raising awareness about the significance of Zakat as a religious obligation, especially during challenging periods like the Covid-19 pandemic, is crucial for societal development. Furthermore, ensuring transparency in Zakat fund management is pivotal to instilling public confidence in the effective utilization of these funds.

A key lesson from MUIS in its Zakat practice lies in the efficient distribution of Zakat funds to the mustahiq (recipient). As noted earlier, the balance between the distribution and the Zakat collection in Singapore for 2022 exhibited minimal variance post-deduction. A prior study underscored a critical concern within Malaysian Zakat institutions, revealing an excess of millions of ringgits in unallocated zakat funds.[82] Reports from 2010 to 2012 on zakat collection and distribution in Malaysia exposed a noteworthy gap, with the rate of zakat distribution significantly trailing behind its collection rate. This underscores the necessity for Malaysia to glean insights from neighboring countries in efficiently managing Zakat distribution. Such improvements are crucial to ensure a more impactful contribution to Malaysia's socio-economic landscape.

---

[77] Salleh, M. C. M., & Chowdhury, M. A. M. (2020). Technological transformation in Malaysian zakat institutions. *International Journal of Zakat*, *5*(3), 44–56.

[78] Ibid.

[79] Ibid.

[80] Yahaya, M. H., & Ahmad, K. (2018). Financial inclusion through efficient zakat distribution for poverty alleviation in Malaysia: using fintech & mobile banking. *Proceeding of the 5th International Conference on Management and Muamalah*, pp. 15–31.

[81] Nor, S. M., Abdul-Majid, M., & Esrati, S. N. (2021). The role of blockchain technology in enhancing Islamic social finance: the case of Zakat management in Malaysia. *Foresight, 23*(5), 509–527.

[82] Ma'ruf, I. R., Jusuf, A. A., Al Jufri, R., Swastria, J., Supriadi, D., Rahayu, P. K., & Arifin, A. (2020). A comparative study on zakat management law practices between Malaysia and Indonesia. *International Journal of Science and Society,* 2(2), 328–341.

As for waqaf, Malaysia can learn the importance of centralized and independent institutions from Indonesia's experience with the establishment of BWI under Section 47(2) of the Waqf Act (2004).[83] This model legitimized BWI to develop and rejuvenate waqf institutions nationwide, ensuring consistency and uniformity in waqf administration.[84] Malaysia can draw valuable lessons on the need for unified governance in managing waqf affairs. Moreover, Indonesia's emphasis on public awareness and intellectual discourse regarding waqf assets and their societal impact showcases the significance of educating the public to strengthen the waqf ecosystem. Malaysia could benefit from similar initiatives to promote understanding and engagement with waqf principles and their broader societal benefits. Furthermore, Malaysia will also benefit in exploring the cash waqaf link sukuk program pioneered by BWI. Embracing such a program could potentially enhance Malaysia's financial landscape, encouraging ethical and socially responsible investments while advancing the development of key societal projects. Such exploration will further be elaborated in the coming chapters.

Taking a cue from Singapore's Waqaf REITS, Malaysia can delve into leveraging its existing waqaf properties to create sustainable income streams, aligning with the fundamental purpose of waqaf, which is to continuously benefit a community. Emulating this strategy could enable Malaysia to optimize the potential of its waqaf properties, ultimately serving the larger goal of community welfare and development. Thus, corporate waqaf in Malaysia, exemplified by Waqaf An-Nur, may consider exploring strategies akin to Singapore's collaboration between MUIS and Warees Investment Pte Ltd. The partnership between Majlis Ugama Islam Singapore (MUIS) and Warees Private Limited has effectively revitalized several low-yielding assets, turning them into high-performing ventures that yield substantial returns. While acknowledging the commendable efforts undertaken by Waqaf An-Nur over the past two decades since its establishment,[85] there remains an opportunity for further enhancement and exploration.

Review Questions

1. Which of the following statements about BWI's role in Indonesia's waqaf development is accurate?
   a. BWI was established to promote the sale of underperforming waqaf properties for profits.
   b. BWI oversees the development and enhancement of waqaf institutions on a national scale.

---

[83] Waqf Governance in Malaysia and Indonesia: A Comparative Analysis Zati Ilham Abdul Manaf, Nor Asiah Mohamad, Zuraidah Ali, Sharifah Zubaidah Syed Abdul Kader & Fahmi M. Nasir. *International Conference on Zakat, Waqf & Islamic Philanthropy ZAWFI'17, 13–14 December 2017.*

[84] Ibid.

[85] Saad, N. M., Kassim, S., & Hamid, Z. (2013). Involvement of corporate entities in waqaf management: experiences of Malaysia and Singapore. *Asian Economic and Financial Review, 3*(6), 736.

c. BWI primarily focuses on the sale and divestment of all waqaf properties in Indonesia.
d. BWI operates as a regulatory body for Islamic finance in Indonesia, overseeing Zakat distribution.

2. What is the primary function of BAZNAS in Indonesia's Zakat management?
   a. Establishing investment strategies for Zakat funds.
   b. Overseeing the collection and distribution of Zakat.
   c. Facilitating technology-based Zakat payments.
   d. Promoting commercial ventures for Zakat funds.
3. How did MUIS in Singapore manage the surplus after Zakat deductions between collection and disbursement?
   a. They redistributed the surplus to other institutions.
   b. They invested the surplus in the stock market.
   c. They maintained a well-handled balance between collected and distributed funds.
   d. They withheld the surplus for future use in Zakat programs.
4. What was the significant impact of the Singapore Fatwa Committee's decision on waqaf properties?
   a. It allowed the waqaf properties to be sold without conditions.
   b. It endorsed the sale of waqaf properties for any purpose.
   c. It permitted the sale of waqaf properties under certain conditions.
   d. It prohibited the sale of waqaf properties under any circumstances.
5. What unique strategy did MUIS employ to enhance waqaf property management in Singapore?
   a. Collaborating with various commercial real estate firms.
   b. Outsourcing property management to private entities.
   c. Setting up a government-owned property management agency.
   d. Establishing a subsidiary for managing waqaf assets.
6. How did the Mosque Building Fund contribute to Singapore's mosques?
   a. It financed the construction and upkeep of several mosques.
   b. It funded the construction of a single mosque in Singapore.
   c. It invested in non-religious community buildings.
   d. It supported the maintenance of religious texts in mosques.
7. What was the core objective of BWI's approach to implementing ZakaTech in Indonesia?
   a. To improve operational efficiency in the tourism sector.
   b. To raise awareness about the significance of waqaf.
   c. To streamline Zakat collections and improve transparency.
   d. To manage investment portfolios for charitable donations.

8. What significant disparity exists between Zakat collection and distribution in Malaysia compared to Singapore and Indonesia?
   a. Malaysia has an excess of unallocated zakat funds.
   b. Singapore and Indonesia exhibit significant surpluses in Zakat collection.
   c. Zakat distribution in Malaysia surpasses collection rates.
   d. The rate of zakat distribution in Malaysia lags behind its collection rate.
9. What lesson can Malaysia learn from Indonesia regarding waqaf management?
   a. The importance of diversifying waqaf assets internationally.
   b. The need for centralized and independent waqaf institutions.
   c. Leveraging religious organizations to manage waqaf affairs.
   d. Prioritizing individual guardianship over centralized governance in waqaf management.
10. What key strategy, akin to Singapore's Waqaf REITS, could Malaysia explore to optimize its waqaf properties?
   a. Embracing corporate waqaf structures for greater community benefits.
   b. Establishing a collaboration between governmental bodies and private entities.
   c. Leveraging technology to digitize waqaf collections.
   d. Developing partnerships between religious councils and commercial enterprises.

Answer

1. b
2. b
3. c
4. c
5. d
6. a
7. c
8. d
9. b
10. a

Chapter 5
Islamic Microfinance

Abstract This chapter provides a comprehensive exploration of Islamic Microfinance, offering readers a nuanced understanding of its key aspects. The chapter begins with an insightful overview of Islamic Microfinance, emphasizing its distinctive features compared to conventional microfinance models. A detailed examination of the legal framework for Islamic Microfinance in Malaysia enhances the reader's comprehension of the regulatory landscape. Real-world case studies enrich the discussion, showcasing practical applications and outcomes. The chapter concludes by addressing the pertinent issues and challenges faced by Islamic Microfinance, providing a well-rounded perspective on this vital component of Islamic Social Finance.

Keywords Islamic microfinance · Conventional microfinance · Regulatory landscape · Malaysia · Financial inclusion · Microenterprise

Learning Outcomes
At the end of this chapter, students must be able to understand.

- an overview of Islamic microfinance,
- the differences between Islamic microfinance and conventional microfinance,
- legal framework for Islamic microfinance in Malaysia,
- case Studies,
- issues and challenges.

S. Kunhibava et al., *Islamic Social Finance*,
https://doi.org/10.1007/978-981-97-1410-0_5

5.1 What is Islamic Microfinance?

Islamic Microfinance is a specialized financial system that combines the principles of microfinance and Islamic finance to provide financial services to individuals and small businesses, particularly those in underserved or marginalized communities.[1] It operates with adherence to Islamic ethical and Sharia-compliant principles. One of its fundamental features is the prohibition of interest (usury) in financial transactions. Instead of charging interest, Islamic Microfinance institutions levy a nominal service fee, and their profit is derived from business and economic transactions that contribute to the real economy.

In Islamic Microfinance, transactions are grounded in real economic activities that create tangible value. These transactions are often backed by tangible assets or services, ensuring that funds are used for productive purposes, thereby fostering economic development. A key distinguishing feature is the active participation of Islamic Microfinance institutions in the transactions and their willingness to share the associated risks with their clients. This risk-sharing approach fosters a sense of partnership between the financial institution and the clients, aligning their interests.

Moreover, Islamic Microfinance institutions have the flexibility to engage in equity-type or venture capital investments, going beyond traditional debt-based financing. This enables them to take an ownership stake in businesses and share in their successes, further promoting economic growth. All financial transactions and investments made by Islamic Microfinance institutions must adhere to Islamic principles and morals. Activities that are considered unethical or non-compliant with Sharia are avoided, ensuring ethical and responsible financial practices.

Islamic Microfinance institutions operate as risk-sharing entities, actively involved in the underlying business transactions rather than simply acting as intermediaries. This departure from conventional banking practices reflects their commitment to supporting economic growth and development. One of their primary objectives is poverty alleviation, with a particular focus on serving poor and vulnerable populations who may not have access to traditional banking services.

Islamic Microfinance institutions have a global presence, operating in various countries worldwide, including Indonesia, Kenya, Afghanistan, Bangladesh, Sri Lanka, Yemen, Egypt, Sudan, Tanzania, Mauritius, South Africa, Malaysia, and Pakistan.[2] They serve a substantial number of clients, often numbering in the millions.

---

[1] Islamic Development Bank. (2016). Empowering the Poor through Islamic Microfinance. Retrieved from https://www.isdb.org/sites/default/files/media/documents/2022-05/Empowering%20the%20Poor%20through%20%20Islamic%20Microfinance_Experience%20of%20the%20Bank%20of%20Khartoum%20Sudan%20in%20Value%20Chain%20Project%20Financing%20.pdf.

[2] Ibid.

In some non-Muslim communities, Islamic Microfinance is introduced as participative microfinance, following the same principles of risk-sharing, ethical standards, and real economic transactions.[3] This approach can attract a broader range of clients interested in ethical and participatory finance.

5.2 Differences Between Islamic Microfinance and Conventional Microfinance

Islamic microfinance and conventional microfinance are two distinct approaches to providing financial services to individuals and small businesses, each with its own set of principles and characteristics. The following Table 5.1 provides the key differences between Islamic microfinance and conventional microfinance in a nutshell.

Table 5.1 Differences between Islamic microfinance and conventional microfinance in a nutshell

Characteristic	islamic microfinance	Conventional microfinance
Source of Funds	External funds, savings of clients, and Islamic charitable sources (e.g., Zakat, Waqf)	External funds, savings of clients, and donor funding are common sources
Mode of Financing	Utilizes Islamic financial instruments and profit-loss sharing (e.g., Mudarabah, Musharakah)	Typically involves interest-based loans (with interest rates) or other forms of debt-based financing
Funds Transfer	Cash is not directly given to clients; instead, goods or assets may be transferred	Cash is directly provided to clients as loans or capital
Deduction at Inception of Contract	No deduction at the beginning of a contract; instead, profits are shared	Often involves deductions from the initial loan amount to cover fees and interest
Target Group	Focus on the whole family as clients, encouraging family participation	Often focuses primarily on women and may not emphasize family participation
Social Development Program	Integrates religious, ethical, and social development into its approach	Emphasizes secular, behavioral, and social development
Interest Rate	Avoids interest (riba) and relies on profit-sharing mechanisms	May involve charging interest rates, which can be relatively high

Source D. Mazur and M. Roayee[4]

[3] Chiara, S. (2005). *Case Study "Islamic Microfinance and Socially Responsible Investments.* University of Torino.

[4] Mazur D., & Roayee M. (2011). Islamic vs. conventional microfinance: A comparative theoretical analysis. *International Journal of Business and Management Tomorrow, 1*(1), 67.

5.3 Legal Framework for Islamic Microfinance in Malaysia

The development of microfinance in Malaysia began with the initiation of "Project Ikhtiar" in 1985, with support from the government and the Science University of Malaysia (Universiti Sains Malaysia).[5] The primary objective of this program was to uplift the economic conditions of the poor by providing them with small loans as seed capital to engage in entrepreneurial activities.

In Malaysia, there are mainly four Microfinance Institutions (MFIs), namely Amanah Ikhtiar Malaysia (AIM), Yayasan Usaha Maju (YUM), Economic Fund for National Entrepreneurs Group (TEKUN Nasional), and People's Credit Cooperation (KKR).[6] AIM, YUM, and TEKUN Nasional receive full government subsidies to cater to the financial needs of the poor across Malaysia, while KKR primarily focuses on serving the poor in Sabah. Besides that, there are also Islamic banks that are licensed under the Islamic Financial Services Act (IFSA) 2016 to offer microfinance services such as Agrobank, Bank Islam, Bank Muamalat and Bank Rakyat.

In its Financial Inclusion Framework 2023–2026 Strategy Paper, Bank Negara Malaysia (BNM) has outlined several key strategies to use microfinancing to improve access to diverse funding sources, providing a 'second chance' for non-viable borrowers, and enhancing support for microenterprises and informal businesses to boost their income and move up the value chain.[7] Specific measures involve reviewing and optimizing the Skim Pembiayaan Mikro (SPM) (Microfinance schemes), establishing a simplified portfolio guarantee scheme in collaboration with strategic partners, promoting the use of alternative data for targeted solutions, and ensuring the ongoing relevance of BNM's Funds. Furthermore, financial institutions are encouraged to offer nano/social/blended finance to help underserved SMEs build a track record and reduce information asymmetry before transitioning to larger, purely commercial microfinancing.

As part of the Framework, BNM has implemented the Micro Enterprises Facility (MEF) which is a financial initiative that is aimed at providing collateral-free financing for eligible micro enterprises and entrepreneurs in Malaysia.[8] Eligible entities include micro enterprises meeting approved definitions, Malaysian micro entrepreneurs (including self-employed individuals and gig workers on digital platforms), and participants of the iTEKAD program. The financing, offered under the SPM, covers working capital and/or capital expenditure, with a maximum funding of RM50,000 per micro enterprise/entrepreneur. The financing rate is determined by

[5] Kassim, S., & Hassan, R. (2008). Issues facing islamic microfinance and their possible solutions: Empirical evidence from Amanah Ikhtiar Malaysia. *Al-Shajarah: Journal of Islamic Thought and Civilization*, special issue, 43–67.

[6] Ibid.

[7] BNM, Financial Inclusion Framework 2023–2026 Strategy Paper. Retrieved from https://www.bnm.gov.my/documents/20124/55792/SP-2nd-fin-incl-framework.pdf.

[8] BNM, Fund for SMEs: Micro Enterprises Facility (MEF). Retrieved from https://www.bnm.gov.my/documents/20124/6025157/mef_broc_en.pdf.

participating financial institutions, and the tenure can extend up to 5 years. Applicants need to apply directly to participating financial institutions, and approval is contingent on the credit assessment of these institutions. The primary objective is to enhance access to financing for micro enterprises without the need for collateral. The initiative is part of BNM's Fund for SMEs, and more information can be obtained through the provided website and contact details.

Over the years, continuous efforts have been made to enhance the sustainability and outreach of these MFIs. Budget allocations for MFIs have increased significantly in recent years, enabling them to expand their operations. For instance, TEKUN Nasional received a higher budget allocation in 2012 compared to the previous year. A 100% stamp duty exemption was also introduced for loan agreements under microfinance schemes to reduce operational costs for microenterprises.[9]

AIM is incorporated under Trustees (Incorporation) Act 1952 (Act 258). Therefore, the legal framework of the Islamic microfinance in Malaysia can be derived from Trustees (Incorporation) Act 1952. In this section of the chapter, salient parts of Trustees (Incorporation) Act 1952 is discussed to understand the legal framework applicable for Islamic microfinance in Malaysia.

The Trustees (Incorporation) Act 1952 is a legal statute enacted on December 30, 1952, in Malaysia.[10] The purpose of this act is to facilitate the incorporation of trustees for specific bodies or associations of individuals. It allows for the creation of a legal entity for such trustees, providing them with distinct legal status and recognition. It is important to note that this Act applies exclusively to Peninsular Malaysia.[11] Essentially, it establishes a legal framework for the incorporation of trustees, ensuring that they have the necessary legal standing to carry out their responsibilities on behalf of the designated bodies or associations.[12]

Section 1A of the Act provides definitions for key terms used within the Act. In this section, "certificate of incorporation" is defined as the certificate of registration granted to trustees when they apply to be recognized as a body corporate under Section 2 of the Act. Section 2 outlines the process by which trustees can be granted a certificate of incorporation as a body corporate. Trustees, who are appointed by any body or association of individuals established for various purposes such as religious, educational, literary, scientific, social, or charitable objectives, may apply to the Minister for this certificate. The Minister, based on factors like the nature and scope of the body or association, has the authority to grant the certificate if incorporation is deemed appropriate. This certificate grants the trustees legal status as a body corporate.

The certificate of incorporation specifies various conditions and directions, including qualifications and the number of trustees, their tenure, appointment procedures for new trustees, use of a common seal, land ownership limits, and land use

[9] Ibid.

[10] See the preamble of the Act.

[11] See: Section 5.1 (2) of the Act.

[12] See the preamble of the Act.

purposes. Once granted, the trustees become a body corporate with perpetual succession and the power to sue and be sued in their corporate name. They can also acquire, manage, and dispose of movable and immovable property in accordance with the conditions and directions outlined in the certificate. Essentially, Section 2 provides the legal framework for the incorporation of trustees and the subsequent management of assets and affairs as a recognized legal entity.

In the context of the Act, it is important to note that Islamic microfinance institutions can fall within the category of associations or bodies established for charitable objectives. Islamic microfinance often serves as a means to provide financial assistance and support to low-income individuals and communities, which aligns with charitable and social welfare objectives. Therefore, Islamic microfinance institutions operating in Malaysia, when established for the purpose of poverty alleviation or economic empowerment in compliance with Shariah principles, can apply for a certificate of incorporation under this Act, subject to the conditions and directions set forth by the Minister. This legal recognition as a body corporate can facilitate their operations and enhance their ability to carry out charitable and developmental activities in a structured and regulated manner.

Section 3 of the Act addresses the vesting of property in the body corporate upon the issuance of the certificate of incorporation. When a body or association of persons is granted a certificate of incorporation as a body corporate under this Act, all property, whether movable or immovable, that is owned by or held in trust for such body or association becomes the property of the newly incorporated body corporate.

Additionally, any person who holds stocks, funds, or securities in trust for the body or association of persons must transfer these assets into the name of the body corporate once it is incorporated. This transfer ensures that the assets are now under the legal ownership and control of the newly established body corporate.

Furthermore, any covenants and conditions that were applicable to immovable property and enforceable by or against the trustees of the body or association of persons before their incorporation continue to be enforceable to the same extent and by the same means after their incorporation as a body corporate. In essence, this section ensures a seamless transition of ownership and responsibilities from the trustees to the newly incorporated body corporate, allowing for the effective management and administration of the assets held for the benefit of the body or association of persons.

Section 4 of the Trustees (Incorporation) Act 1952 provides a comprehensive framework for the application process when seeking a certificate of incorporation under the Act. The Act mandates that all applications be submitted in written form and must bear the signature of the applicant. These applications must meticulously adhere to the specifics outlined in the Schedule annexed to the Act. This Schedule enumerates crucial particulars pertaining to the case, such as the objectives of the body or association of persons, the governing rules and regulations, any pertinent legal documents involved (including their creation details and parties involved), land descriptions or interests held by the body or association, and the names, residential addresses, and qualifications of the trustees representing the entity.

To ensure the accuracy and integrity of the information provided, the Minister possesses the discretionary power to request additional evidence, such as a statutory declaration, for the purpose of verification. It is important to underscore that the Minister wields the authority to refuse the issuance of a certificate of incorporation if it is ascertained that the application does not align with the provisions stipulated within the Act or any associated regulations. Effectively, this section of the Act serves as the cornerstone for establishing the requisite formalities and verification procedures that applicants must meticulously follow to secure legal recognition as a corporate entity under the Act.

Section 5 of the Trustees (Incorporation) Act 1952 outlines the procedures for appointing trustees and addressing vacancies within a body corporate seeking incorporation. It stipulates that before a certificate of incorporation can be granted, trustees must be appointed to the satisfaction of the Minister of Finance, adhering to the organization's constitution, settlement, or relevant conditions. Once incorporation is approved, any trustee vacancies that occur in accordance with the organization's rules must be filled using legal means as if no incorporation had taken place, or as specified by the relevant conditions. The appointment of new trustees should be certified by the Minister upon completion. Furthermore, this section mandates an annual reporting requirement, with the current trustees obligated to provide the Minister with a list of trustees, including their names, residences, and descriptions, within one month after each year following incorporation or as requested by the Minister. Section 5 ensures the proper governance and maintenance of the trustee body within the incorporated entity.

Section 6 of the Act addresses the liability of trustees and others, even after the incorporation of a body or association of persons. It establishes that following the issuance of a certificate of incorporation under the Act, all trustees, despite their incorporation, remain accountable and responsible for the property under their control. They are held liable for their own actions, receipts, omissions, and defaults, as well as for the proper management of the body or association of persons and its assets. This liability is equivalent in nature and scope to what it would have been if the incorporation had not occurred.

Importantly, this section clarifies that the Act does not diminish or impair the control or authority exercised by the Attorney General under Section 9 of the Government Proceedings Act 1956 over the trustees who have been incorporated. Such trustees continue to be subject jointly and individually to the control and authority of the Attorney General as if they had not undergone incorporation. In essence, Section 6 underscores that the legal responsibilities and obligations of the trustees persist even after the incorporation process, ensuring accountability for the management of the entity's assets and affairs.

Section 6A of the Act establishes specific disqualifications that prevent individuals from becoming or continuing as trustees once a certificate of incorporation has been granted under the Act. These disqualifications encompass various criteria, including criminal convictions resulting in a fine of at least one thousand ringgit or imprisonment for a minimum of one year, security-related measures such as detention or deportation orders, undischarged bankruptcy status, and being declared of unsound mind. These stringent provisions are put in place to ensure that individuals with certain legal, security, financial, or mental health issues are ineligible to hold trustee positions within an incorporated body or association. Such measures aim to maintain the suitability and integrity of trustees in the effective management of the entity's affairs.

Section 7 of the Act states that a certificate of incorporation, once granted under the Act, serves as conclusive evidence that all the preliminary requirements and requisitions stipulated for the incorporation have been met. This certificate's validity remains in force unless it is revoked by relevant authorities. Additionally, the date of incorporation specified in the certificate is deemed to be the official date when the incorporation formally occurred. In essence, Section 7 underscores the importance and legal validity of the certificate of incorporation as proof of compliance with the prerequisites for incorporation and the establishment of the incorporation date.

Section 8 of the Act mandates that the Minister, in a manner deemed appropriate, shall ensure the maintenance of a record encompassing all applications for certificates of incorporation and the granted certificates themselves. Furthermore, all documents submitted to the Minister in accordance with the Act shall be preserved in a similar manner. Any individual may request a certified copy or extract of any such document, and such a copy or extract shall be authenticated by the designated person appointed by the Minister for this purpose. The Act permits the imposition of a prescribed fee for obtaining these certified copies or extracts. In essence, Section 8 emphasizes the importance of documentation and record-keeping in the context of applications for incorporation, ensuring transparency and accessibility of relevant information to the public.

Section 9 of the Act establishes that all conditions and directions included in a certificate of incorporation are legally binding upon the trustees responsible for managing the body or association of persons. These conditions and directions must be faithfully performed or adhered to as part of the trustees' duties. Furthermore, these stipulations are subject to enforcement by the Attorney General or other interested parties in accordance with the provisions outlined in section 9 of the Government Proceedings Act 1956.

Additionally, Section 10 of the Act specifies that every application seeking a certificate of incorporation and every issued certificate is subject to a stamp duty of thirty ringgit. To denote the payment of this duty, an appropriate stamp indicating the fee's payment must be either impressed upon or affixed to the application or certificate. In essence, Section 9 underscores the enforceability of conditions and directions in certificates of incorporation, while Section 10 addresses the stamp duty requirement for such applications and certificates.

Section 11 of the Act outlines the legal effect of donations, gifts, and dispositions of land or interests therein made to an association or body of persons that has been incorporated under the Act. Any such donation, gift, or disposition, whether made before or after the incorporation, shall take effect as if it had been made directly to the body corporate or for the same purposes.

Section 12 pertains to the common seal of the body corporate. It stipulates that the common seal shall feature a design approved by the Minister. In the absence of such a common seal, the Minister may authorize the use of an individual's seal as the common seal of the body corporate. Any instrument bearing the common seal, in accordance with the conditions or directions specified in Section 2, will be legally binding on the body corporate, even if there are defects or issues with the seal's execution.

Section 13 addresses contracts entered into by the trustees of a body or association of persons. It specifies that contracts made by the trustees, which would be considered valid and binding under the organization's constitution, settlement, or rules and regulations, remain valid and binding, even if they were not executed under the common seal of the trustees. Section 14 safeguards individuals who make or allow transfers or payments in good faith relying on instruments bearing the common seal of a body corporate formed under this Act. Such individuals shall be indemnified and protected regarding these transfers or payments, regardless of any defects or circumstances affecting the execution of the instrument. These sections collectively establish the legal framework for the incorporation, operations, and legal protections associated with entities formed under the Act.

Section 15 of the Act establishes the financial management and reporting requirements for trustees of a body or association that has been incorporated under this legislation. It mandates that these trustees maintain accurate records of all financial transactions, including income and expenditures, in dedicated books. Annually, or as specified by the Minister, the trustees are obligated to prepare financial accounts that encompass gross income from endowments, starting balances, receipts, and payments. These accounts must be certified and, if applicable, audited by the organization's auditor. Copies of these financial accounts are to be submitted to the Minister within a set timeframe, allowing for public inspection, subject to regulations and fees. Furthermore, trustees must report on endowments and any changes in property ownership. This section ensures proper financial management, transparency, and accountability for incorporated bodies and associations.

Section 16 of the Act outlines the process for resolving disputes regarding a person's membership in a body corporate incorporated under the Act. If there is a question about whether someone is a member of such a body corporate, any interested party can petition the High Court for a ruling on the matter. The Court's opinion on this question is binding not only on the individual in question but also on all members of the body corporate and other concerned parties who were duly notified of the hearing.

Section 17 of the Act empowers the Minister to revoke a certificate of incorporation under certain circumstances. These circumstances include fraud, misrepresentation, unlawful purposes, pursuing objectives different from the original purpose, willful contravention of the Act or regulations, or violations of other laws punishable by fines or imprisonment. Before revoking a certificate, the Minister must notify the body corporate and provide an opportunity for it to show cause why the certificate should not be revoked. During this process, the Minister can suspend the body corporate's activities if it is in the public interest or to prevent further violations. The revocation of a certificate is final upon communication to the trustees.

Section 18 of the Act outlines the voluntary dissolution of a body corporate incorporated under the Act. It can occur either upon the occurrence of a specific event specified in the trust deed that leads to dissolution or by the unanimous agreement of the trustees, testified by the signature of the trustee constituting the body corporate on an instrument of dissolution and with the consent of the body or association of persons that appointed the trustees. The trustee must inform the Minister when either of these dissolution methods is invoked, and the Minister will then make an order to revoke the certificate of incorporation, effectively dissolving the body corporate.

Section 19 discusses the consequences of the revocation of the certificate of incorporation, whether through voluntary dissolution or other grounds. Upon revocation, the body corporate is dissolved, and any assets or liabilities of the body or association of persons that vested in the body corporate will be transferred to trustees appointed by the body or association or, in the absence of such appointment, to Amanah Raya Berhad in trust for the body or association of persons. Legal proceedings related to these assets or liabilities may continue or be initiated against the new trustees.

Section 20 provides for the appointment of a Registrar, Deputy Registrars, and Assistant Registrars by the Minister to administer the provisions of the Act. These officials perform specified functions to execute the Act's provisions, are considered public servants under the Penal Code, and are protected from legal action for acts or omissions performed in good faith while executing their duties.

Section 21 of Act which is the final section, grants the Minister the authority to create regulations that are necessary or expedient for implementing the Act effectively and ensuring its provisions are carried out. These regulations can cover various aspects, including the procedures for applying to register a trustee as a body corporate, the specific registration process, the information required to be submitted to the Minister, and the fees that can be levied and collected in connection with the Act's implementation. These regulations are essential for providing guidance and structure to the processes and procedures outlined in the Act.

In sum, the Trustees (Incorporation) Act 1952 in Malaysia provides the legal framework for the incorporation of trustees, outlining procedures for obtaining corporate status and defining their powers and responsibilities. While not directly addressing microfinancing institutions, the act is relevant insofar as these institutions may choose to incorporate as trustees or need to comply with legal requirements related to asset management and regulatory compliance. The act indirectly impacts microfinancing institutions by influencing the legal structure they adopt, particularly if they operate as trusts, and by emphasizing the importance of accelerating innovation and digital transformation, which can affect how these institutions evolve in the context of technology-driven financial services. Thus, understanding the provisions of the Trustees (Incorporation) Act becomes crucial for microfinance institutions in Malaysia to ensure lawful and effective operation within the broader legal landscape.

5.4 Case Studies

5.4.1 Amana Ikhtiar Malaysia (AIM)[13]

Amana Ikhtiar Malaysia (AIM) is a prominent financial institution in Malaysia, specializing in microcredit financing schemes that target individuals engaged in various economic activities. AIM's primary goal is to alleviate poverty and enhance the economic well-being of low-income households in Malaysia by providing microcredit financing for income-generating ventures. AIM has been in operation for over three decades, and its exceptional performance is evident through the distribution of more than RM21.47 billion in microcredit to over 300 thousand borrowers across the country, maintaining a commendable non-performing loan (NPL) rate of less than 2%.

AIM plays a pivotal role in fostering entrepreneurship within the low-income segment of the population. Beyond financial support, AIM offers guidance, training, and continuous support to empower entrepreneurs. As of the latest update, AIM has provided its services to more than 732 thousand borrowers, with over RM22 billion in capital distributed through 4,830,204 loans.

Under the leadership of YBhg. Junaidah Kiting as the Chairman of the Board, AIM has undergone significant developments. Notable achievements include strengthening the Board of Trustees with independent members and government representatives, forging critical partnerships, and reevaluating management charges while eliminating hidden costs. Furthermore, AIM has enhanced its internal and external structures, empowering regional managers and decentralizing operations by absorbing 30% of headquarters staff into regional and branch offices.

To secure AIM's future sustainability and independence, several entities were established, including Koperasi Sahabat, a cooperative for investment purposes, Staff Cooperative to provide various benefits to employees, and AIM Sdn Bhd (AIMSB) focusing on investment activities. AIM engaged KPMG for a forensic audit of AIMSB, leading to changes in its senior management for improved governance.

AIMSB has embarked on diversifying into new business areas including cooperatives through its Koperasi Sahabat Amanah Ikhtiar Malaysia (Koop Sahabat) division which announced a dividend payout amounting to RM6.5 million to its 452,728 members for the financial year ending December 31, 2022.[14]

The restructuring of the Employee Cooperative, AIM Berhad, with a new board marks a significant shift in activities and opportunities for growth, contributing to AIM's profitability and project exploration.

---

[13] Information derived from Amana Ikhtiar Malaysia, (2019). Bulletin. Retrieved from https://www.aim.gov.my/pdf/BULETIN_AIM_FINAL_22_AUG_2019.pdf.

[14] MalayMail, Koop Sahabat announces 10pc dividend payout (18 June 2023). Retrieved from https://www.malaymail.com/news/money/2023/06/18/koop-sahabat-announces-10pc-dividend-payout/75039

5.4.2 TEKUN Nasional[15]

TEKUN Nasional, a prominent financial institution in Malaysia, has made significant strides in adopting Shariah-compliant financing solutions. This recognition came in 2017 when the institution received accolades from the Syariah Center of Excellence at Bank Islam Malaysia Berhad for its steadfast commitment to Shariah-compliant practices. Presently, TEKUN proudly declares that all its financing products adhere to the principles of Shariah. This case study delves into TEKUN Nasional's unwavering commitment to Shariah compliance, outlining the financing concepts and contracts it employs, and underscoring the advantages of Shariah-compliant financing.

TEKUN Nasional has embraced Shariah compliance across its entire spectrum of financing products. The fundamental concept that underpins TEKUN's financing products is Tawarruq, characterized by Murabahah commodity trading transactions founded on residual payments. Tawarruq, in essence, amalgamates a range of contracts, including:

- Bai' Murabahah: This contract governs the sale and purchase of goods, with agreed-upon cost and profit rates. Payment can be made in full or installments.
- Wakalah: It involves one party delegating another to perform Shariah-compliant tasks, either voluntarily or with wage payments.
- Ta'widh: Indemnities are imposed to cover actual losses sustained by TEKUN due to customer delays in repayment. This serves as a source of income for TEKUN.
- Gharamah: Fine or penalties are levied on customers who default in paying debts. Notably, these fines do not constitute income for TEKUN but are directed toward charitable or baitulmal purposes.
- Ibra': TEKUN extends rebates to customers who choose to settle their financing ahead of schedule. The presence of Ibra' clauses in agreements mitigates uncertainties (gharar) concerning customer rights.

Since 1998, TEKUN Nasional has been providing financing products aligned with the Tawarruq concept including TEKUN Niaga, TEMAN TEKUN, TemanNita, Kontrak-i, and various special programs tailored to different target groups. Moreover, TEKUN incorporates the Qard concept in products such as the Special Programme (Azam Tani, PERHEBAT, DVS Johor, UKAS). Qard entails a loan contract where repayment mirrors the borrowed amount.

TEKUN extends AR-RAHNU products characterized by Shariah-compliant concepts, including:

- Qard: This loan contract ensures that the repayment amount equals the borrowed sum.
- Rahn: Gold serves as collateral or mortgage, securing loans for borrowers. The deposited gold is disbursed in case the borrower cannot meet the loan obligations.

[15] Information is taken from: TEKUN Nasional. (n.d). TEKUN Nasional Shariah Concept. Retrieved from https://www.tekun.gov.my/en/tekun-nasional-shariah-concept/

- Wadi'ah: Wadi'ah signifies a savings contract where the owner entrusts their gold to a safekeeping entity.
- Ujrah: Ujrah encompasses fees charged for gold storage services provided.

Shariah-compliant financing delivers several advantages, including:

- Ethical Practices: It upholds Shariah principles, steering clear of sinful and usurious activities.
- Halal Income: Ensures that TEKUN earns a halal income, aligning with Islamic financial ethics.
- Blessed Livelihood: Elevates the blessedness of livelihoods earned by entrepreneurs.
- Peace of Mind: Provides peace of mind to both TEKUN and entrepreneurs, fostering financial tranquility.

TEKUN Nasional extends Shariah-compliant financing to all entrepreneurs, regardless of their religious beliefs. This inclusivity ensures that the profit generated adheres to Shariah principles and upholds the institution's ethical standards. While the profit rates may not necessarily be lower than conventional loan interest rates, Shariah-compliant financing serves as a viable solution for those seeking to avoid usury, a practice prohibited by Shariah.

TEKUN Nasional has embraced terminological adjustments in its financing operations to align with Shariah-compliant concepts. Notable changes include substituting "loans" with "financing," "charges" with "profit rates," "insurance" with "takaful," "rebate" with "ibra" "borrowers" with "financing receivers" or "entrepreneurs," "loan balances" with "financing balances," and "fees" with "wakalah fees."

TEKUN Nasional's unwavering dedication to Shariah-compliant financing underscores its commitment to ethical and inclusive financial practices. By providing accessible and Shariah-compliant financing solutions to entrepreneurs, TEKUN contributes to their economic well-being while adhering to Islamic principles, ensuring a halal income stream, and nurturing peace of mind. This case study portrays TEKUN Nasional as a leading financial institution that wholeheartedly embraces Shariah-compliant finance, setting a commendable precedent in the industry.

5.5 Issues and Challenges

Islamic microfinance faces several critical issues and challenges that impact its effectiveness and sustainability. Addressing these challenges is crucial to ensure that Islamic microfinance institutions (MFIs) can fulfill their mission of promoting financial inclusion and poverty alleviation while adhering to Shariah-compliant principles. Below is an overview of the major issues and potential solutions in the context of Islamic microfinance[16]:

[16] Abdul Rahman, R., & Dean, F. (2013). Challenges and solutions in Islamic microfinance. *Humanomics, 29*(4), 293–306.

1. Market Penetration: One of the significant challenges faced by Islamic MFIs is their limited market penetration, especially in remote and underserved areas. The lack of a physical branch network and inadequate infrastructure can hinder their ability to reach potential clients. To address this issue, Islamic MFIs can explore innovative solutions, such as partnerships with postal systems digital banking or mobile banking services. These collaborations can provide a cost-effective channel to extend their services to rural populations.
2. Sustainability of Islamic MFIs: Many Islamic MFIs struggle with sustainability due to high administrative costs, inadequate fund mobilization, and heavy reliance on external funding sources. To ensure sustainability, Islamic MFIs should diversify their funding streams. This may involve leveraging waqf (endowment) funds, forming partnerships with Islamic banks, and exploring alternative funding mechanisms. Moreover, product diversification is essential to generate a more stable income stream and reduce reliance on external financing.
3. High Transaction Costs: Like conventional microfinance, Islamic MFIs face high transaction costs, particularly in rural and remote areas. These costs can erode the benefits of microfinance for clients. To mitigate this challenge, Islamic MFIs can embrace technological solutions, such as mobile banking and digital financial services, which can reduce the cost of reaching and serving clients. Additionally, group-based lending methodologies can help distribute monitoring costs among borrowers, making the process more efficient and cost-effective.
4. Effectiveness in Alleviating Poverty: The effectiveness of Islamic microfinance in poverty alleviation remains a subject of debate. Some studies suggest that one-time, one-year credit may be less effective than multiple loans over a more extended period. To enhance effectiveness, Islamic MFIs can focus on providing longer-term loans and prioritize financial education and training for clients. Responsible borrowing practices and comprehensive financial literacy programs can empower clients to make informed financial decisions.
5. Shariah Compliance and Education: Ensuring strict adherence to Shariah principles is a fundamental challenge for Islamic MFIs. The lack of Shariah-compliant products and services, as well as a shortage of trained personnel, can hinder their operations. Islamic MFIs should invest in Shariah-compliant product development and education for their staff and clients. Collaborations with religious leaders and scholars can also provide valuable guidance on Shariah compliance.

Review Questions

1. What is one of the fundamental features of Islamic Microfinance that distinguishes it from conventional microfinance?

    a. High-interest rates
    b. Prohibition of interest (usury)
    c. Direct cash transfer to clients
    d. Use of donor funding

2. In Islamic Microfinance, where do institutions derive their profit from?

   a. Interest charges
   b. High service fees
   c. Business and economic transactions
   d. Donor contributions

3. Which section of the Act allows for the Minister to create regulations necessary for its implementation?

   a. Section 6
   b. Section 11
   c. Section 16
   d. Section 21

4. What is the penalty for individuals who are disqualified from becoming or continuing as trustees under Section 6A of the Act?

   a. Fine of one thousand ringgit
   b. Imprisonment for one year
   c. Deportation
   d. All of the above

5. Which section of the Act specifies the legal effect of donations, gifts, and dispositions of land made to an incorporated body or association?

   a. Section 6
   b. Section 11
   c. Section 16
   d. Section 21

6. What is the primary purpose of the Trustees (Incorporation) Act 1952?

   a. To regulate financial institutions
   b. To facilitate the incorporation of trustees for specific bodies or associations
   c. To establish a legal framework for corporations
   d. To govern foreign investments

7. What is the primary goal of AIM (Amana Ikhtiar Malaysia)?

   a. Achieving high profitability
   b. Providing microcredit for income-generating ventures
   c. Maximizing market penetration
   d. Offering interest-based loans

8. What can enhance the effectiveness of Islamic microfinance in poverty alleviation?

   a. Providing one-time, one-year credit
   b. Offering shorter loan terms
   c. Prioritizing financial education and longer-term loans

   d. Avoiding financial education programs

9. How can Islamic MFIs address the issue of high transaction costs?
   a. Expand their physical branch network
   b. Introduce more complex financial products
   c. Embrace technological solutions like mobile banking
   d. Ignore the issue as it's unavoidable

10. What is one of the significant challenges faced by Islamic microfinance institutions (MFIs)?
    a. Lack of trained personnel
    b. High profitability
    c. Overreliance on external funding
    d. Excessive market penetration

Answers:

1. b
2. c
3. d
4. d
5. b
6. b
7. b
8. c
9. c
10. c

Chapter 6
Social Sukuk

Abstract This chapter delves into the intricate realm of Social Sukuk, providing readers with a profound understanding of these financial instruments. The chapter begins by elucidating the concepts of social bonds, social Sukuk, and SRI Sukuk, unraveling their unique characteristics. A comparative analysis with other Islamic financial tools such as Sadaqah, Zakat, Waqf, Microfinance adds depth to the discussion. The legal framework for Social Sukuk in Malaysia is explored, shedding light on the regulatory dimensions. Real-world case studies offer practical insights, showcasing the application and impact of Social Sukuk. The chapter concludes by addressing the prevalent issues and challenges in the realm of Social Sukuk, contributing to a holistic perspective on these instruments within the landscape of Islamic Social Finance.

Keywords Sukuk · Waqf link sukuk · Social sukuk · Bond

Learning Outcomes
At the end of this chapter, readers will be able to:

- describe what a social bond, social sukuk and SRI sukuk is,
- explain the differences between sadaqah, zakat, waqf, microfinance, and social sukuk
- apply the legal framework for social sukuk in Malaysia,
- understand the use-case studies on social sukuk,
- and access the issues and challenges on social sukuk.

6.1 What is Social Sukuk?

Social sukuk involves issuing certificates for social and environmental purposes, but what exactly is sukuk? Sukuk is a certificate representing a debt owed to an investor or ownership of an investor in Shariah-approved assets. It acts as a financial investment instrument allowing corporations, municipalities, governments, and other entities

S. Kunhibava et al., *Islamic Social Finance*,
https://doi.org/10.1007/978-981-97-1410-0_6

to raise funds in the Islamic capital market. The Securities Commission Malaysia defines sukuk as "certificates of equal value indicating undivided ownership or investment in assets using Shariah principles endorsed by the Shariah Advisory Council (SAC)".[1] Sukuk, an innovative financial instrument, was designed as a substitute for bonds. Unlike bonds, which are interest-bearing debt instruments similar to loans and commonly utilized in capital markets for fundraising, the inaugural sukuk was introduced in 1990 by Shell Bhd in Malaysia.[2]

A sukuk framework eliminates interest (riba) and simultaneously ensures profits for investors by involving the exchange of a Shariah-approved asset for financial consideration. This is achieved through the application of various Shariah contracts, including ijarah (leasing contract), tawarruq (buy and sell contract), bai' bithaman ajil (BBA) (deferred sales contract), Musharakah (profit and loss sharing), Mudarabah (partnership), and others. Consequently, each sukuk will be backed by a tangible underlying asset, and the nature of this asset determines the specific type of sukuk.

Commonly, the underlying assets pose challenges as they are illiquid and not easily transferable or divisible into smaller units. To address this, sukuk relies on the process of securitization. Securitization involves bundling financial promises into tradable parts, allowing numerous investors to participate. This mechanism facilitates the acquisition and sale of assets, such as immovable property, in equal and smaller units. Consequently, a single asset valued at USD$ 6 million can be transferred and collectively owned by 20 or more investors through the securitization process, with each investor holding an undivided ownership stake in the asset.

The intricacies of sukuk structuring are shaped by a multitude of factors that collectively contribute to a well-crafted financial instrument. Paramount among these considerations is a meticulous assessment of the obligor's specific needs and financial obligations. Additionally, the choice of assets available for inclusion in the sukuk, coupled with the obligor's credit rating, plays a pivotal role in determining the overall structure. Legal frameworks in the jurisdiction where the sukuk is intended to be issued introduce another layer of complexity, requiring careful navigation to align with regulatory requirements. Moreover, tax implications further influence the structuring process, necessitating a comprehensive approach to ensure compliance and optimal financial outcomes. In essence, the formulation of a sukuk involves a strategic orchestration of these factors to create a robust and Shariah-compliant financial instrument.[3]

Sukuk can be classified as asset based sukuk where the beneficial interest in the underlying assets is transferred to the investors, or an asset backed sukuk where a true sale occurs, and the legal ownership of the assets are transferred to the investors.

---

[1] Securities Commission. (2019). Guidelines on Seasoned Corporate Bonds and Sukuk. Retrieved from https://www.sc.com.my/api/documentms/download.ashx?id=9f708d2e-0db0-4c19-850d-272cae0f1922.

[2] International Islamic Financial Market. (2012). Sukuk report: A comprehensive study of the global sukuk market, http://iifm.net/media/pdf/iifm_suku_report_2.pdf.

[3] Kunhibava, S., Mustapha, Z., Muneeza, A., Sa'ad, A.A. & Karim, M.E. (2021). Ṣukūk on blockchain: A legal, regulatory and Sharī'ah review. *ISRA International Journal of Islamic Finance, 13*(1), 118–135. https://doi.org/10.1108/IJIF-06-2020-0120.

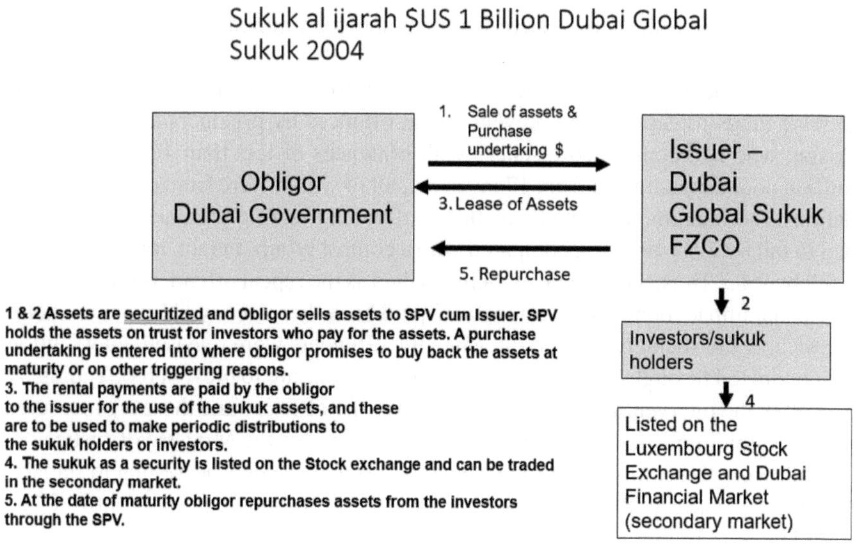

Fig. 6.1 Sukuk Al-Ijara (*Source* Authors' own)

In an asset based sukuk the profit is paid by the obligor and recourse in the event of default is with the obligor. Whereas in an asset backed sukuk the assets generate the profits and the assets are legally owned by the investor.[4]

Another classification of the types of sukuk is debt based sukuk or equity based sukuk. Debt based Sukuk are Sukuk issued based on debt related contracts, while equity based sukuk is based on partnership and profit sharing between the investor and the originator, where both contribute the capital and/or labour according to the contract setting.[5]

Commonly sukuk structures will require a special purpose vehicle (SPV) whose function is to act on behalf of the investors and hold assets for them through trust. Also necessary is a purchase undertaking where the obligor promises to re-purchase the sukuk assets.

A simple asset-based sukuk with an ijara contract is explained and illustrated below in Fig. 6.1:

Understanding social sukuk involves starting with its traditional counterpart—the social bond or social impact bond. Social bonds are essentially financial tools designed to raise money for addressing social issues. They work by setting specific social goals or Key Performance Indicators (KPIs). If these goals are met, investors receive their invested money back along with interest payments from the government. However, if the goals aren't achieved, investors stand to lose their money. This

[4] Securities Commission Malaysia (2009). *Sukuk,* Abdul Kader Thomas (Ed.). Kuala Lumpur: Sweet and Maxwell.

[5] Ibid.

unique structure reflects a creative financial approach aimed at addressing societal challenges.[6]

The first social bond was launched in 2010.[7] Here a social impact bond was issued to raise funds to support and prevent repeat offences by prisoners at Peterborough Prison, who had committed offences with sentences of less than 12 months.[8] Five million pounds was raised from 17 investors, all of whom were from charitable foundations.The outcome expected was that reoffending among prisoners participating had to fall by 7.5% or more, compared with a control group. In fact, it is reported that it fell by 9%.[9] Thus, the objectives were reached as the repeat offenders reduced, so in this social impact bond the investors were paid back their money.[10] Figure 6.2 below shows how the social bond worked, when the offenders were released, interventions are conducted through the funding, these interventions are to prevent reoffending. As a result of the interventions some commit no further offences and these are measured, if the reoffending is reduced, savings maybe created for the Ministry of Justice.

Following this initial effort more social bonds were issued, according to statistics the amount raised globally through social bonds from the year 2018 until 2022 is from US$14.3 billion to US$164 billion.[11]

A social sukuk's objective is the same as that of a social bond, that is, to provide funding for an environmental or social problem, and through the funding, impact the environment or social issue in a positive way. One of the first documented social sukuk, although not known as social sukuk, was issued in 2015 under the name SRI (sustainable and responsible investment) sukuk by Malaysia's Sovereign Wealth Fund Khazanah. It was known as Ihsan SRI Sukuk and had as its objective improving

[6] Arena, M., Bengo, I., Calderini, M., & Chiodo, V. (2016). Social impact bonds: Blockbuster or flash in a pan? *International Journal of Public Administration.* https://doi.org/10.1080/01900692.2015.1057852, p. 2.

[7] Rand Corp. (2016). Evaluating the World's First Social Impact Bond. Retrieved from https://www.rand.org/randeurope/research/projects/social-impact-bonds.html.

[8] Disley, E., Giacomantonio, C., Kruithof, K., & Sim, M. (2015). The payment by results Social Impact Bond pilot at HMP Peterborough: Final process evaluation report. Santa Monica, CA: RAND Corporation. https://www.rand.org/pubs/research_reports/RR1212.html.

[9] The Economist. (2017). Britain is a pioneer when it comes to social-impact bonds. Retrieved from https://www.economist.com/britain/2017/08/03/britain-is-a-pioneer-when-it-comes-to-social-impact-bonds?utm_medium=cpc.adword.pd&utm_source=google&ppccampaignID=18156330227&ppcadID=&utm_campaign=a.22brand_pmax&utm_content=conversion.direct-response.anonymous&gclid=Cj0KCQjwiIOmBhDjARIsAP6YhSVGG2-o7iCKv2aEpqqrLrJ0xN7RzAzY-acuxR9_fmRZTO5OD5YWrT8aAq82EALw_wcB&gclsrc=aw.ds.

[10] Disley, E., Giacomantonio, C., Kruithof, K., & Sim, M. (2015). The payment by results Social Impact Bond pilot at HMP Peterborough: Final process evaluation report. Santa Monica, CA: RAND Corporation. https://www.rand.org/pubs/research_reports/RR1212.html.

[11] BNPparibas. (2023, June). Social bonds: Financing positive change in society. Retrieved from https://cib.bnpparibas/social-bonds-financing-positive-change-in-society/.

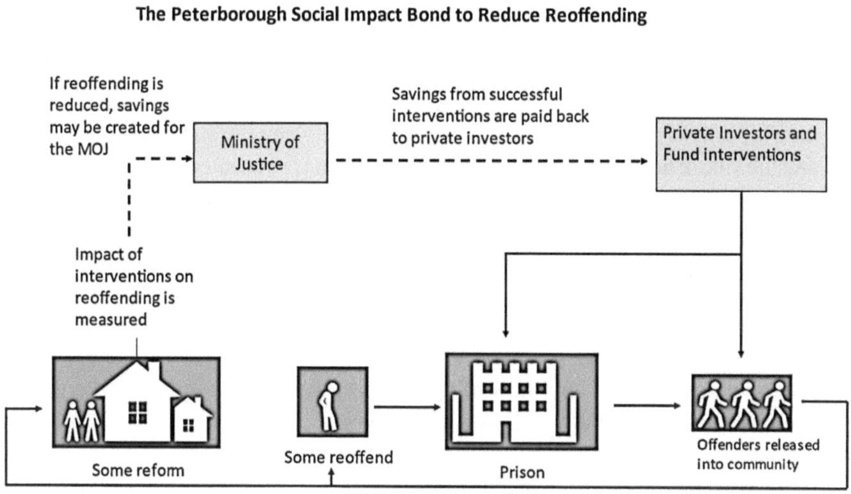

Fig. 6.2 First social bond (*Source* Modified from Rand Corporation)[12]

access to quality education in government schools in Malaysia.[13] Similar to the social impact bond of Peterborough Prison, this sukuk is based on a pay for success principle. Where if the KPIs are met the investors would get 4.2% profit rate per annum, however if the KPIs were not met the investors would get 4.6% annual profit rate per annum. In other words the investors forego a certain portion of the profit rate as part of their social obligation and instead gain through non-monetary value of benefiting the society.[14] Investors were also given the option to donate their investment for the social cause if they chose to do so. The KPIs included the increase in number of schools under Khazanah's trust foundation, and increased performance in terms of student outcome and teachers and school senior leadership performance.[15]

The Ihsan SRI sukuk was based on the Shariah contract of Wakalah (agency) Bi Al Istithmar (with investment). Basically, an SPV (Ihsan) was the wakeel (agent) who collected funds from the investors to invest. Ihsan as wakeel appointed Khazanah as sub-wakeel to invest in Shariah compliant business ventures. The proceeds from the

---

[12] Rand Corporation. (2015). Evaluating the World's First Social Impact Bond. Retrieved from https://www.rand.org/randeurope/research/projects/social-impact-bonds.html.

[13] Syed Azman, S.M.M., Ismail, S., Haneef, M.A., & Engku Ali, E.R.A. (2022). An empirical comparison of sustainable and responsible investment ṣukūk, social impact bonds and conventional bond. *ISRA International Journal of Islamic Finance 14*, 3, https://doi.org/10.1108/IJIF-04-2021-0074.

[14] Khazanah Nasional. (2015). Khazanah to issue first Ringgit-denominated sustainable and responsible investment sukuk. Retrieved from https://www.khazanah.com.my/media/uploads/2020/03/Khazanah-to-issue-first-Ringgit-denominated-sustainable-and-responsible-investment-sukuk.pdf.

[15] Kareem, M. (2022). Khazanah issues world's first ringgit-denominated SRI Sukuk: A shift toward retail. Islamic Sustainable Investment and Finance. Retrieved from https://islamicsustainable.com/khazanah-issues-worlds-first-ringgit-denominated-sri-sukuk-a-shift-toward-retail/.

sukuk investment are given to Yayasan AMIR, which is a Non-Profit Organisation which manages the school program.

Explanation of above diagram according to CIMB's Information memorandum:

1. (a), (b), (c), & (d). under a wakalah agreement between the sukuk trustee (CIMB) and the sukuk holders (investors) and Ihsan, Ihsan is appointed as wakeel to invest the funds to be collected from the investors. Ihsan then appoints Khazanah as sub-wakeel to invest the funds on behalf of the investors. Ihsan then issues the sukuk Ihsan to the investors, who in turn subscribes to the Sukuk Ihsan by paying the issue price.
2. Khazanah will invest in and manage the sukuk fund investments in Shariah compliant investments.
3. Periodic payments (if any) according to the terms of the agreement are paid to Ihsan who will distribute to the sukuk holders.
4. On the dissolution date Khazanah will exercise the purchase undertaking and purchase the underlying assets from the investors, and sukuk is dissolved.[16]

While the above figure does not show proceeds flowing to the social cause, other literature documents that at maturity if KPI's are met then the investors will forego a pre-agreed percentage of the nominal amount.[17]

The above SRI Ihsan sukuk, is for all intends and purposes a social sukuk, though not named social sukuk, because the structure, characteristics, and aims are the same as social bond.[18]

The question arises then what is an SRI sukuk?

According to the SC's Sustainable and Responsible Investment Sukuk Framework[19]:

> SRI sukuk is where the sukuk proceeds will be applied exclusively for funding of any activities or transactions relating to the eligible SRI projects.

SRI projects are those that are green, social, or waqf based as shown in Fig. 6.3.

The SRI eligible projects listed in the diagram above clearly align with the objectives of a social bond. All the SRI projects tie in with the United Nations SDGs, and at the same time further the Maqasid al-Shariah. We can thus infer that SRI sukuk is

---

[16] Ibid.

[17] Khazanah. Khazanah Nasional. (2015). Khazanah to issue first Ringgit-denominated sustainable and responsible investment sukuk. Retrieved from https://www.khazanah.com.my/media/uploads/2020/03/Khazanah-to-issue-first-Ringgit-denominated-sustainable-and-responsible-investment-sukuk.pdf.

[18] Syed Azman, S.M.M., Ismail, S., Haneef, M.A. & Engku Ali, E.R.A. (2022). An empirical comparison of sustainable and responsible investment ṣukūk, social impact bonds and conventional bond. *ISRA International Journal of Islamic Finance, 14*, 3. https://doi.org/10.1108/IJIF-04-2021-0074; RAM Ratings. (2015). Credit FAQs: Rating Khazanah's Sukuk Ihsan. In S.S. Ming & T. H. Nee (Eds.). RAM Holdings.

[19] Securities Comission. (2019). Sustainable and Responsible Investment Sukuk Framework An Overview. Retrieved from https://www.sc.com.my/api/documentms/download.ashx?id=84491531-2b7e-4362-bafb-83bb33b07416.

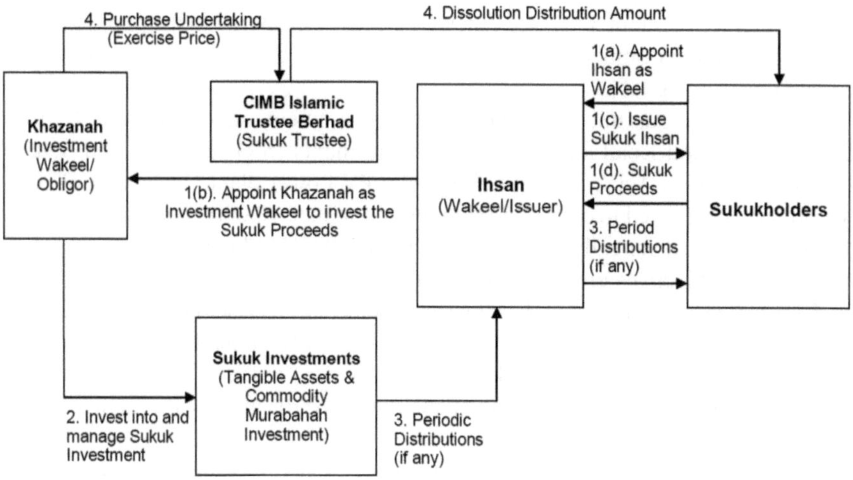

Fig. 6.3 SRI Ihsan sukuk (*Source* CIMB [2015])[20]

a social bond, but the Shariah compliant version of it, and includes green and waqf based objectives as well.

An example of a Green SRI sukuk would be the Quantum Solar Park (Semenanjung) sukuk. In this sukuk Quantum Solar Park (Semenanjung), the SPV, issued a 1 billion solar project linked sukuk in 2017 (October). The assets were bought and sold under a commodity murabaha and tawarruq structure through agency agreements at Bursa Suq al-sila.[21]

The funds generated were allocated for the construction of three significant solar photovoltaic (PV) facilities in Kedah, Melaka, and Terengganu states within Malaysia. These environmentally-friendly power stations were anticipated to provide approximately 282,000 megawatts of electricity each year to Malaysia's electric utility firm, Tenaga Nasional, as part of their respective Power Purchase Agreements, spanning a duration of 21 years. 'In terms of social impact as well as the sustainability aspects of the projects, it is expected to reduce 193,000 tons of carbon per year. This is enough to power up about 90,000 over homes as well as create 3,000 jobs.'[22]

[20] CIMB. (2015). Principal Terms and Conditions of the Sukuk Programme. Retrieved from https://fast.bnm.gov.my/fastweb/public/PublicInfoServlet.do?fileId=2017071700017&fileName=Ihsan%20Sukuk%20Programme%20PTC%20%28Revised%29.pdf&mode=DOWNLOAD&dlTbl=m&module=News.

[21] Bursa Suq al-sila is a commodity trading platform specifically dedicated to facilitate Islamic liquidity management and financing by Islamic financial institutions- Bursa. (2023). Bursa Suq al-sila. Retrieved from https://www.bursamalaysia.com/trade/our_products_services/islamic_market/bursa_suq_al_sila.

[22] World Bank. (n.d.). Case Studies on Islamic Finance for Asset Recycling. Retrieved from https://ppp.worldbank.org/public-private-partnership/case-studies-islamic-finance-asset-recycling.

This green SRI sukuk provided renewable and clean energy to the population and thus furthered environmental conservation objectives, and also included the social element of creating jobs.

More recently in mid-2023 Malaysian government announced the National Energy Transition Road and that Islamic instruments (SRI sukuk) would be used to fund South East Asia's largest hybrid solar PV power plant.[23] The first phase of the project is expected to create 23,000 jobs and reduce 10,000 gigagrams of carbon dioxide equivalent annually.[24] The sukuk that will be issued would be an SRI sukuk, having as its objectives green and social goals.

To conclude, a social sukuk has the same objectives as a social bond, except that a social sukuk is Shariah compliant. In Malaysia an SRI sukuk that raises capital for green and social projects and the development of waqf assets is a social sukuk.

A case study of a waqf asset type of sukuk will be discussed later in this chapter under Section 6.4.2.

Having explained and understood what a social sukuk is, next this chapter will explain the differences between sadaqah, zakat, waqf, microfinance and social sukuk, and then move on to explain the regulatory framework of social sukuk in Malaysia.

6.2 Differences Between Sadaqah, Zakat, Waqf, Microfinance and Social Sukuk

Sadaqah, zakat and waqf are philanthropic, unilateral advances that an individual or Islamic organisation provides for a social benefit. Sadaqah and waqf are wholly voluntary, while zakat is mandatory and binding on every eligible Muslim and only directed to specific categories of recipients.

As for microfinance and social sukuk, they are not charities nor unilateral contracts. Both are bilateral contracts that require the consent of the counter party, and both often provides a return on investment. Microfinance and social sukuk do however have as their objective the alleviation of the disadvantaged condition of the recipients, just like sadaqah, zakat and waqf. Microfinance provides tiny or small capital that is a loan or a joint venture, whereas social sukuk, through the issuance of sukuk certificates raises large amounts of capital for social, green or waqf projects. Thus, each of these Islamic social financing products have unique characteristics that differentiate them from one another and caters for a variety of different social needs (Fig. 6.5).

---

[23] Kareem, M. (2023). Malaysia announces National Energy Transition Roadmap; Islamic instruments to fund SEA's largest hybrid solar PV power plant. Islamic Sustainable Investment and Finance. Retrieved from https://islamicsustainable.com/malaysia-announces-national-energy-transition-roadmap-islamic-instruments-to-fund-seas-largest-hybrid-solar-pv-power-plant/.

[24] Business Today. (2023). National Energy Transition Roadmap Secures RM25 Billion Investment Creating 23,000 Jobs. Retrieved from https://www.businesstoday.com.my/2023/07/27/national-energy-transition-roadmap-secures-rm25-billion-investment-creating-23000-jobs/.

Table 6.1 Legal framework for social sukuk

Guideline	Purpose
"Guidelines on Issuance of Corporate Bonds and Sukuk to Retail Investors (revised 2021)"	This guideline provides the requirements for the issue of bonds or sukuk to retail investors
"Guidelines on Unlisted Capital Market Products Under the Lodge and Launch Framework (revised 2022)"	This guideline provides the requirements for unlisted capital market products including bonds and sukuk to sophisticated investors and other high net worth persons described in paragraph 1 of Part 1, Schedule 5 of the Capital Market and Services Act 2007
"Guidelines On Seasoned Corporate Bonds and Sukuk (revised 2019)"	This guideline was created by the SC to allow retail investors to invest in seasoned corporate bonds and sukuk that were offered to sophisticated investors (and other high net worth investors) in the primary market (as stated in the above row). The sophisticated investors (and other high net worth investors) buy the sukuk in large denominations in the primary market and then later it is divided into smaller denominations for retail investors to buy in the secondary market
"SRI Sukuk Framework" The framework falls under either the Lodge and Launch Framework or the Guidelines on Issuing Corporate Bonds and Sukuk to Retail Investors, both of which are related to Unlisted Capital Market Products	These guidelines are for issuers that want to offer SRI Sukuk. Issuers are required to adhere to either the Guidelines on Unlisted Capital Market Products as part of the Lodge and Launch Framework or the Guidelines on the Issuance of Corporate Bonds and Sukuk to Retail Investors
"Guidelines on Islamic Capital Market Products and Services (issued 2022)"	These guidelines provide additional requirements for Islamic Capital Market products including the issuance of sukuk

Source Authors' own

6.3 Legal Framework for Social Sukuk in Malaysia

Under Section 377 of the Capital Markets and Services Act 2007 the SC is empowered to issue guidelines in relation to the capital markets. The guidelines within the legal framework of sukuk must be complied with, in addition to Guidelines on SRI sukuk for social sukuk. In relation to sukuk the SC has issued several guidelines, the relevant ones that will be covered in this chapter are as shown in Table 6.1:

Prior to going into the various guidelines let's understand certain terms in the Islamic capital market.[25]

[25] BIX Malaysia. (2020). SRI Sukuk: The Journey Towards Sustainable and Responsible Investment. Retrieved from https://www.bixmalaysia.com/learning-center/articles-tutorials/sri-sukuk-the-journey-towards-sustainable-and-responsible-investment.

Securities Commission Malaysia (SC) serves as the regulatory body for capital markets, encompassing the Islamic capital market. Section 15 of the Securities Commission Act 1993 outlines its functions, which include advising the finance minister on capital market matters, regulating all capital market-related affairs, and ensuring compliance with securities laws. Section 16 grants SC the necessary powers for performing its functions under securities laws.

Primary Issuance involves the initial sale of securities like bonds or sukuk to investors through a principal dealer, facilitated by the Fully Automated System for Issuing/Tendering (FAST), approved by BNM. The issuance occurs through tender or private placement.

Secondary Market is where investors trade securities, either through exchanges like Bursa or over-the-counter. Bursa Malaysia, a major exchange holding company in ASEAN, offers Main, ACE, and LEAP marketplaces. Secondary trading of sukuk can take place through Bursa's stock market as Exchange Traded Bond and Sukuk (ETBS).

Over-the-counter (OTC) involves trading securities, including bonds and sukuk, through a dealer or bank network. Unlike formal exchanges like Bursa, OTC allows for the buying or selling of unlisted bonds or sukuk, known as OTC bonds and sukuk.

Retail Investors are ordinary individuals making investments, while Sophisticated Investors are institutions, businesses, entities, or high-net-worth individuals legally defined under the Capital Market and Services Act 2007.

Next this chapter will delve into the main provisions of the Guidelines outlined in Table 6.1.

6.3.1 Guidelines on Issuance of Corporate Bonds and Sukuk to Retail Investors

According to paragraph 4 of the guidelines, an issuer is required to meet eligibility criteria to issue sukuk. This implies that the issuer must fall into one of the following categories: a public company, a licensed Islamic bank, or other specified types of public companies as listed in paragraph 4.[26]

The sukuk issued under these guidelines must meet specific criteria to ensure compliance. These are: it should be denominated in Malaysian Ringgit, it should have a tenure surpassing one year, and feature a fixed term with principal and accrued returns or profits payable upon maturity. The return or profit rate may be either fixed

[26] '(c) Cagamas Bhd; (d) Danajamin Nasional Bhd; (e) Khazanah Nasional Bhd; or (f) A public company whose shares are not listed and quoted on a stock exchange, provided that—(i) the corporate bonds or sukuk are irrevocably and unconditionally guaranteed in full by any of the entities referred to in the above subparagraphs (a), (b), (c), (d), (e) or the Credit Guarantee and Investment Facility; or (ii) the sukuk are issued by a public company established by any of the entities referred to in the above sub-paragraphs (a), (b), (c), (d) or (e), with full recourse to the establishing entity in its capacity as obligor.' Para 4.01 Guidelines on Issuance of Corporate Bonds and Sukuk to Retail Investors.

or variable, with periodic payments at specified intervals. Importantly, the sukuk's ranking should be equal to amounts owed to unsecured and unsubordinated creditors, and it should not incorporate derivatives. These stringent conditions aim to uphold the integrity and stability of sukuk offerings within the market.[27]

According to Chapter 5 of the Guidelines, it is mandatory for the sukuk to undergo a rating process by a credit agency. The obtained credit rating must be included in the application submitted to the Securities Commission (SC) for the issuance of the sukuk. A credit agency, responsible for assessing the creditworthiness of individuals and businesses, assigns a score indicative of the issuer's ability to meet debt repayment obligations. This requirement emphasizes the importance of transparency and risk assessment in the sukuk issuance process.

The mode to offer corporate sukuk is through the FAST system for issuance or tendering and it is conducted in a scripless manner. Furthermore, they should be deposited and settled through the Real-Time Electronic Transfer of Funds and Securities System (RENTAS), overseen by Bank Negara Malaysia. This mode applies unless the issuer is seeking to list and quote the sukuk on a stock exchange, such as Bursa Malaysia. If the corporate sukuk is listed on Bursa, compliance with continuous disclosure requirements, as per Bursa's listing standards, is mandatory. In the case of OTC offered corporate sukuk, ongoing disclosure of material information is essential. Any corporate sukuk approved by the SC under these guidelines is required to be implemented within one year or within two years for a sukuk program. A sukuk program refers to a facility that enables multiple issuances, offers, or invitations to subscribe or purchase Islamic Medium-Term Notes (MTNs) during a disclosed availability period reported to the Securities Commission (SC) and sukuk holders. This definition is provided in the Guidelines on Issuance of Corporate Bonds and Sukuk to Retail Investors.

Apart from the previously mentioned conditions, corporations intending to issue SRI sukuk must adhere to the stipulations outlined in Chapter 21 of the guidelines. To be classified as SRI Sukuk, the funds raised through the sukuk issuance must be dedicated solely to financing eligible SRI projects. As illustrated in Fig. 6.4, an eligible SRI project encompasses green projects, social projects, or those involved in the development of waqf assets.

The SRI Sukuk Framework incorporates four fundamental principles. Firstly, the funds generated from SRI sukuk must be dedicated solely to financing activities or transactions associated with eligible SRI projects. Secondly, issuers of SRI sukuk are required to establish internal processes for the evaluation and selection of these eligible SRI projects. Thirdly, there is an obligation for proper management of proceeds, signifying that funds allocated for eligible SRI projects must be credited into a designated account or meticulously tracked. Lastly, issuers are mandated to

[27] Para 4.02—'except in the case of convertible or exchangeable corporate bonds or sukuk where:
(i) The option is to convert or exchange the corporate bonds or sukuk into shares;
(ii) The option to convert or exchange the corporate bonds or sukuk into shares is at the discretion of the investor; and
(iii) The underlying shares are listed and quoted on a stock exchange.'

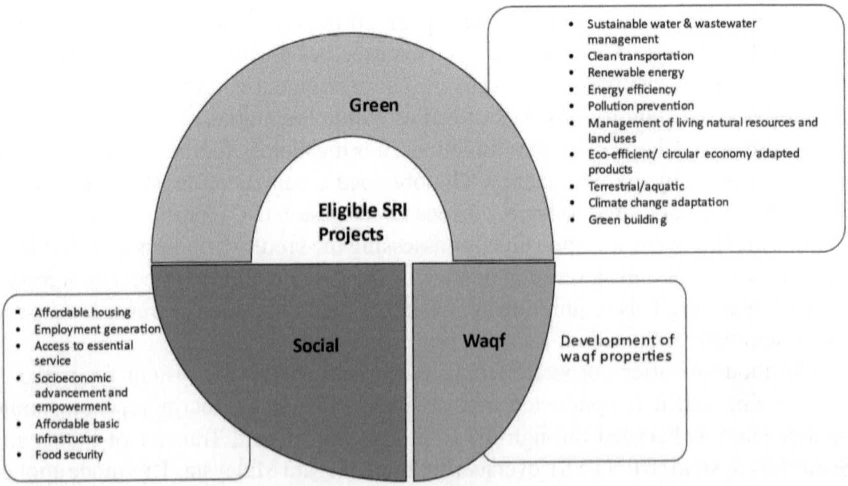

Fig. 6.4 SRI eligible projects (*Source* Modified from Securities Commission [2019])[28]

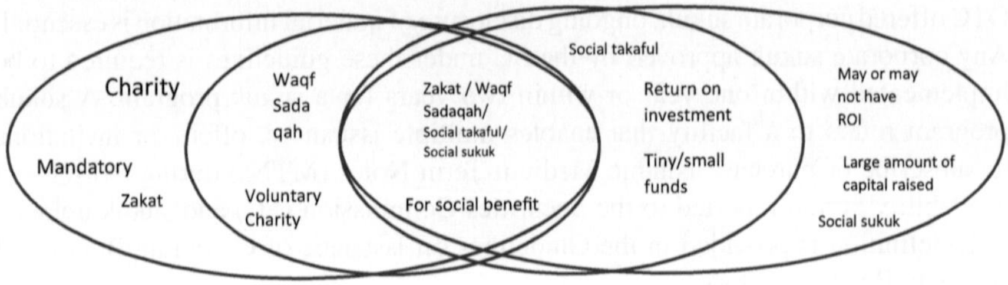

Fig. 6.5 Comparing the tools of Islamic social finance (*Source* Authors' own)

provide annual reports through a designated website to investors, containing pertinent information such as the original amount of proceeds allocated for eligible SRI projects. Paragraph 21.14 stipulates specific disclosure requirements, including: (a) the initial amount allocated for the Eligible SRI projects; (b) the amount expended on the Eligible SRI projects; (c) the remaining unused amount and its placement or investment pending utilization; and (d) a comprehensive list of the Eligible SRI projects, along with a concise description of each project and its impact or anticipated impact. This disclosure should encompass the key underlying methodology or assumptions employed in determining the impact or expected impact.

Moreover, there are stringent disclosure requirements pertaining to the issuer and details of the SRI sukuk that must be publicly accessible through a designated website. This information is mandated to be available at the point of issuance and must remain accessible throughout the tenure of the SRI sukuk. Paragraph 20.16 outlines the comprehensive information that must be accessible on the designated website,

[28] Ibid.

including: (a) the overarching SRI objectives sought by the issuer; (b) the utilization of proceeds from the SRI sukuk issuance, with specific details if used for refinancing; (c) the identified Eligible SRI projects for fund allocation; (d) detailed information on the Eligible SRI projects and, where feasible, their impact objectives; (e) the issuer's processes for evaluating and selecting Eligible SRI projects; (f) criteria employed to identify and manage environmental or social risks related to the projects; (g) the issuer's processes for managing SRI sukuk proceeds; and (h) an assertion of the issuer's compliance with relevant environmental, social, and governance standards or recognized best practices pertaining to the Eligible SRI projects.

An external reviewer may be appointed to assess and furnish a report on the eligible SRI projects or the issuer's adherence to the relevant requirements outlined in the SC's guidelines. The report generated by the external reviewer is obligated to be accessible on the designated website.

6.3.2 Guidelines on Unlisted Capital Market Products Under the Lodge and Launch Framework

These guidelines are applicable to unlisted capital market products exclusively offered to sophisticated investors in Malaysia or persons outside Malaysia.

They are structured into various sections, encompassing general requirements for all unlisted products, specific requirements for each type of unlisted product, additional requirements for Shariah-compliant unlisted capital market products, and transitional provisions for products approved or authorized by the Securities Commission (SC) before the Lodge and Launch framework.

This current chapter focuses on the specific provisions pertaining to SRI sukuk under the Lodge and Launch Framework. Section B, Part 3 of these guidelines outlines the specific requirements for corporate bonds or sukuk issuance, including eligibility criteria for issuers, the appointment of a Shariah adviser, publication of a credit rating report, proper utilization of sukuk proceeds, and adherence to Shariah-compliant purposes. The mode of sukuk issuance aligns with the guidelines on corporate bonds and sukuk for retail investors, utilizing the FAST system and settling on RENTAS or listing on an exchange (Bursa). Chapter 7 of these guidelines details the specific requirements for SRI sukuk, mirroring those explained in the Guidelines on Issuance of Corporate Bonds and Sukuk to Retail Investors above.

6.3.3 Guidelines on Seasoned Corporate Bonds and Sukuk

These guidelines delineate the stipulations for offering seasoned corporate bonds or sukuk to retail investors. In Chapter 3, eligibility criteria for distributors and eligible corporate bonds or sukuk are detailed. Eligible distributors for sukuk must be a licensed Islamic bank, hold a Capital Markets and Services Licence for dealing in securities, or possess a restricted Capital Markets and Services Licence for over-the-counter bonds. The eligible corporate bonds or sukuk for distribution encompass those issued by a licensed bank, licensed investment bank, or licensed Islamic bank; a publicly listed company; Cagamas Bhd; Danajamin Nasional Bhd; Khazanah Nasional Bhd; or a non-listed public company guaranteed by the mentioned entities. Characteristics of eligible corporate bonds or sukuk include being denominated in Malaysian ringgit, having a tenure exceeding one year, possessing a minimum 'A' rating by a credit rating agency, and completing the full seasoned period. Additionally, they must have an information memorandum, a trust deed, and, for sustainable and responsible investment (SRI) sukuk, an independent expert report on eligible SRI projects following the Lodge and Launch Framework Guidelines. Chapters 4 and 5 outline compliance requirements for distributors, covering employee qualification and investor disclosure. Chapter 6 addresses notification and reporting, while Chapter 7 underscores the duty of eligible distributors to prevent false or misleading statements or material omissions to the SC.

6.3.4 Guidelines on Islamic Capital Market Products and Services

These set of guidelines has been established for Islamic capital market products and services, introducing Shariah compliance requirements specific to these offerings. These guidelines provide a comprehensive overview of the roles and responsibilities of Shariah advisors registered with the SC. In the context of sukuk, these guidelines cover various critical aspects. Firstly, an issuer is required to obtain the endorsement of the SAC prior to lodgement, adhering to the mandates outlined in the Lodge and Launch Framework Guidelines. Additionally, the guidelines stipulate that the proceeds from sukuk issuance must be utilized exclusively for Shariah-compliant purposes. This Shariah compliance extends beyond sukuk issuance to encompass related ventures, investments, or securitizations.

Asset identification and utilization must align meticulously with Shariah principles, ensuring a robust adherence to ethical and Islamic financial standards. The guidelines also specify that various aspects, including asset pricing, ibra (release of rights), ta'widh (compensation), kafalah (guarantee), tanazul (waiver), Shariah-compliant designated accounts, and the naming of ringgit-denominated sukuk, must strictly adhere to the provided guidelines. Furthermore, Shariah rulings for different sukuk types such as sukuk ijarah, sukuk mudarabah, sukuk musharakah, and sukuk wakalah bi al-istithmar must align with the guidelines, ensuring a comprehensive and uniform Shariah compliance framework.

This regulatory framework is paramount for issuers looking to issue SRI sukuk in Malaysia, ensuring that their financial instruments are in strict adherence to Shariah principles.

Next two case studies of social sukuk will be explained in detail.

6.4 Use of Innovation in Social Sukuk—Case Studies

Under this section two innovative case studies on social sukuk offered will be reviewed. The first one Sukuk Prihatin in Malaysia and the second one Sukuk Waqf Indonesia.

6.4.1 Sukuk Prihatin (Malaysia)

Sukuk Prihatin is a Malaysian government sukuk[29] and response to economic hardship following the Covid-19, it was issued as part of the National Economic Recovery Plan termed in the national language as *Pelan Jana Semula Ekonomi Negara* (PENJANA). PENAJA aimed at propelling businesses, empowering individuals and stimulating economic growth.[30] Sukuk Prihatin allowed contribution and participation of Malaysians to help the economy. It was created in response to calls of various public parties' desire to contribute.[31]

The proceeds generated from the sukuk issuance were channelled into a Covid-19 Consolidated Fund, which was subsequently utilized for various development initiatives. These initiatives encompassed enhancing connectivity in rural schools, providing financial support for small and micro enterprises, and offering grants for research into infectious diseases.[32] The Sukuk was Structured using the Shariah

---

[29] Cheong, A. P. Y. (2020). Government Launches Malaysia's First Digital Sukuk, Sukuk Prihatin With 2% p.a. Profit Rate. RinggitPlus. Retrieved from https://ringgitplus.com/en/blog/investment/government-launches-malaysias-first-digital-sukuk-sukuk-prihatin-with-2-p-a-profit-rate.html.

[30] Ministry of Finance Malaysia. (2020). PENJANA: Building the Economy together—Short-term Economic Recovery Plan June–December 2020. Retrieved from https://penjana.treasury.gov.my/pdf/PENJANA-Booklet-En.pdf, accessed 22 October 2020.

[31] Cheong, A. P. Y. (2020). Government Launches Malaysia's First Digital Sukuk, Sukuk Prihatin With 2% p.a. Profit Rate. RinggitPlus. Retrieved from https://ringgitplus.com/en/blog/investment/government-launches-malaysias-first-digital-sukuk-sukuk-prihatin-with-2-p-a-profit-rate.html.

[32] Ibid.

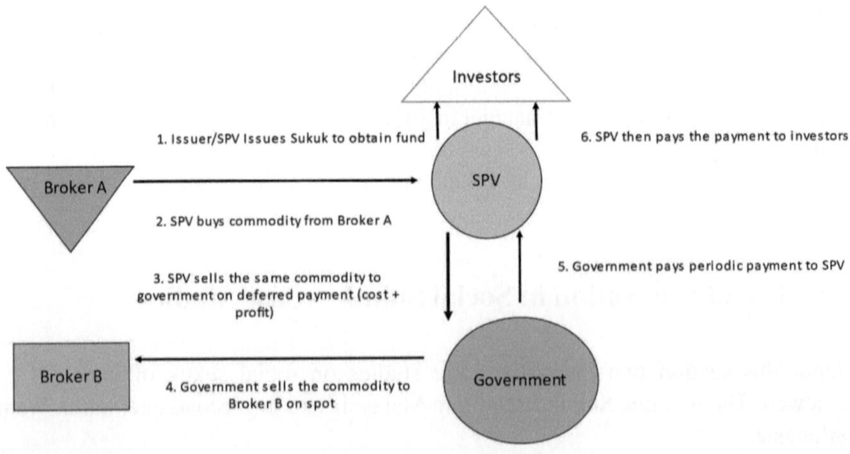

Fig. 6.6 Tawarruq via commodity Murabaha for Sukuk Prihatin (*Source* Modified from Razak et al. [2019])[34]

contract of tawarruq which is also known as commodity Murabahah as can be seen in Fig. 6.6.[33]

The structure of the sukuk involved 6 main steps. Step 1 the issuer or SPV issues the sukuk to investors who provides funds which is used in step 2 to buy commodity from Broker A. This commodity is sold to the government on deferred basis (cost + profit) in step 3, payment to be deferred. Then in step 4 government sells the commodity to Broker B and obtains capital which it uses for various social recovery needs. In step 5 the government makes periodic payment to SPV who in step 6 pays the investors.

Upon the issuance of Sukuk Prihatin, there was a remarkable oversubscription of RM166 million. As a result, the government decided to increase the issuance size from the initial RM500 million to RM666 million.[35] Sukuk Prihatin was made available to both retail and corporate investors, with a minimum subscription requirement of RM500. The subscription period for the sukuk took place from August 18, 2020,

[33] Tawarruq is a tripartite Islamic financing technique that involves buying of a Shariah-compliant commodity on deferred payment basis with a mark-up price from a seller and, on spot payment basis, the same commodity is sold by the buyer to a third party.

[34] Razak, S.S., Saiti, B., Dinç, Y. (2019). The contracts, structures and pricing mechanisms of sukuk: A critical assessment. *Borsa Istanbul Review, 19*(1). S21–S33. Retrieved from https://www.sciencedirect.com/science/article/pii/S2214845018301765.

[35] Ministry of Finance Malaysia. (2020). Sukuk Prihatin: From RM500 million to more than RM666 million; Proof of Malaysians' Solidarity in Supporting Economic Recovery Efforts. Media Release, September 20. Retrieved from https://www.treasury.gov.my/index.php/en/gallery-activities/press-release/item/6984-media-release-sukuk-prihatin-from-rm500-million-to-more-than-rm666-million-proof-of-malaysians%E2%80%99-solidarity-in-supporting-economic-recovery-efforts.html. See also The Star. (2020, September 20). Subscription to Sukuk Prihatin hits RM666m. Retrieved from https://www.thestar.com.my/business/business-news/2020/09/20/subscription-to-sukuk-prihatin-hits-rm666m.

until September 17, 2020, and it was officially issued on September 22, 2020. This sukuk offered an annual profit rate of 2%, paid on a quarterly basis, and had a two-year maturity period, set to mature on September 22, 2022. Importantly, it was a non-tradable, non-assignable, and non-transferable sukuk.[36]

The Sukuk Prihatin issuance was entirely digital and could be invested in through the internet and mobile banking services provided by the distribution banks. Investors could use Malaysian national payment networks such as JomPay and DuitNow to participate in this sukuk issuance.[37]

Investors interested in the sukuk were required to maintain an account with any of the authorized distribution banks, which had to include mobile and/or internet banking access. Additionally, they needed to provide an email address and contact number as part of the subscription process. To facilitate subscription and payment via JomPay, the sukuk was assigned two biller codes: 14,076, used for subscription and waiver of principal at maturity, and 28,670, exclusively for subscription. In the case of DuitNow, the sukuk was associated with two Business Registration Numbers (BRN): SUKUKP20SUM, used for both subscription and waiver of principal at maturity, and SUKUKP20PEL, designated for subscription only. This setup allowed applicants to choose whether they wanted to contribute a portion of their investment as charity, as depicted in Fig. 6.7. Depending on the applicants' preferences, their bank accounts were debited for the applicable amount corresponding to the requested sukuk units.[38]

The success of the issuance of Sukuk Prihatin and its oversubscription is a model for the global community to follow in times of national distress whether due to climate change or a pandemic. The dual role of investment and social benefit truly featured in Sukuk Prihatin and showed investor interest.[39] The objective of the issuance of Sukuk Prihatin is within the Maqasid al-Shariah[40] which is to cater for social benefit. The

---

[36] Ministry of Finance Malaysia. (2020). PENJANA: Sukuk Prihatin Knowledge Pack. Retrieved from https://av.sc.com/my/content/docs/my-gom-sukuk-prihatin-knowledge-pack.pdf.

[37] JomPay is a bill payment scheme that enables customers to pay any registered biller through mobile or internet banking by drawing money from savings, current and credit card accounts. By signing up with one bank, JomPay enables billers to be assigned a biller code and receive payments through 42 banks. DuitNow, for its part, enables instant payment to any bank account in Malaysia using a DuitNow ID which include mobile number, passport number, National Registration Identity Card (NRIC) number and other nationally approved means of identification—PayNet. (n.d.). Who we are. Retrieved from https://paynet.my/about-paynet.html.

[38] Ministry of Finance Malaysia. (2020). PENJANA: Sukuk Prihatin Knowledge Pack. Retrieved from https://av.sc.com/my/content/docs/my-gom-sukuk-prihatin-knowledge-pack.pdf.

[39] Bin-Nashwan, S.A., Muneeza, A., & Kunhibava, S. (2022). What motivates retail investors to invest in government-issued digital sukuk during COVID-19? *Journal of Islamic Accounting and Business Research, 13*(3) 393–424. Retrieved from https://doi.org/10.1108/JIABR-12-2020-0387.

[40] Saada, M.A., & Mohamed Fisol, W.N. (2020). Rebuilding The National Economy By Issuance Of The First Malaysia Digital Sukuk (Sukuk Prihatin) And Its Distribution Through Fintech Services: A View From The Perspective Of Maqasid Alshari'ah. Presented at International Conference on Contemporary Issues in Islamic Finance (e-ICCIIF 2020). Retrieved from https://www.researchgate.net/publication/344944232_REBUILDING_THE_NATIONAL_ECONOMY_BY_ISSUANCE_OF_THE_FIRST_MALAYSIA_DIGITAL_SUKUK_SUKUK_PRIHATIN_AND_ITS_DISTRIBUTION_THROUGH_FINTECH_SERVICES_A_VIEW_FROM_THE_PERSPECTIVE_OF_MAQASID_AL-_SHARI%27AH.

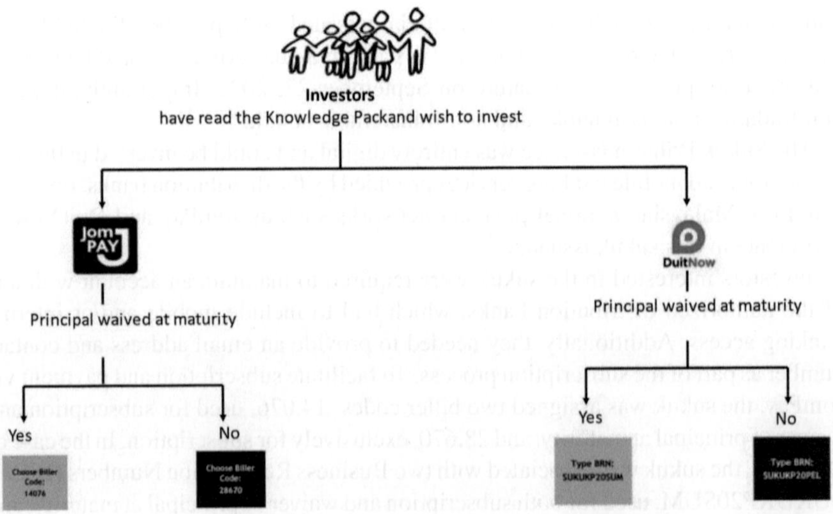

Fig. 6.7 Investing in Sukuk Prihatin (*Source* Modified from Cheong [2020])[41]

success of Sukuk Prihatin can be seen from the Ministry of Finance Press Release[42] which recorded that the Sukuk was fully redeemed on 22 September 2022 and that the funds raised was used for the following:

> Proceeds from the issuance were channeled to the COVID-19 Fund to finance, among others, micro credit loans under Bank Simpanan Nasional and TEKUN Nasional, special assistance for students of higher education institutions, e-Commerce campaigns for SMEs and micro enterprises as well as public healthcare expenses in addressing COVID-19 pandemic.

The press release also recorded the multiple awards won by Sukuk Prihatin and that 95 investors chose to donate their principle, which totalled RM2,599,400. This amount was transferred to a Trust Account for Disasters, 'which will support, among others, the repair of damaged infrastructure and public facilities, as well as financial relief for victims of natural disasters.'[43]

[41] Cheong, A. P. Y. (2020). Government Launches Malaysia's First Digital Sukuk, Sukuk Prihatin With 2% p.a. Profit Rate. RinggitPlus. Retrieved from https://ringgitplus.com/en/blog/investment/government-launches-malaysias-first-digital-sukuk-sukuk-prihatin-with-2-p-a-profit-rate.html.

[42] Ministry of Finance. (24 September, 2022). Full Redemption of Award-Winning Sukuk Prihatin, Malaysia's First Digital Sukuk. Press Release. Retrieved from https://www.mof.gov.my/portal/en/news/press-release/full-redemption-sukuk-prihatin-digital-sukuk

[43] Ibid.

6.4.2 *Sukuk Wakaf Indonesia (Cash Waqf Linked Sukuk Indonesia)*

The Sukuk Wakaf Indonesia, also recognized as Cash Waqf Linked Sukuk, made its inaugural issuance on March 1, 2020,[44] in Indonesia. This significant financial instrument was introduced with the primary aim of fostering social investment and contributing to the advancement of the National Waqf movement in Indonesia. The Sukuk played a pivotal role in addressing the short-term investment requirements of the Indonesian government, specifically directed towards the development of social facilities and infrastructure.[45] By aligning financial objectives with social and national development goals, the Sukuk Wakaf Indonesia emerged as a strategic instrument in channelling funds for impactful initiatives and supporting the overall welfare of the Indonesian society.

The Cash Waqf Linked Sukuk involved the co-operation and collaboration of a multitude of parties, which were the National Waqf body in Indonesia, Central Bank of Indonesia, Ministry of Finance, and the Ministry of Religious Affairs, and Islamic financial Institutions, for this purpose a Memorandum of Understanding was signed by the relevant parties.[46] Table 6.2 summarises the role of the collaborating parties.

Each party had their distinct role, however some roles overlapped. The overlapping roles was the collaboration and cooperation between the different bodies. Next, we view in detail the structure of Sukuk Wakaf Indonesia in Fig. 6.8.

From the structure above the following is the sequence of events:

1. a & b: Donations or investments are made by the waqif (donor of waqf) depending on whether they choose the permanent or temporary cash waqf option respectively. Islamic financial institutions and non- Islamic financial institutions are the nazir partners who collect the cash Waqf from the waqifs (nazir is the Indonesian Waqf Board that holds the waqf property as trustee).
2. a & b: The nazir partners enters into a MOU with the nazir,[47] and places the funds with Indonesian Waqf Body.

---

[44] See Bank Indonesia, (2021). *Cash Waqf Linked Sukuk Annual Report 2021*. Retrieved from https://www.bi.go.id/id/edukasi/Documents/Laporan-Tahunan-Cash-Waqf-Linked-Sukuk-2021.pdf. Two issues were made one private and one retail.

[45] Fad, M. F. (2021). Waqf Linked Sukuk Dalam Perspektif Maqashid Syari'ah, *Journal of Islamic Studies and Humanities*, *6*(1), 44–62. Retrieved from https://journal.walisongo.ac.id/index.php/JISH/article/view/8150/pdf. Hafandi, A., & Handayati, P. (2021). Is Cash Waqf Linked Sukuk (CWLS) Less Than Ideal According to Islamic Laws? *Studies of Applied Economics*, *39*(12), 1–16.

[46] "CWLS was developed with government support and commitment along with other relevant authorities in relation to the Islamic social finance sector in Indonesia. The joint commitment was contained in a Memorandum of Understanding (MoU) between the Ministry of Finance, Ministry of Religious Affairs, Bank Indonesia and BWI concerning cash waqf asset management through development of waqf-linked sukuk on 1st November 2018, which facilitated collaborative management and development of cash waqf through Government Islamic Securities (SBSN)." See Bank Indonesia, (2021). *Cash Waqf Linked Sukuk Annual Report 2021*. Retrieved from https://www.bi.go.id/id/edukasi/Documents/Laporan-Tahunan-Cash-Waqf-Linked-Sukuk-2021.pdf.

[47] Ibid.

Table 6.2 Role of different parties[48]

Institution	Role
Indonesia Waqf Body	Single buyer Sukuk Wakaf Indonesia Transaction operationalisation with Ministry of Finance and Islamic financial Institutions Design of sukuk business model Determining *nazir* partner and the allocation of the sukuk returns Formulated marketing program
Central Bank of Indonesia	Recording Sukuk Wakaf Indonesia- as Scripless Securities Settlement System (BISSSS) Design of sukuk business model Facilitator for product marketing and trainer development, responsible for liaising with the Indonesian Council of Ulama to address the Shariah perspective of the inaugural sukuk issuance
Ministry of Finance	Issuer of Sukuk Wakaf Indonesia Design of sukuk business model Setting the corpus benefit of waqf Facilitator of product marketing and training of trainers
Islamic financial institutions	Settlement of waqif (donor)/investor transactions Facilitation of investment in Sukuk Wakaf Indonesia Sukuk Wakaf Indonesia product marketing

Source Adopted from Bank Indonesia (2021)[49]

[48] See Bank Indonesia. (2021). *Cash Waqf Linked Sukuk Annual Report 2021*. Retrieved from https://www.bi.go.id/id/edukasi/Documents/Laporan-Tahunan-Cash-Waqf-Linked-Sukuk-2021.pdf, p. 30

[49] Bank Indonesia. (2021). *Cash Waqf Linked Sukuk Annual Report 2021*. Retrieved December 14, 2022, from https://www.bi.go.id/id/edukasi/Documents/Laporan-Tahunan-Cash-Waqf-Linked-Sukuk-2021.pdf.

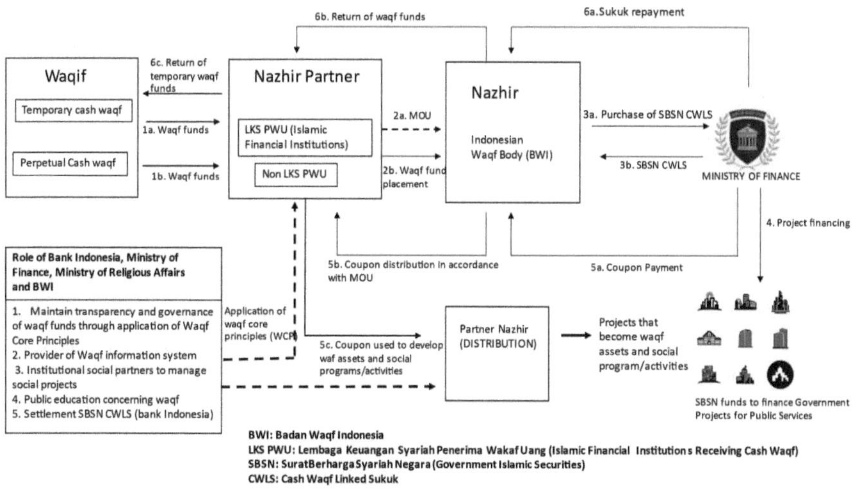

Fig. 6.8 The structure of CWLS[50] (*Source* Modified from Bank Indonesia [2021])[51]

3. a & b: Indonesian Waqf Board buys the sukuk (Government Islamic Securities) from the Ministry of Finance with a private placement mechanism; sukuk ownership documents are delivered to Indonesian Waqf Board.
4. The funds received are subsequently used to fund government projects for public services. At this stage, in its capacity as the sukuk administrator, Central Bank of Indonesia records the ownership and engages in sukuk clearing and settlement.[52]
5. a, b & c: The government paid the return to Indonesian Waqf Board in the form of a discount or coupon, which was distributed to the nazir partners to fund social projects or activities.
6. a, b & c: Finally, the Ministry of Finance, at maturity, repays the cash to the Indonesian Waqf Body. The Indonesian Waqf Board pays the temporary cash waqfs to the *nazir* partners who will return it to the donors who opted for temporary waqf, or it is further managed by Indonesian Waqf Board in the case of a permanent cash waqf.

Reports show that the returns received from the Sukuk Wakaf Indonesia series was and is continually being used for medical equipment and building development for an eye hospital in Serang, Banten, development of madrasahs, Islamic boarding schools, social programs in education, health, economy, social development and also

[50] Badan Wakaf Indonesia. (2021). *Risk Management in Cash Waqf Linked Sukuk Based on the Waqf Core Principle: A Preliminary Study—BWPS No. 07 2021.* Retrieved December 14, 2022, from https://www.bwi.go.id/7342/2021/09/30/risk-management-in-cash-waqf-linked-sukuk-based-on-the-waqf-core-principle-a-preliminary-study-bwps-no-07-2021/.

[51] Bank Indonesia. (2021). *Cash Waqf Linked Sukuk Annual Report 2021.* Retrieved December 14, 2022, from https://www.bi.go.id/id/edukasi/Documents/Laporan-Tahunan-Cash-Waqf-Linked-Sukuk-2021.pdf.

[52] Ibid.

other various social needs and projects.[53] The success of this sukuk is tied to the cooperation and collaboration of all parties involved, in fact this sukuk won the 2023 IsDB Prize for Impactful Achievement in Islamic Economics.[54]

6.5 Issues and Challenges

Social sukuk is relatively a new innovation that raises funds from investors for social, and environmental causes or for the development of waqf assets. However, there are some issues or challenges that have to be considered and overcome for future impactful social sukuk.

When developing the social sukuk it is important to clearly define the social benefit or KPI that is to be achieved. Also, the potential impact needs to be studied beforehand. While Sukuk Prihatin's and Sukuk Waqf Indonesia's benefit and impact on society during the pandemic was obvious, this may not be the situation in all cases of social sukuk. It is opined that to have effective impact and efficiency, social sukuk needs to be properly evaluated and its potential impact needs to be objectively and possibly professionally accessed before it is structured and issued.[55]

Additionally, how the social benefit or KPI will be measured needs to be formulated upfront. The underlying asset too must be identified along with the relevant Shariah contract when structuring the social sukuk.

Currently the need for an external reviewer for SRI sukuk is just voluntary and not compulsory, but moving forward it is opined that it should be made mandatory to ensure proper verification of the social or environmental impacts of the social sukuk and to avoid greenwashing.[56]

To become truly impactful, social sukuk requires the collaboration and cooperation of all the relevant stakeholders of that particular social or environment cause or for the development of waqf property. This would include non-governmental organisers, the relevant Ministry, Islamic religious councils, Islamic financial institutions,

[53] See also Badan Wakaf Indonesia. (2021). Risk Management in Cash Waqf Linked Sukuk Based on the Waqf Core Principle: A Preliminary Study—BWPS No. 07 2021. Hosen, M.N., Maulana, A., Farhand, & Rahman, M. H. (2022). Evaluating The Fundraising Process of The World's First Cash Waqf-Linked Sukuk In Indonesia. *Qudus International Journal of Islamic Studies (QIJIS), 10*(1), 175–214. See also Dompet Dhufa. (2022). The Government Intensively Invites Sukuk Waqf, What is Sukuk Waqf? Retrieved from https://www.dompetdhuafa.org/en/the-government-intensively-invites-sukuk-waqf-what-is-sukuk-waqf/.

[54] Islamic Sustainable Finance and Investment. (2023). Indonesian Government's Cash Waqf-linked Sukuk Initiative Wins 2023 IsDB Prize for Impactful Achievement in Islamic Economics. Retrieved from https://islamicsustainable.com/indonesian-governments-cash-waqf-linked-sukuk-initiative-wins-2023-isdb-prize-for-impactful-achievement-in-islamic-economics/.

[55] Mustapha, Z., Kunhibava, S., Muneeza, A., Khalid, M., & Thong, M.S. (2023). Social Sukuk for Sustainable Development—Review of Sukuk Prihatin, Ihsan Sukuk (Malaysia) and Cash waqf linked Sukuk (Indonesia). Presented at *The 10th International Islamic Economic System Conference (I-iECONS2023) 14–15 August 2023, Mecca-Medina, Saudi Arabia.*

[56] Ibid.

the regulatory bodies, and expert agencies to evaluate the projects. This collaboration and co-operation are especially needed for social sukuk because it involves the community and real-world issues not just the financial sector of the economy.

Another important area that needs to be furthered is research. Especially research through academia and industry collaborations, these collaborations need to be funded and carried out to further develop this area. Cross border collaborations and research with international bodies should also be explored. As there is currently a lack of international standardised impact assessment methodology to access the impact of social sukuk this will need to be developed to ensure investor confidence and increase in issuance of social sukuk.[57]

Review Questions

1. Sukuk is
   a. a bond
   b. a loan
   c. an obligation
   d. a certificate
2. Securitisation
   a. Allows many investors to have undivided ownership in assets
   b. allows liquid assets to be illiquid
   c. Involves interest based calculations
   d. creates assets
3. In an asset based sukuk
   a. assets generate income
   b. assets are owned by sukuk holders
   c. sukuk holder have undivided beneficial ownership in the assets
   d. True sales occur
4. Which of the following are **untrue** of a social bond
   a. Social bond does not have interest
   b. social bond is a debt instrument
   c. social bond is used for raising funds for social issues
   d. social bond is security
5. An SRI sukuk is a social sukuk whose projects are green, social, or waqf based:
   a. True
   b. False

---

[57] Morea, D., & Poggi, L.A. (2017). An innovative model for the sustainability of investments in the wind energy sector: The use of green sukuk in an Italian case study. *International Journal of Energy Economics and Policy, 7*(2), 53–60.

6. Social sukuk issuance for retail investors must comply with all the following regulations, **except**
   a. Guidelines on Issuance of Corporate Bonds and Sukuk to Retail Investors
   b. Guidelines on Unlisted Capital Market Products Under the Lodge and Launch Framework
   c. Guidelines On Seasoned Corporate Bonds and Sukuk
   d. Guidelines on Islamic Capital Market Products and Services
7. An external reviewer report of SRI projects must be placed in the annual report of all SRI sukuk
   a. True
   b. false
8. A sophisticated investor includes high-net worth-individuals
   a. true
   b. false
9. All the following is true about Sukuk Prihatin **except**
   a. It was issued on assist in Covid 19 related hardships
   b. It was oversubscribed
   c. It was offered to only institutional investors
   d. It was redeemed in 2022
10. The Sukuk Waqf Indonesia required the collaboration of all the following parties **except**
    a. Ministry of Finance
    b. Central Bank of Indonesia
    c. Islamic Financial institutions
    d. Ministry of Home Affairs

Answers:

1. d
2. a
3. c
4. a
5. a
6. c
7. b
8. a
9. c
10. d

Chapter 7
Social Takaful

Abstract This chapter provides a comprehensive exploration of Social Takaful, offering readers insights into this crucial aspect of Islamic Social Finance. The chapter commences with an overview of Social Takaful, unraveling its fundamental principles and significance. A comparative analysis distinguishes Social Takaful from other Islamic financial tools like Sadaqah, Zakat, Waqf, Microfinance, and Social Sukuk, highlighting their unique contributions. The legal framework governing Social Takaful in Malaysia is thoroughly examined, providing readers with a clear understanding of regulatory nuances. Real-world case studies elucidate the practical application and impact of Social Takaful, offering valuable lessons. The chapter concludes by delving into the prevalent issues and challenges within the realm of Social Takaful, fostering a nuanced comprehension of this critical aspect of Islamic financial practice.

Keywords Takaful · Islamic insurance · Micro takaful · Financial inclusion

Learning Outcomes
At the end of this chapter, readers will be able to:

- describe an overview of social takaful,
- explain the differences between Sadaqah, zakat, Waqf, Microfinance, Social Sukuk and Social Takaful,
- apply the legal framework for Social takaful in Malaysia,
- understand the use-case s tudies,
- and access the issues and challenges.

S. Kunhibava et al., *Islamic Social Finance*,
https://doi.org/10.1007/978-981-97-1410-0_7

7.1 What is Social Takaful?

In Arabic, "takaful" translates to insurance and embodies the principle of "mutually guaranteeing each other" against unforeseen calamities, disasters, or injuries through collaborative cooperation and solidarity among participants in a takaful scheme.[1]

The essence of a takaful lies in a formal agreement between an individual and a takaful company, wherein a financial transfer occurs in case of a loss, in exchange for a fee. The core concept of takaful centers around collective assurance, where a group of individuals unite to provide indemnification to a member of the group facing a specified calamity or loss.

Within a takaful scheme, all participants commit to supporting each other financially when a fellow member encounters a defined risk. Moreover, they pool their funds for investment purposes, guided by the principle of ta'awun (mutual assistance). This collaborative approach ensures that members collectively contribute funds to achieve a shared objective of providing mutual financial aid to fellow group members in times of specific risks or losses.

The practice of takaful, also known as "mutual guaranteeing," has historical roots dating back to early Arab societies during the time of the Prophet S.A.W. The concept of takaful, similar to "'aqilah," (collective compensation of blood money), involved tribes collectively supporting each other in times of tragedy or loss. This concept extended to the first Constitution of Madinah, which incorporated provisions for social insurance, reflecting the values of mutual assistance and aid to the needy, ill, and poor.

The notion of takaful evolved over time, with various scholars holding different perspectives on its legality. Some scholars deemed it permissible, provided it avoided elements of riba (interest), while others limited its application to certain areas, such as property insurance, citing concerns about maysir (gambling) and gharar (uncertainty). Despite the differing opinions, misconceptions arose among Muslims regarding takaful, leading to debates on its compatibility with Islamic principles.

Misconceptions included the belief that takaful contained elements of riba, gharar, and maysir due to perceived uncertainties in the contractual agreement. However, takaful deals with the risk associated with future events, not the exact timing of those events, and does not promote speculative gains. Additionally, concerns were raised about takaful's impact on Islamic inheritance principles and the concept of tawakkal (reliance on Allah). Nonetheless, takaful's design allows for the appointment of nominees, acting as trustees to distribute benefits to the deceased's legal heirs.

Takaful, the Islamic concept of insurance, is characterized by several distinctive features that set it apart from conventional insurance practices. Firstly, policyholders collaborate collectively to ensure the protection of their shared interests. Secondly, each participant contributes their premium to provide assistance to those in need within the community. This contribution is made under the tabarru' contract, which aims to distribute losses and liabilities fairly among the members through a pooling system. By adopting the tabarru' principle, uncertainty is eliminated regarding both

---

[1] Hassan, R. (2011). *Islamic Banking and Takaful*. Selangor: Pearson.

subscription payments and compensation. Moreover, the essence of takaful lies in not seeking advantage at the expense of others, fostering a spirit of mutual aid and solidarity among all participants involved.

Social takaful, also known as solidarity takaful, is a significant concept within the realm of Islamic finance. At its core, social takaful represents an inclusive and community-driven approach to insurance and financial protection. Unlike traditional takaful schemes that rely on participants contributing to a shared pool to cover potential losses, social takaful is specifically designed to cater to the needs of financially excluded or marginalized individuals who may not have the means to participate in regular takaful schemes.[2]

The primary objective of social takaful is to promote financial inclusion and social welfare. By providing affordable contribution options or covering contributions on behalf of beneficiaries, social takaful ensures that even the economically disadvantaged members of society have access to essential financial protection. This concept aligns with the principles of Islamic finance, which emphasizes mutual cooperation and support among community members.

One of the key mechanisms of social takaful is micro-takaful, a specialized form of takaful tailored to low-income populations. Micro-takaful enables financially marginalized individuals to participate by offering affordable contribution amounts, ensuring that they, too, can benefit from the protective measures provided by the takaful scheme.

In many instances, social takaful schemes involve third-party contributions. This means that the contributions required to cover the beneficiaries' protection are paid by external entities, such as the government or corporations. This approach further enhances accessibility and ensures that those who cannot afford to contribute directly can still receive the necessary financial support.

While social takaful remains a relatively less common practice compared to traditional takaful schemes, some countries have implemented notable initiatives. For instance, the mySalam takaful scheme in Malaysia, supported by the government, provides financial aid to low-income individuals facing critical illnesses. Additionally, in Egypt, a program called "Takaful and Karama" acts as a national-focused social safety net, offering income support to financially vulnerable citizens.

In a nutshell it can be said that social takaful represents a fundamental aspect of Islamic social finance, emphasizing inclusivity and solidarity within communities. It serves as a powerful tool to assist those who are financially incapable of protecting themselves against unforeseen adversities. By bridging the gap between financially capable individuals and the economically vulnerable, social takaful embodies the values of Islamic ethics, fostering a more compassionate and supportive society. As

---

[2] Hassan, M., & Muneeza, A. (2022). *COVID-19 and Islamic Finance (Elements in the Economics of Emerging Markets)*. Cambridge: Cambridge University Press. https://doi.org/10.1017/9781009189484; Hassan, M.K., Muneeza, A., & Sarea, A.M. (Eds.). (2021). *COVID-19 and Islamic social finance*. Abingdon, Oxon: Routledge; Hassan, M.K., Muneeza, A., & Sarea, A.M. (Eds.). (2021). *Towards a Post-Covid Global Financial System Lessons in Social Responsibility From Islamic Finance*. United Kingdom: Emerald Publishing Limited.

the concept evolves, its potential to uplift marginalized populations and promote social well-being continues to gain recognition within the realm of Islamic finance.

7.2 Differences Between Sadaqah, Zakat, Waqf, Microfinance, Social Sukuk and Social Takaful

In Islamic finance, there are several concepts that promote charitable giving and financial inclusivity. Sadaqah represents voluntary acts of charity, driven by compassion and generosity, with no specific obligations or guidelines on the amount to be given. On the other hand, zakat is an obligatory form of charity, constituting a fixed percentage of a Muslim's wealth, which is directed to specific categories of recipients defined in Islamic law. Waqf is a philanthropic concept where an individual dedicates an asset or money for a charitable purpose, and its benefits are utilized for specific causes in perpetuity.

Moving beyond charitable giving, microfinance is a financial service tailored to financially excluded individuals or entrepreneurs who lack access to traditional banking services. The aim is to empower them by providing small loans, savings accounts, and insurance, allowing them to start businesses and improve their financial well-being.

Social sukuk, or Islamic bonds, stand out as financial instruments funding projects with a social impact. Investors in social sukuk may not receive financial returns but instead contribute to projects that benefit society, such as those related to education, healthcare, and affordable housing.

Lastly, social takaful, also known as solidarity takaful, represents an important Islamic cooperative insurance concept focused on providing financial protection to economically vulnerable individuals. Social takaful emphasizes mutual support and community solidarity, enabling those who cannot afford regular takaful contributions to access essential financial protection. By offering support to the financially marginalized, social takaful promotes financial inclusion and social welfare.

The following Table 7.1 provides the differences between sadaqah, zakat, waqf, microfinance, social sukuk and social takaful in a nutshell.

7.3 Legal Framework for Social Takaful in Malaysia

In Malaysia, there is no specific legal framework dedicated solely to social takaful. Instead, the country follows the general takaful framework to regulate all takaful operations, including social takaful initiatives. Takaful, which is a Shariah-compliant insurance, was introduced in response to the demand for an Islamic alternative to

Table 7.1 Differences between Sadaqah, zakat, Waqf, microfinance, Social Sukuk and Social Takaful in a nutshell

Concept	Description
Sadaqah	Voluntary charity based on compassion and generosity, given without any specific guidelines or obligations
Zakat	Obligatory charity representing a specific percentage of a Muslim's wealth, given to designated categories of recipients in Islamic law
Waqf	Charitable endowment where an asset is dedicated to support specific causes in perpetuity
Microfinance	Financial services provided to financially excluded individuals or entrepreneurs to support small-scale businesses and improve financial well-being
Social Sukuk	Islamic bonds that fund projects with a social impact, allowing investors to contribute to socially beneficial initiatives
Social Takaful	Islamic cooperative insurance concept aimed at providing financial protection to the economically vulnerable or marginalized individuals, promoting financial inclusion and community solidarity

Source Authors' own

conventional insurance and to complement the establishment of Islamic banks in the early 1980s.[3]

The Malaysian National Fatwa Committee's decree played a significant role in inspiring the development of the takaful industry. The committee ruled that conventional life insurance contracts were void due to the presence of elements like uncertainty (gharar), usury (riba'), and gambling (maisir). In response to this ruling, the Government formed a Special Task Force in 1982 to explore the viability of establishing an Islamic insurance company.

Following the Task Force's recommendations, the Takaful Act was enacted in 1984, paving the way for the incorporation of the country's first takaful operator in November of the same year. The core concept of takaful lies in participants contributing money to a common fund, which is used to provide mutual assistance against defined losses or damages.

The takaful operator manages the fund on a commercial basis, seeking profit as a business venture. Sources of income for the operator include profit from investments, agency or wakalah fees, a share of investment profits from takaful funds, and surplus from takaful funds.

Takaful operations in Malaysia are based on three underlying concepts:

- Takaful: Derived from an Arabic word meaning joint guarantee, participants agree to jointly guarantee each other against defined losses.
- Tabarru': This refers to the act of donation, gift, or contribution by the participants. They agree to contribute a portion of their contributions into the takaful fund to

[3] Bank Negara Malaysia. (2004). Takaful Annual Report 2004. https://www.bnm.gov.my/documents/20124/792371/booklet.en.pdf.

assist other participants facing difficulties. It forms the core of the takaful system, allowing for uncertainty elements to be permissible under the takaful contract.
- Mudharabah/Wakalah: The takaful operator acts as the fund's administrator and manages it in trust on behalf of the participants. The contract between the participants and the operator is governed by mudharabah (profit-sharing) or wakalah (agency). Under mudharabah, the contracting parties share the profit, while participants bear the losses. In the wakalah model, the takaful operator earns a fee for services rendered, and losses are borne by the participants.

There are differences between in insurance and takaful. Insurance and takaful, two risk coverage mechanisms, differ significantly in their fundamental principles and contractual structures. Insurance operates on an exchange contract between the insurer and the insured, where policyholders pay premiums to secure coverage for potential risks. On the other hand, takaful incorporates a unique combination of two essential concepts. Firstly, there is the concept of tabarru' or donation, where participants contribute a certain proportion of their contributions into a takaful fund. This fund is designed to assist other participants in times of need, reflecting the essence of mutual cooperation and shared responsibility. Secondly, takaful involves an agency or profit-sharing contract with the takaful operator, who manages the fund on behalf of the participants.

The responsibilities of policyholders and participants also diverge between insurance and takaful. In the case of insurance, policyholders pay premiums to the insurer, establishing a bilateral contractual relationship. In contrast, takaful participants make contributions to the scheme, laying the foundation for mutual assistance within the takaful pool. Participants jointly guarantee each other against defined losses, creating a system based on collective protection and support.[4]

The liability of the insurer/operator represents another key distinction between insurance and takaful. In insurance, the insurer assumes the responsibility to pay out the insurance benefits as promised in the insurance contract. These payments are typically made from the insurer's funds, which may include insurance premiums and shareholders' funds. Conversely, in takaful, the takaful operator does not bear the liability for takaful benefits. Instead, the operator serves as the administrator of the takaful scheme, managing the fund on behalf of the participants.[5] Takaful benefits are directly paid from the takaful funds, which remain separate from the operator's assets. Moreover, in the event of a deficiency in the takaful funds, the takaful operator provides an interest-free loan to rectify the shortfall. This arrangement ensures that participants' interests are safeguarded and aligns with the principles of mutual cooperation and support within the takaful system.

Another crucial aspect where insurance and takaful differ is in the investment of their respective funds. Insurance companies may invest their funds with relatively few restrictions, subject to prudential regulations. Conversely, takaful funds are invested exclusively in Shariah-compliant instruments, adhering to Islamic ethical

[4] Section 7.2 IFSA.

[5] Section 90 IFSA.

and legal guidelines. By avoiding investments in industries and activities deemed non-compliant with Shariah principles, such as those related to alcohol, gambling, or interest-based transactions, takaful funds reflect their commitment to upholding Islamic values and ethical considerations.[6]

The Takaful framework under the Islamic Financial Services Act (IFSA) 2013 encompasses several key aspects which is provided below.

- Takaful Funds Requirement: The IFSA mandates clear segregation of Takaful participants' funds from shareholders' funds.[7] In cases of deficits in the risk fund, Takaful operators are required to provide a compulsory interest-free loan (Qard)[8] to rectify the shortfall, fostering the spirit of mutual assistance.
- Exclusive License for Family and General Takaful Businesses: The IFSA strictly prohibits licensed Takaful operators (except professional Retakaful operators) from conducting both family and general Takaful businesses.[9] Entities have been given a grace period of five years to separate their family and general Takaful operations into distinct entities.
- Form of Business Entity: All Takaful operators are now required to be established as public companies, in compliance with the Companies Act 1965.[10,11] Existing Takaful operators registered under the repealed Takaful Act 1984 must convert into public companies within 12 months from the IFSA's enactment date, with a possibility of extension upon application.
- Additional Fiduciary Duties of the Board of Directors: The IFSA imposes greater fiduciary duties on the Board of Directors (BOD) of Takaful operators.[12] BODs are responsible for ensuring effective internal controls, compliance, and risk management. They must also balance the interests of shareholders and third-party consumers (Takaful participants).
- Shari'ah Governance Matter: The IFSA gives significant powers and authority to the Shari'ah Committee (SC) of Takaful operators.[13] The SC is responsible for ensuring Shari'ah compliance in all aspects of Takaful operations, and any ruling made by the SC is deemed compliant with Shari'ah principles.
- Consumer Protection: The IFSA emphasizes consumer protection by requiring Takaful operators to provide clear disclosure of contract terms and relevant information to Takaful participants.[14] Conversely, consumers must take reasonable care not to misrepresent information to Takaful operators.

[6] Section 28 IFSA.

[7] Section 91 IFSA.

[8] Section 95 IFSA.

[9] Section 16 IFSA.

[10] In the Act the reference is made to the previous Act. Companies Act 2016 is the current legislation.

[11] Section 287 IFSA.

[12] Section 58 IFSA.

[13] Section 28 & 29 IFSA.

[14] Section 141 IFSA.

- Insolvency Framework: In terms of the insolvency framework, the IFSA specifies provisions for winding up Takaful operators.[15] It aims to safeguard the interests of stakeholders, especially Takaful participants.

Although the IFSA introduces stringent requirements, it also seeks to enhance the overall credibility, trust, and sustainability of the Takaful industry. While Takaful operators may face operational challenges and increased costs, they must adapt to the new regulatory framework to maintain competitiveness and ensure sustainable growth in the market.

Recently, Malaysia introduced the Value-based Intermediation for Takaful (VBIT) initiative[16] with the aim of encouraging Takaful Operators (TOs) to achieve sustainable and meaningful growth that positively impacts all stakeholders. The framework provides TOs with guidelines for implementing VBIT and outlines industry best practices. VBIT is aligned with the principles of Corporate Value Intent (CVI), which expresses the specific desirable future that TOs are committed to achieving while ensuring value creation for all stakeholders.

The underpinning thrusts of VBIT encompass financial resilience, good self-governance, community empowerment, and best conduct. These thrusts serve as guiding principles for TOs to adopt VBIT and create positive value and sustainable impacts for stakeholders. Key implementation strategies include inclusive stakeholder engagement, impact-based assessment, constructive collaboration, and value-driven solutions. These strategies assist TOs in executing their CVI and implementing value-based initiatives effectively.

Performance measurement is crucial in assessing the progress and effectiveness of VBIT initiatives. It addresses both financial and non-financial indicators under the four underpinning thrusts, providing quantifiable measurements of VBIT implementation. Enhanced disclosure demonstrates TOs' accountability and commitment to VBIT, providing stakeholders with relevant impact-focused information and promoting informed decision-making.

Value creation under VBIT extends to various stakeholders. Society benefits from improved Takaful offerings, transparency, and awareness. Regulators and government authorities experience better alignment with national agendas and financial stability. TOs benefit from enhanced operational efficiency, new business opportunities, and increased competitiveness. The effective Takaful ecosystem enhances corporate image and reputation.

The future landscape of Takaful under VBIT envisions shared prosperity and value, with performance measurement and disclosure of financial returns and value. Innovation in products and services caters to diverse consumer needs, and meaningful involvement from stakeholders drives positive impacts in various focus areas. In essence, the VBIT initiative in Malaysia aims to foster a sustainable and socially responsible Takaful industry, promoting the well-being of society and enhancing collaboration among stakeholders.

---

[15] Sections 212–218 IFSA.

[16] Malaysian Takaful Association. (n.d.). *Value Based Intermediation for Takaful*. http://migration.malaysiantakaful.com.my/vbit/#faq.

7.4 Case Studies

7.4.1 mySalam (Malaysia)[17]

The mySalam national health protection scheme is a groundbreaking initiative initiated by the Malaysian Government to provide essential takaful protection to financially vulnerable citizens. With the goal of offering comprehensive coverage and financial support during critical health situations, mySalam Takaful aims to uplift the lives of 6.8 million eligible individuals.

The target group for mySalam Takaful comprises recipients of the Bantuan Sara Hidup (BSH) program, including individuals aged between 18 and 65 and their spouses, single individuals aged between 40 and 65 earning less than RM24,000 per annum, and OKU (Orang Kurang Upaya, disabled persons) individuals aged between 18 and 65 earning less than RM24,000 per annum.

The scheme's coverage benefits are designed to address the specific needs of the target group. One of the key components is the provision of critical illness coverage. Eligible BSH recipients who are diagnosed with one of the 45 specified critical illnesses are entitled to a one-time RM8,000 cash payout. This financial support serves as a crucial safety net, helping to alleviate the financial burden associated with expensive medical treatments and allowing beneficiaries to focus on their recovery and well-being. No registration is required as eligible recieipients are automatically covered under the scheme. Approximately 2 million individuals from the B40 group, protected under the mySalam Public Health Protection Scheme, have received approved claims, totaling nearly RM800 million since its launch in 2019 until now.[18] As mySalam is a government-initiated free health protection takaful scheme, the contributions come from the government and are dispensed through the mySalam Trust Fund.[19]

In addition to critical illness coverage, mySalam Takaful offers hospitalisation income replacement benefits. BSH recipients are eligible to receive RM50 daily income replacement, up to a maximum of RM700 per annum, during hospital stays at any government, military, or university hospital. This income replacement feature ensures that beneficiaries have access to financial assistance to cover daily expenses while undergoing treatment, thus relieving them of additional worries about managing their basic needs during hospitalisation.

The mySalam Takaful scheme has had a significant impact on the lives of eligible BSH recipients. By offering free takaful protection, the initiative provides a safety net for those who are financially vulnerable, ensuring that they have access to essential health coverage during critical times. The cash payout upon critical illness diagnosis

---

[17] mySalam. (n.d.). About mySalam. https://www.mysalam.com.my/b40/info/?url=main_EN.

[18] Utusan Malaysia, mySalam beri sinar harapan kepada hampir 2 juta rakyat (16 January 2023). Retrieved from https://www.utusan.com.my/nasional/2023/01/mysalam-beri-sinar-harapan-kepada-hampir-2-juta-rakyat/.

[19] mySALAM, FAQs about mySalam. Retrieved from https://www.mysalam.com.my/b40/info/?url=FAQ-BM.

provides much-needed financial assistance, helping beneficiaries manage medical expenses and maintain their quality of life. Moreover, the hospitalisation income replacement eases the financial strain for those undergoing hospital treatments, allowing them to focus on recovery without additional financial worries.

In a nutshell it can be said that mySalam Takaful scheme exemplifies the Malaysian Government's commitment to promoting financial inclusivity and providing essential health protection to its citizens. Through this initiative, millions of BSH recipients gain access to critical illness coverage and hospitalisation income replacement, fostering a sense of security and well-being in times of need. mySalam Takaful stands as a powerful example of the potential of social takaful in safeguarding the financial health of the nation's most vulnerable populations, fostering a more resilient and caring society.

Takaful and Karama (Egypt)[20]

Egypt's Takaful and Karama program, a key component of the Strengthening Social Safety Net project, has been instrumental in providing crucial support to the country's most vulnerable citizens. Since its inception in 2015, the program has successfully enrolled 3.1 million households, benefiting a total of 11.1 million individuals, with an impressive 75 percent of them being women. With a focus on women's empowerment and human capital development, Takaful and Karama have made significant strides in improving the lives of the disadvantaged population across all 27 governorates of Egypt.

Targeting the most marginalized groups, the program extends both conditional (Takaful) and unconditional (Karama) cash transfers. The conditional component aims to break the cycle of poverty and foster human capital accumulation. In response to the challenges posed by the COVID-19 pandemic, the program was further expanded to include additional beneficiaries. To mitigate the risk of dependency on cash transfers, the government introduced the Forsa (opportunity) program. This complementary initiative not only paves the way for beneficiaries to graduate from Takaful but also facilitates productive inclusion by providing opportunities for livelihood creation through asset transfers and skill development.

The Takaful program aims to provide financial support to impoverished families with children in various educational stages, from kindergarten to secondary school.[21] The program offers 60 pounds per primary school pupil, 80 pounds per preparatory school pupil, and 100 pounds per secondary school pupil. To receive these amounts, families must ensure their children attend school for at least 80% of actual school

---

[20] The World Bank. (2020). Takaful and Karama: A Social Safety Net project that Promotes Egyptian Women Empowerment and Human Capital. https://www.worldbank.org/en/results/2020/11/17/takaful-and-karama-a-social-safety-net-project-that-promotes-egyptian-women-empowerment-and-human-capital.

[21] State Information Service, Takaful & Karama Program. Retrieved from https://www.sis.gov.eg/Story/173372/Takaful-%26-Karama-Program?lang=en-us

days. Additionally, the health aspect of the program provides cash assistance to families with children under six years old and pregnant mothers, contingent on adhering to health care programs outlined by the Ministry of Health. The Karama program targets two groups: elderly individuals over 65 who are unable to work and lack fixed income, and disabled individuals with inhibiting conditions verified by medical certificates. Karama offers financial assistance ranging from EGP 325 to EGP 550 based on the number of eligible members within the family. The overall project cost is estimated at 5.6 billion pounds, approved by the Council of Ministers, and aims to support three million poor families over four years through three implementation phases. The Ministry of Finance provides cash support to beneficiaries according to the plan set by the Ministry of Solidarity.

Efficient targeting is achieved through a Proxy Means Testing Questionnaire, cross-referenced with a Unified National Registry linked to unique IDs. The conditional cash transfers under Takaful are strategically utilized to enhance income, increase food intake, and alleviate poverty. Coupled with health and education conditions, these transfers encourage families to prioritize their children's education and healthcare needs.

In parallel, the unconditional cash transfer program, Karama, provides vital support to vulnerable citizens above the age of 65, as well as those with severe disabilities, including poor orphans and widows.

Recognizing the significance of economic inclusion, the Ministry of Social Security launched the Forsa program, which emphasizes job placement, asset transfer, training, and skill development, ensuring that beneficiaries are not left unemployed.

Leveraging the Takaful and Karama database Management Information System, the Ministry of Social Security integrates beneficiaries into other social protection services, fostering literacy promotion, family planning, improved housing, and overall well-being.

An independent impact evaluation conducted by the International Food Policy Research Institute (IFPRI) reveals the program's impressive outcomes. Takaful beneficiaries experienced an increase in household consumption, reducing the likelihood of falling below the poverty line. The program's positive effects extended to improved nutritional status among children and increased investments in education. Notably, women's empowerment and sense of dignity were significantly enhanced, leading to greater involvement in household decision-making and financial choices.

Driven by its success, the Takaful and Karama program has been formally institutionalized as a national initiative, with yearly fiscal allocations steadily increasing within the national budget, affirming the government's steadfast commitment and ownership.

The World Bank Group has played a pivotal role in supporting the program, providing financial investments and grants, and collaborating closely with the Ministry of Social Solidarity and other relevant ministries to ensure effective implementation and coordination.

Moving forward, the government aims to enhance the program's overall efficacy by integrating the old Social Solidarity Pension system into Takaful and Karama. Emphasis will be placed on closely monitoring and implementing conditionalities for children's education and health, further strengthening human capital development within participating families. The focus will shift from pure protection to fostering economic productivity, enabling beneficiaries to generate their own livelihoods and achieve financial independence.

Uplift Mutuals Biradaree (India)[22]

The introduction of Uplift Mutuals Biradaree, a not-for-profit health assurance scheme, has brought an innovative alternative to formal takaful to India's Muslim-majority localities. Launched in April 2018 in two of Mumbai's Muslim-majority areas, Kurla and Malad, this unique scheme operates on the principles of mutual assurance, adhering to the concepts of takaful and Shariah-compliant finance. The underlying idea revolves around mutual cooperation, where individuals pool their resources by contributing an agreed amount into a common fund to support and protect each other from various risks.

The distinguishing feature of this mutual health assurance model is that there is no trading of risk involved, eliminating any potential conflict of interest between the insurer and the insured. The scheme aims to promote the principle of "prevention is better than cure," emphasizing proactive measures to prevent illnesses in the first place. To achieve this, monthly clinics are organized in the localities, and doctors are made available 24/7 for consultation and medical assistance.

Unlike traditional insurance, Uplift Mutuals Biradaree goes beyond financial coverage and acts as a comprehensive health service provider. The scheme is not limited to a specific religious community; it is designed to be affordable and open to all financially vulnerable families, regardless of their religious background.

Uplift Mutuals, the driving force behind this health assurance scheme, is a well-established community-owned mutual health assurance model that has been serving the urban and rural poor in Maharashtra and Rajasthan for fifteen years. However, one challenge that emerged during the creation of this new scheme was the need to find a solution for the funds raised that would comply with Shariah principles, as India does not have any Islamic banks. To address this, the funds are placed in a separate current account, and any incidental interest earned is purged to ensure Shariah compliance.

The success of Uplift Mutuals Biradaree is further bolstered by the involvement of external funding from the International Cooperative and Mutual Insurance Federation (ICMIF). As part of its 5-5-5 Mutual Microinsurance Strategy for India, ICMIF has partnered with Uplift India Association to extend mutual assurance coverage to half a million people over the next five years. This support has helped keep the annual contribution affordable—700 Indian rupees ($10) for a single member and 1,400

[22] Kadar, S.A. (2018). India's Muslims develop mutual health insurance scheme as alternative to Takaful. https://www.zawya.com/en/business/indias-muslims-develop-mutual-health-insurance-scheme-as-alternative-to-takaful-wcycmj2k.

rupees per year for a family of four—making it accessible to financially vulnerable families.

Beyond its financial viability, the scheme has also garnered significant interest and enrollment from the local community. Uplift Mutuals Biradaree represents a compelling case study for social takaful, addressing the need for a Shariah-compliant insurance alternative in a country where formal takaful initiatives face regulatory obstacles. The mutual model's ability to offer affordable coverage without transferring risk places it outside the purview of the Insurance Regulatory and Development Authority (IRDA), making it an accessible and inclusive option for financially vulnerable families. With strong community support and strategic partnerships, the scheme has the potential to expand to cover more people from different income categories, contributing to the overall development of social takaful in India.

7.5 Issues and Challenges

Social takaful, as a form of Islamic insurance aimed at providing coverage and protection to individuals and communities facing social and economic challenges, holds great potential for societal welfare. However, to fully realize its transformative impact, several issues and challenges must be addressed. Ensuring accessibility and affordability of social takaful products for economically disadvantaged or marginalized beneficiaries is a fundamental concern. This requires careful product design, pricing and assessments of risks, as well as the establishment of effective distribution channels to reach underserved areas. Moreover, measuring the social impact of these initiatives becomes crucial in assessing their effectiveness in achieving intended objectives, such as poverty alleviation and community empowerment. Financial sustainability is also vital, necessitating a delicate balance between social goals and sound business practices to ensure long-term viability. Raising awareness and promoting financial literacy among potential beneficiaries are equally essential to empower them to make informed decisions about their insurance needs. The regulatory framework must foster the growth of social takaful while upholding Shariah principles and consumer protection requirements. Additionally, forging collaborations and partnerships with various stakeholders will be instrumental in addressing social challenges effectively and maximizing the positive impact of social takaful programs. Tackling these issues head-on is imperative to unlock the full potential of social takaful as a force for positive change and social welfare enhancement. The issues and challenges in this regard are further explained below:

- Accessibility and Affordability: One of the primary challenges for social takaful is ensuring that the products and services are accessible and affordable for the targeted beneficiaries. Many of the potential beneficiaries of social takaful are economically disadvantaged or marginalized, and they may face financial constraints in accessing insurance coverage. Designing and pricing social takaful products in a way that caters to the affordability and needs of the target population is essential. Additionally, developing distribution channels that reach out to underserved areas or communities can enhance accessibility.

- Social Impact Measurement: Measuring the social impact and effectiveness of social takaful programs is crucial to evaluate their success in achieving intended social objectives. Establishing robust frameworks and methodologies for social impact measurement is necessary to assess outcomes related to poverty alleviation, community empowerment, and social welfare improvement. This data-driven approach helps in refining social takaful initiatives and maximizing their positive impact.
- Financial Sustainability: Social takaful operators must balance their social objectives with financial sustainability and viability. While the focus is on providing coverage and support to the needy, managing risks and maintaining adequate capital and reserves are crucial for the long-term stability of social takaful operations. Achieving a sustainable business model ensures that the operators can continue fulfilling their social responsibilities effectively.
- Consumer Awareness and Education: Enhancing consumer awareness about the concept and benefits of social takaful is essential. Many potential beneficiaries may not be familiar with Islamic insurance and the advantages it offers. Promoting financial literacy and education can empower individuals to understand the coverage, benefits, and obligations of social takaful. Outreach efforts, educational programs, and consumer protection measures can aid in building consumer confidence and trust.
- Regulatory and Supervisory Framework: Creating a supportive regulatory and supervisory framework is crucial for the development and growth of social takaful. The framework should be conducive to Islamic principles, while also ensuring consumer protection and transparency. Addressing regulatory challenges, providing clear guidelines, and fostering accountability in the operation and governance of social takaful operators are essential for building trust among stakeholders.
- Collaboration and Partnerships: Collaborative efforts between various stakeholders, including social takaful operators, government agencies, NGOs, and community organizations, are essential for effective addressing of social issues. By fostering partnerships and leveraging resources, social takaful initiatives can benefit from shared expertise, increased reach, and more extensive impact. Sharing best practices and lessons learned can further enhance the success of social takaful programs.
- Innovation and Technology: Embracing technology and innovation can significantly benefit social takaful operations. Leveraging digital platforms, mobile applications, and data analytics can streamline processes, reduce costs, and reach out to a broader audience. Investing in technological advancements can enhance the efficiency and effectiveness of social takaful initiatives. In November 2022, Bank Negara Malaysia (BNM) issued the Licensing and Regulatory Framework

for Digital Insurers and Takaful Operators Exposure Draft which sets out a regulatory framework for digital insurers and takaful operators (DITOs) in Malaysia.[23] The framework aims to facilitate the entry of DITOs with innovative business models by outlining licensing and regulatory requirements that consider differences in their operations. It covers applicants, licensed DITOs, and relevant shareholders. Legal provisions, effective upon the final issuance, are detailed under specific sections of financial acts. The eligibility criteria focus on value propositions, urging applicants to contribute to financial inclusion, competition, and efficiency. The document seeks feedback on challenges and clarity. Business models can involve assuming risks or adopting risk-sharing protection, excluding intermediaries. Criteria for risk-sharing models stress consumer suitability, effective risk management, and transparency, with the possibility of additional requirements by BNM.

Addressing these issues and challenges will help promote the growth and impact of social takaful, allowing it to serve as an effective social safety net for vulnerable communities and individuals in need. As the industry evolves, continuous evaluation and adaptation will be necessary to ensure that social takaful remains relevant and impactful in addressing societal challenges.

Review Questions

1. What does "takaful" mean in Arabic?
   a. Mutual assistance
   b. Insurance
   c. Collaboration
   d. Solidarity
2. What is the core concept of takaful?
   a. Profit-sharing among participants
   b. Eliminating uncertainty in contracts
   c. Gambling for potential gains
   d. Individual protection against losses
3. Under a takaful scheme, what do participants do to support each other?
   a. Financially assist each other in times of risk
   b. Compete for the highest contributions
   c. Invest independently for personal gain
   d. Withhold contributions for personal savings

[23] BNM, Licensing and Regulatory Framework for Digital Insurers and Takaful Operators Exposure Draft. Retrieved from https://www.bnm.gov.my/documents/20124/948107/ED_DITO_Licensing_and_Regulatory_Framework.pdf.

4. Which historical practice resembles the concept of takaful?
   a. Tabarru' contribution for the needy
   b. Trading in uncertain financial contracts
   c. Tribes supporting each other in times of loss
   d. Speculative gambling among individuals
5. What is the primary objective of social takaful?
   a. Maximizing profit for participants
   b. Promoting financial inclusion and social welfare
   c. Offering luxury insurance products
   d. Encouraging individualism and self-reliance
6. What is micro-takaful?
   a. Takaful for large corporations
   b. Takaful with no contribution requirements
   c. Takaful tailored to low-income populations
   d. Takaful for government employees
7. How are contributions for social takaful schemes often covered?
   a. By participants' personal savings
   b. Through external contributions by the government or corporations
   c. By borrowing funds from Islamic banks
   d. Through profits from speculative investments
8. What values does social takaful emphasize within communities?
   a. Individualism and competition
   b. Inclusivity and solidarity
   c. Risk-taking and speculation
   d. Profit maximization for participants
9. What is the primary difference between Sadaqah and Zakat?
   a. Sadaqah is obligatory, while Zakat is voluntary.
   b. Sadaqah requires a fixed percentage of wealth, while Zakat is a voluntary donation.
   c. Sadaqah has specific guidelines on the amount to be given, while Zakat does not.
   d. Sadaqah benefits specific categories of recipients defined in Islamic law, while Zakat is directed to anyone in need.
10. What is the focus of Social Takaful in Islamic finance?
    a. Providing small loans to entrepreneurs
    b. Obligatory form of charity

c. Financial protection for economically vulnerable individuals
d. Funding projects with a social impact

Answers:

1. b
2. b
3. a
4. c
5. b
6. c
7. b
8. b
9. c
10. c

Chapter 8
Contemporary Issues and Challenges in Islamic Social Finance

Abstract This chapter serves as a culmination of the exploration into Islamic Social Finance, focusing on Contemporary Issues and Challenges within this dynamic landscape. Readers will gain a profound understanding of the nuanced complexities and emerging concerns that shape the trajectory of Islamic social finance. The chapter delves into an in-depth analysis of these contemporary challenges, offering insights into their multifaceted nature. Strategies for overcoming these challenges are meticulously examined, providing readers with practical approaches to navigate the intricacies of Islamic social finance. Furthermore, the chapter illuminates potential pathways for future development in this vital field, fostering a forward-looking perspective on the evolution of Islamic social finance.

Keywords Standardization · Challenges · Social finance · Way forward

8.1 Contemporary Issues

Globally countries have been aligning their efforts to fulfill the United Nations 17 Sustainable Development Goals (SDGs) since 2012. These universal goals were created to address the urgent challenges facing the world in relation to the environment, economy, and politics. In the Islamic world fulfilling Maqasid al-Shariah, giving zakat, waqf, and sadaqah have been part of the fabric of Islamic history since 1400 years, and as earlier explained in chapter one, SDGs are fulfilled by the instruments of Islamic social finance.[1] These Islamic social finance tools are part of the theory of Islamic economics which ensures the balance between wealth creation and

[1] Rosman, R., Redzuan, N.H., Mokhtar, N.Z.N., Engku Ali, E.R.A., & Mohammed, M.O. (2022). Islamic social finance and sustainable development goals: Issues and challenges. *Journal of Islamic Finance*, *11*(2), 56–67. Retrieved from https://journals.iium.edu.my/iiibf-journal/index.php/jif/article/view/690.

S. Kunhibava et al., *Islamic Social Finance*,
https://doi.org/10.1007/978-981-97-1410-0_8

fair distribution.[2] However, reports shows that Muslim countries are the among the poorest, economically backward and most politically challenged.[3]

Reasons given for this has ranged from imposition of wars, economic embargoes, governmental incompetence, and corruption.[4] However, is it possible that in addition to those reasons the tools of Islamic social finance are not being properly applied or there are other challenges preventing its efficient use?

This chapter will discuss the contemporary issues and challenges facing Islamic social finance.

8.1.1 The Need for Integration Between Islamic Finance Institutions and Traditional Islamic Social Finance Organizations

One of the important contemporary issues which is a hurdle to the development of Islamic social finance is the barrier between, or separation of Islamic finance from Islamic social finance. Islamic finance growth and development has been impressive, however it has focused extensively on the for-profit financing contracts and tools, this is not unexpected or wrong in agenda, since wealth creation is required and encouraged in Islamic economics. Nevertheless, in the pursuit of these commercial financing instruments, well-known social contracts and tools have been sidelined and ignored. This focus on for-profit contracts, such as murabaha, tawarruq, salam, istisna, mudarabah and musharakah, has diminished the power of Islamic economics as a whole, as the scale of wealth creation and wealth distribution is not balanced. When one views the five objectives of Shariah, Maqasid al-Shariah, they encompass wealth preservation and wealth distribution, there is no emphasis on one objective over the other.

Another point to take note of is that the commercial side to Islamic financing is no longer enough to overcome the inherent problems plaguing society, such as poverty, climate change, mass migration and so forth. There is therefore a need to overcome emphasis on for-profit contracts and solutions and combine the positive traits of Islamic finance with Islamic social finance to serve the society and environment. It is therefore essential to integrate Islamic social finance with Islamic finance to achieve higher agendas which cannot be achieved through Islamic finance alone.[5]

---

[2] Ibid.

[3] Bala, A.A. (2022). Chapter 12: The role of Zakat in addressing poverty: An analysis of Sokoto State Zakat and Waqf (Endowment) Commission. In Qadri H.M., Bhatti, M.I. (Eds.). *Contemporary Issues in Islamic Social Finance* (pp. 185–193). Routledge.

[4] Qadri, H.M., & Bhatti, M.I. (2022). In Qadri H.M, Bhatti, M.I. (Eds.), *Contemporary Issues in Islamic Social Finance* (pp. 1–10). Routledge.

[5] Tahiri Jouti, A. (2019). An integrated approach for building sustainable Islamic social finance ecosystems. *ISRA International Journal of Islamic Finance, 11*(2), 246–266.

Tahiri Jouti[6] lists four ways of integrating Islamic finance with Islamic social finance:

The first is through the collaboration of Islamic finance institutions with Islamic social finance institutions.

- An example of this was the Memorandum of Understanding signed by Bank Islam Bhd and the Wilayah State Religious Council (MAIWP) in 2022, whereby Bank Islam would provide microfinancing to those who are eligible from the pool of zakat payers, this initiative is known as iTekad.[7]

The second way is through Islamic finance institutions providing funds for Islamic social institutions.

- An example of this would be the myWakaf initiative, where Bank Negara Malaysia through the Association of Islamic Banking and Financial Institutions (AIBIM) invited Islamic banks to participate in creating and maintaining a standardized Waqf fund that would be used to fund social projects under the purview of the State Religious Councils. The waqf fund would be pooled from endowments of individuals and corporations. There are currently six Islamic banks participating in this initiative namely: Affin Islamic Bank Berhad, Bank Islam Malaysia Berhad, Bank Muamalat Malaysia Berhad, Bank Rakyat, Maybank Islamic Berhad and RHB Islamic Malaysia Berhad. The following sectors are targeted for the Waqf fund: education, health and healthcare, investment and community empowerment.[8] One successful project which used the funds from MyWakaf through Bank Rakyat was the creation of the Maida, Hemodialysis Center on waqf land in Trengganu. The amount raised was RM952,740.00 in 2020 which was used to renovate a bunglow on waqf land to become the hemodialysis center and to buy the required equipment.[9]

The third way is through the co-financing or re-financing of Islamic social finance projects by Islamic finance institutions and Islamic social finance institutions.

- An example of this is the collaboration of Bank Islam Bhd with the Kedah State Zakat Board (LZNK) to provide housing for asnaf Kafa (religious) teachers who were unable to buy a home with the allowances they receive. The scheme, named i-Asnaf Personal Financing, involves the joint provision of financing from Bank Islam Bhd and LZNK, where 50% is financed by LZNK through zakat funds and the remaining 50% is financed through a personal loan from Bank Islam Bhd. With

---

[6] Ibid.

[7] Aman, A.S. (2022, December). Bank Islam to lend more to micro-entrepreneurs with PPZ-MAIWP help. *The News Straits Times*. Retrieved from https://www.nst.com.my/business/2022/12/863848/bank-islam-lend-more-micro-entrepreneurs-ppz-maiwp-help.

[8] MyWakaf. (2019). About Us. Retrieved from https://www.mywakaf.com.my/about-us/#1519010542854-4f88995a-f56e.

[9] MyWakaf. (2019). Our Projects. Retrieved from https://www.mywakaf.com.my/our-projects/?project=37.

this fund a house is built for around RM45,000 for the Kafa teacher's family.[10] The Kafa teacher will then pay monthly RM260 for 10 years to Bank Islam Bhd, and eventually own the house.[11]

The fourth way is through Islamic social finance institutions being guarantors for commercial financing. MSMEs usually find it difficult to obtain financing from commercial Islamic banks because of the credit risk and lack of collateral as security.[12] To assist MSMEs to get microfinancing the concept of kafalah could be used, where Islamic social finance institutions could provide a guarantee for the performance of an MSME who has obtained a microfinance from an Islamic bank.

All these four methods should be further explored to maximize the impact of Islamic social finance.

8.1.2 Inefficient Management and Ineffective Attitude of Recipients

Rosman et al.[13] identified in their research that notwithstanding having the Islamic social finance tools of zakat, waqf and sadaqah, SDG 1 elimination of poverty goal is not being achieved due to the **inefficient management** of Islamic social finance projects and institutions and the **attitude of recipients of the benefits**.

Following this finding, let us discuss the first issue which is inefficient management. There is a need for those who manage Islamic social projects and institutions to have the right skills to manage funds under their responsibility. The necessary skills include financial knowledge and know-how of the latest innovations in technology such as fintech. Discussions with collaborators with State Islamic Religious Councils have highlighted that there is a knowledge gap between the individuals in the management of Islamic social finance projects and those working in the State

[10] Lembaga Zakat Negeri Kedah. (2020). LZNK Laksanakan Projek Perintis Bersama Bank Islam Bantu Penjawat Awam Tidak Bergaji Miliki Rumah Sendiri. Retrieved from https://www.zakatkedah.com.my/lznk-laksanakan-projek-perintis-bersama-bank-islam-bantu-penjawat-awam-tidak-bergaji-miliki-rumah-sendiri/

[11] World Zakat and Waqf Forum. (2021). Kafa Teachers in Malaysia Now Able to Own A House With LZNK's Special Collaboration Scheme With Bank Islam Malaysia Berhad (BIMB). Retrieved from https://wzwf.org/asia/257-kafa-teachers-in-malaysia-now-able-to-own-a-house-with-lznk%E2%80%99s-special-collaboration-scheme-with-bank-islam-malaysia-berhad-bimb.html.

[12] AIBIM. (2023). Islamic Social Finance a Viable Way to Assist MSMEs. Retrieved from https://aibim.com/news/islamic-social-finance-a-viable-way-to-assist-MSMEs.

[13] Rosman, R., Redzuan, N.H., Mokhtar, N.Z.N., Engku Ali, E.R.A., & Mohammed, M.O. (2022). Islamic social finance and sustainable development goals: Issues and challenges. *Journal of Islamic Finance*, *11*(2), 56–67. Retrieved from https://journals.iium.edu.my/iiibf-journal/index.php/jif/article/view/690.

Islamic Religious Councils when compared to practitioners.[14] It is important therefore to continuously update the knowledge of the management of Islamic social finance projects and other stakeholders on latest innovations and possible ways of raising and distributing funds to the right recipients. Another important requirement for the management of Islamic social finance projects and those working in the State Islamic Religious Councils is to have the correct updated data to identify which cause or who are most eligible for the benefits (more on this will be discussed below).

Further, State Islamic Religious Councils should employ advisory members who are practitioners in Islamic finance to advise them on how to manage their funds efficiently. For example the Selangor State Religious Council (MAIS) has as their committee members academicians on Islamic studies from a number of local universities, this is a progressive development. Another example is the Federal State Wilayah's Federal Territory State Religious Council (MAIWP) chairman[15] who is Tan Sri Dr. Mohd Daud Bakar, a well-known Shariah scholar in Islamic finance. As the chairman Tan Sri Dr. Mohd Daud Bakar can use his knowledge to improve the ways on how to invest and distribute zakat, waqf and sadaqah and also introduce other collaborations between Islamic finance and Islamic social finance. This is also an excellent development which all State Religious Councils should try to adopt. At the very least practitioners who understands the financial market should be employed as advisors, where these advisors could enable them to efficiently manage the Islamic social finance assets.

On the second issue of recipients' attitude, there are cases of the recipients being in debts[16] which they are unable to manage, many are even plagued with generational liabilities and are therefore in a continuous cycle of poverty. It is therefore crucial that recipients themselves have the requisite education on how to use the benefits handed to them and the financial skills on how to manage money, how to pay off debts and invest. These skills are crucial for their survival, to enable proper impact of the social benefits provided and the eventual independence from the cycle of poverty. Thus, there is a need for the support of recipients in the form of awareness and education on how to efficiently use the benefits that are given to them.

8.1.3 Lack of Standardized Reporting

Reporting by State Religious Councils and other related stakeholders responsible for zakat, waqf and sadaqah has been under scrutiny for several years by researchers.

[14] From interview with Mr Hamid Rashid and Mr Sree Charan, Finterra. Thursday, 21 July 2021 at 11:00am online.

[15] MAIWP. (2023). Barisan Ahli Sesi 2021–2024. Retrieved from https://www.maiwp.gov.my/i/index.php/en/mengenai-kami/ahli-majlis-agama-islam-wilayah-persekutuan-maiwp.

[16] Rosman, R., Redzuan, N.H., Mokhtar, N.Z.N., Engku Ali, E.R.A., & Mohammed, M.O. (2022). Islamic social finance and sustainable development goals: Issues and challenges. *Journal of Islamic Finance*, *11*(2), 56–67. Retrieved from https://journals.iium.edu.my/iiibf-journal/index.php/jif/article/view/690.

There is an abundance of literature detailing the lack of proper reporting and transparency on financial and non-financial disclosures, such as impact, governance, performance and sustainability.[17] Reporting enables better public trust in establishments responsible for managing zakat, waqf and sadaqah assets, it also ensures accountability and integrity from those same establishments. It increases possibilities of collaborations with Islamic financial institutions and other stakeholders and thus benefits the recipients indirectly. Lack of proper reporting deprives donors of knowledge on the outcome and impact of their donation. Lack of knowledge on how their donation impacts society will prevent further donations.

Kamaruddin et al.[18] found that there are five reasons why there are weak waqf reporting practices in waqf institutions in Malaysia. These findings it is believed can be applied to zakat and sadaqah reporting too. The reasons include—the absence of standardized reporting standards, lack of awareness on what to disclose and how to disclose to the public by the institutions, there are limited ways of reporting from the state to the federal authority, different ways of governance and practice of the institutions at the state level influences how reporting is done and its unstandardized nature. Finally, the reluctance of the administration of the waqf to report. On the other hand the Kamaruddin et al. found that good leadership, good cultural setting, positive political will, better qualified personnel and visibility of the report is important for good reporting practices.

Following this it is recommended that there should be created a standardized manner of reporting for Islamic social financing projects on both financial and non-financial disclosure. Awareness of why correct reporting is essential, how to report and what to report must be established within the responsible establishments. Further qualified personnel who are proficient in the right knowledge should be employed and tasked with reporting to the public. Also, better collaboration between the federal and state authorities in charge of zakat, waqf and sadaqah should be pursued where the federal authority should have the mandate to check the practices of the state authority.

---

[17] See for example: Kamaruddin, M.I.H., Hanefah, M.M., & Masruki, R. (2022). Challenges and prospects in waqf reporting practices in Malaysia. *Journal of Financial Reporting and Accounting*. https://doi.org/10.1108/JFRA-01-2022-0018; Kamaruddin, M.I.H., Masruki, R., & Hanefah, M.M. (2018). Waqf management practices: Case study in a Malaysian waqf institution. *World Journal of Social Sciences, 8*(3), 1–12; Adnan, M.A., Sulaiman, M., & Mohd Nor, P.N.S.M. (2007). Some thoughts about accounting conceptual framework and standards for a waqf institutions. *Indonesian Management and Accounting Research, 6* (1): 43–56; Arshad, R., & Mohd Zain, N. (2017). Performance measurement and accountability of waqf institutions in Malaysia. *SHS Web of Conferences, 36*(5), 1–15; Chowdhury, M.S.R., Chowdhury, I.A., & Muhammad, M.Z. (2012). Problems of waqf administration and proposals for improvement: A study in Malaysia. *Journal of Internet Banking and Commerce, 17* (1), 1–8; Daud, D. (2019). The role of Islamic governance in the reinforcement waqf reporting: SIRC Malaysia case. *Journal of Islamic Accounting and Business Research, 10*(3), 392–406.

[18] Kamaruddin, M.I.H., Hanefah, M.M., & Masruki, R. (2022). Challenges and prospects in waqf reporting practices in Malaysia. *Journal of Financial Reporting and Accounting*. https://doi.org/10.1108/JFRA-01-2022-0018.

8.1.4 *Outdated Regulation and Governance*

An updated and comprehensive regulatory and policy environment needs to exist for Islamic social finance to be efficient and have an impact, in other words, correct regulatory environment is a crucial enabler for the sustainability and longevity of Islamic social finance projects.[19] Many of the state enactments are in need of amendments and updates including clear guidelines, standards, and oversight mechanisms to ensure the current socio-economic environment are factored in.

There is a need for principles that promote transparency, accountability, and recipient protection in the operations of Islamic social finance institutions. The role and co-operation between the regulatory bodies or specialized entities in the supervision and monitoring of the activities of Islamic social finance institutions has to be mandated and also stated clearly for the benefit of all stakeholders. It is thus of crucial importance that firstly the relevant state regulations and enactments are updated and modernized and secondly the operations, accountability and transparency of Islamic social finance institutions are clearly included in standards or principles.

8.1.5 *Need for Sharing of Resources*

In Malaysia according to article 74 of the Federal Constitution, states have the power to legislate on matters listed in List II of the ninth schedule. List II enumerates among others—Islamic law, waqf, zakat and charities (sadaqah). This means that states have the exclusive power for the collection, distribution and management of zakat, waqf and sadaqah.

Cheng[20] highlighted that as a result of this division of powers between the state and federal government on Islamic matters, some states may have a higher collection of cash waqf, sadaqah and zakat as compared to other states. For example in 2022, RM923,284,151.65 zakat on wealth was collected in Kuala Lumpur as reported by the MAIWP[21] while RM122,498,456.57 zakat on wealth was collected by the Sabah State Religious Council (MUIS).[22] There is definitely a huge difference in the amount collected. This means in 2022 MAIWP was able to distribute way more than MUIS. One of the reasons for the difference in amounts collected is because of the larger

---

[19] Uddin, T., & Mohiuddin, M. (2020). Islamic social finance in Bangladesh: Challenges and opportunities of the institutional and regulatory landscape. *Law and Development Review*, *13*(1), 265–319.

[20] Cheng, K. (2023). The breadth of Islamic social finance in Malaysia and its institutionary and legal challenges. Unpublished Project paper for Masters of Commercial Law.

[21] MAIWP. (2022). Laporan Tahunan. Retrieved from https://drive.google.com/file/d/1fGckNDMIXFgy3YkeC0v0h962D5WXrhho/view?pli=1.

[22] MUIS. Statistik Pungutan 2022. Retrieved from https://appszakat.sabah.gov.my/statistik_pungutan.php.

number of Muslims and Islamic institutions in Kuala Lumpur as compared to in Sabah.

There is no federal control on the resources of zakat, waqf and sadaqah and thus there would not be a sharing of resources and therefore not an equal distribution of wealth. Some states that have more poverty would have less to distribute. It is therefore recommended that there should be an ability to share resources between different states, so that states with lower collections can obtain funds from 'richer' states thus ensuring more equal distribution of wealth.

8.1.6 *Need for a Digital Database*

Migdad[23] upon analyzing zakat management, collection and distribution in Malaysia recommended that there is a need to establish a comprehensive and holistic database on recipients of all welfare systems and reliefs provided by non-governmental organizers, charities and other stakeholders to reduce double spending. In this way zakat and other donations can be efficiently distributed to all those who are genuinely in need. This database has to be updated periodically so that recipients' details and status are correct. This job is definitely a mighty task and will need the collaboration of a number of stakeholders. It is opined that work should be handled at a state level but coordinated at the federal level so that there is one database where all state religious authorities can refer to and have access to.

This can be achieved with blockchain. Since blockchain is the digital version of a ledger. In a blockchain data once verified remains in the blockchain for the viewing pleasure of the public or those permissioned, with slim chances of being deleted or falsified because the records are immutable. If blockchain can be used to store data of the needy then it would be easier to share resources between states as the recipients and their needs can easily be viewed. Distribution of the donations would be more efficient and maximum impact can be achieved.

8.2 The Way Forward for Digital Islamic Social Finance

Malaysia introduced the Shared Prosperity Vision 2030 in 2019, which aims to enable all Malaysians to have a decent standard of living by 2030. To accomplish this, 16 key economic activities were proposed, the first two are 'Islamic finance hub' and 'digital economy' respectively. Following this, new innovative investments of Islamic social finance through digital tools will support this shared prosperity vision and

[23] Migdad, A. (2019). Managing Zakat through institutions: Case of Malaysia. *International Journal of Islamic Economics and Finance Studies, 3*, 28–44. Retrieved from https://dergipark.org.tr/en/download/article-file/868357.

enable long-term social improvements and sustainability that will increase the socio-economic well-being of the country.[24] The potential of leveraging digital technology to enhance the efficiency, accessibility, and effectiveness of Islamic social finance initiatives is obvious following the case-studies presented in the above chapters.

There is no way to escape the digitalization paradigm, as long as it is to promote Maqasid al Shariah, technology should be embraced. For this purpose, we need experts who can apply successfully the relevant technology, for example digital platforms, fintech solutions and other technological tools that could facilitate and scale up Islamic social finance initiatives in a digitally-driven world Thus improving accessibility, efficiency, and impact of such initiatives.

For this to be successful collaboration is paramount, collaboration of the State Religious Council with tech expert firms, academia and Islamic finance practitioners.

Review Questions

1. Fill in the gaps:

   Research shows that there are four ways of integrating Islamic finance with Islamic social finance, these are: a..............................., b................................., c........................, d.................................

2. Integration of Islamic finance and Islamic social finance is recommended.

   a. True
   b. false

3. There is a focus on for-profit contracts in Islamic social finance:

   a. True
   b. False

4. Wealth creation should be balanced with:

   a. Wealth transfer
   b. Risk mitigation
   c. Wealth distribution
   d. Wealth hoarding

5. Knowledge of the stakeholders is paramount for the success of the Islamic social finance projects.

   a. True
   b. False

[24] Rosman, R., Redzuan, N.H., Mokhtar, N.Z.N., Engku Ali, E.R.A., & Mohammed, M.O. (2022). Islamic social finance and sustainable development goals: Issues and challenges. *Journal of Islamic Finance, 11*(2), 56–67. Retrieved from https://journals.iium.edu.my/iiibf-journal/index.php/jif/article/view/690.

6. Integration of Islamic finance with Islamic social finance can be achieved through:

   i. Colloration
   ii. Co-financing
   iii. Proft focus
   iv. Guarantor role
      a. All of the above
      b. i & ii
      c. ii. & iv
      d. i, ii & iv

7. Reporting in a transparent manner by State Islamic Religious Councils and other stakeholders is important because

   i. increases public trust
   ii. ensures accountability and integrity
   iii. Increases collaboration with Islamic financial institutions
   iv. Beneficial for recipients
      a. All of the above
      b. i & ii
      c. iii only
      d. i only

8. Sharing of resources between State Islamic Religious Councils is encouraged by art. 74 of the Federal Constitution

   a. True
   b. False

9. A digital database is needed

   a. For prevention of corruption
   b. To identify the right recipient
   c. To encourage donations
   d. To ensure data protection

10. Blockchain is suitable technology to use to create a recipient database because it is virtual

    a. True
    b. False

Answers:

1. a. through the co-financing or re-financing of Islamic social finance projects by Islamic finance institutions and Islamic social finance institutions; b. through Islamic finance institutions providing funds for Islamic social institutions; c. through the collaboration of Islamic finance institutions with Islamic social finance institutions; d. through the collaboration of Islamic finance institutions

2. a
3. b
4. c
5. a
6. d
7. a
8. b
9. b
10. b

Index

S. Kunhibava et al., *Islamic Social Finance*, https://doi.org/10.1007/978-981-97-1410-0

MIX
Papier aus verantwortungsvollen Quellen
Paper from responsible sources
FSC® C105338

If you have any concerns about our products,
you can contact us on
ProductSafety@springernature.com

In case Publisher is established outside the EU,
the EU authorized representative is:
Springer Nature Customer Service Center GmbH
Europaplatz 3, 69115 Heidelberg, Germany

Printed by Libri Plureos GmbH
in Hamburg, Germany